Forget English!

Forget English!

ORIENTALISMS AND

WORLD LITERATURES

Aamir R. Mufti

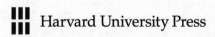 Harvard University Press

Cambridge, Massachusetts
London, England

First Harvard University Press paperback edition, 2018
First printing

Library of Congress Cataloging-in-Publication Data

Mufti, Aamir, author.
   Forget English! : Orientalisms and world literatures / Aamir R. Mufti.
      pages cm
   Includes bibliographical references and index.
   ISBN 978-0-674-73477-7 (alk. paper)
   ISBN 978-0-674-98689-3 (pbk.)
   1. Literature and society.   2. Politics and literature.   3. English
literature—History and criticism.   4. Literature—History and criticism.
5. Oriental literature (English)—History and criticism.   6. Developing
countries–Intellectual life.   I. Title.
   PN98.P64M84 2015
   809-dc23

2015034400

قطرے میں دجلہ دکھائی نہ دے اور جزو میں کل
کھیل لڑکوں کا ہوا دیدۂ بینا نہ ہوا م

For Bhaiyya

(Khalid R. Mufti)

Contents

Preface   ix

Prologue: The Universal Library
of World Literature   1

1   Where in the World Is World Literature?   56

2   Orientalism and the Institution of Indian
Literature   99

3   Global English and Its Others   146

4   "Our Philological Home Is the Earth": World
Literature from Auerbach to Said   203

Epilogue: "For a Ruthless Criticism
of Everything Existing"   243

Notes   255

Acknowledgments   279

Index   285

Preface

No MATTER HOW FAR you travel from home today, you can be pretty sure about some of the things to expect if you are told that you will be meeting someone who is a writer of some renown in that country. Any linguistic difficulties of such a meeting might be overcome by recourse to one or the other of the "world" languages of European origin, such as English, above all, but also French or Spanish, either directly or through an intermediary. You would likely meet a person familiar with the worlds of literary magazines and literary publishing, and you both may have read some of the same magazines or reviews or might at least be familiar with some of the same ones. The two of you could most probably exchange views about favorite authors, maybe even discover that you like the same ones, whom each of you may have read in the original or in translation. On the other hand, you may come to form an opinion of the person's literary tastes as somewhat poor or even shocking. The person may stiffen visibly if you are introduced as a "literary critic"—he or she is a "writer," after all. You might discuss the recent film adaptation of an important novel you both like. And, thinking back on the encounter, you might even come to believe that you may have recognized in this person one or another of a distinct "type" of literary or writerly personality familiar to you from other places in the world.

A mere hundred years ago—and that is a relatively short interlude in the history of the modern world—your encounter would have been far less predictable, even in a place like India, whose languages and cultures had already undergone dramatic change under the violent impact of foreign rule by the British Empire for well over a century. Another fifty or hundred years earlier, the experience might have proved simply undecipherable. A recent European arrival requesting such an encounter might have discovered, first of all, many distinct cultures of poetic composition even in the same town or city, based in a variety of languages and dialects with no clear connection to ideas about the language of a people, let alone a nation. Some of these bodies of writing may have been alien or opaque and even possibly unknown to each other even in the same locale. In other cases, the same individual may have written in more than one language or dialect according to the very different aesthetic standards that were extant in each of them. Some persons who were introduced to the visiting European as composers of verse might have seemed more like musicians or even mystics or religious functionaries. Others may have been busy writing odes to landlords, petty princes, kings, or even officers of the British colonial administration according to regimented rules for singing the praise of benefactors specific to the language. On the one hand, such scenarios are part of the concern of the intellectual and scholarly activity called world literature; on the other, the social and cultural transformations from the older scenario to the contemporary one can be described as the *emergence* of world literature, the transformation of literature into a world-encompassing reality. It is with such matters that we shall be concerned in this book.

The idea of world literature seems to exercise a strange gravitational force on all students of literature, even on those whose primary impulse is to avoid or bypass it entirely, forcing on them involuntary and unwanted changes of course and orientation. Its promise of a unified perspective on world culture brooks no possibility of strong repudiation. It hardly seems viable to say in response, "Back to national literatures!" And yet the ongoing institutionalization of world literature in the academic humanities and in publishing cannot quite dispel a lingering sense of unease about its supposed overcoming of antagonisms and a reconciliation and singularity that is too easily achieved. More bluntly put, it is hard not to wonder if all this talk of world literature might not be an intellectual correlate of the happy talk that accompanied globalization over the past couple of decades, until the financial crash and its ongoing global aftermath, which has taken the form of a new Great Depression in some countries, introduced a certain reality check into the public discourse. How do we ensure what we might call the *critical intelligence* of the concept, which after all has had a presence in the work of so diverse a set of critical thinkers as Karl Marx and Friedrich Engels, Erich Auerbach, and Edward Said but which at the same time seems susceptible to easy commodification in the literary marketplace, broadly conceived?

It will have been noticed that in the opening paragraphs, I more or less implicitly assumed "you" to be Euro-American. Could it be that the latter is always at the "center" of the discourse whenever we talk about world literature? What would a discourse look like in which that was not the case? Could I have written a preface in which the native of an Asian or African society, for instance, was invited to imagine a historical encounter with a European writer as a means of discovering the alienness of *European* "literature"? The very difficulty of imagining this reverse mode of address is a sign of the *success* of "world literature." Concepts and categories of European origin are at the core of literature as a worldwide "space" or reality, including long-established ways of thinking about the alien, the exotic, or the other. And European "world" languages, above all English, seem to be the not-quite-invisible ether that permeates this space. But what is the nature of this space, exactly, and by what means did it get established? How are we to understand its expansion and "success" worldwide? And what is its relationship exactly to modes of writing and expressivity that belong to places that are non-Western, "global southern," or of the "underdeveloped" world? James Joyce's great image in *Ulysses* for the predicament of culture in a colonized society was reflections in the "cracked looking glass of a servant." The image of the native that the world threw back at her was a broken and disfigured one. How can we characterize the predicament in a postcolonial society? A great deal more is at stake in the question of world literature than some of its leading contemporary elaborators seem to recognize: the origins of bourgeois modernity—that is, the culture of capitalist society—within a history of worldwide imperial violence; the persistence into our times, albeit in altered forms, of the racial and cultural antagonisms of the colonial world; and the ongoing struggle over the right and the ability to define the contours of human experience. The discourse of world literature today often seems to consider itself immune to questions concerning such problems. In this book, I attempt to develop ways of thinking that might hazard answers to at least some of them.

Prologue: The Universal Library
of World Literature

IN THE HISTORY OF modern language and literature, the enticing
and irresistible thought of literature as a single and world-extensive
reality—*world literature*—has often found an echo in the literary
image of a library that contains everything of value that has ever been
written—a *universal* library containing *universal* literature. Among
the highlights of these interlinked preoccupations might be the following moments and scenarios. On January 31, 1827, at his home in
Weimar, Johann Wolfgang von Goethe surprised an acolyte with the
intimation that he had been reading a "Chinese novel" and went on
to ruminate that "National literature is now an unmeaning term; the
epoch of World-literature [*Weltliteratur*] is now at hand, and everyone
must strive to hasten its approach." But then, as if to mitigate the effects of the dizzying prospect such a statement opened up, he went
on to reassure his friend that "if we really want a pattern, we must
always return to the ancient Greeks, in whose works the beauty of
mankind is constantly represented. All the rest we must look at only
historically; appropriating to ourselves what is good, so far as it goes."
Eight years later, in the midst of the historical process of the colonial
modernization of elites in India in the mid-nineteenth century,
Thomas Babington Macaulay, then a member of the governing
council of the East India Company administration in Calcutta, in
recommending that "a small class" of Indians be educated not in their
own language and tradition but instead in those of another continent,

1

imagined "a good European library," a "single shelf" of which could subsume all that was worthwhile in "the whole native literature of India and Arabia"—as precise an encapsulation as any of the cultural logic of colonial rule. In a lecture delivered in Calcutta in 1907 to an audience concerned with developing an indigenous form of education to replace the colonial one, Rabindranath Tagore asserted that "our goal is to view universal humanity in universal literature by freeing ourselves from rustic uncatholicity . . . and . . . in this totality we shall perceive the interrelations among all human efforts at expression"—attempting to use ideas of national particularity in order to undermine nationalism as such. Writing three decades later (and over a century after Macaulay) in Argentina at the threshold of the transition to a postcolonial world, as European global dominance was coming to an end in an intra-European conflagration, Jorge Luis Borges expanded the limits of the ("good European") library until it became coextensive with the universe itself. Borges imagined this world as the "Library of Babel"—an infinitely expansive labyrinth, a world of bookshelf-lined hexagonal cells and passageways populated by itinerants and pilgrims, librarians, esoteric cults, mystics and fanatics, rival sects fiercely devoted to opposing doctrines about the nature of the library, and rumors about the existence of the one book that contains all the other books that have ever been written or that might be written in the future: a library that encompasses the work of humanity in all its infinitesimal complexity. Composing a novel in England in Arabic a quarter century later, the Sudanese writer Tayeb Salih placed his universal library in a padlocked room in a farmer's home in a sunbaked village on the banks of the Upper Nile, a perfect replica of a private English library—down to author-signed books, framed pictures and mementos on the mantelpiece, carpets, and shawl-draped armchairs—whose existence is unknown to all in the village but its owner and which contains only books in English, "not a single Arabic book," with even "*The Qur'an* in English": this room is a stark encapsulation of the alienated fate of an African and Arab society that has undergone colonization, permanently set on a "migration" toward the North—the central image of Salih's novel. And finally, in Orhan Pamuk's Nobel Prize acceptance speech—written, in the new millennium, in the same apartment building in a bourgeois neighborhood of Istanbul in which he, as he tells us, has lived for most of his life—the author recalled from his childhood his father's library of mostly European and Republican Turkish works, a record of the disorientations of a Muslim society undergoing state-enforced Europeanization, suddenly cut off from the entire literary heritage produced until just a few decades earlier in a version of the same language but in another script.[1]

Goethe and Macaulay's remarks might differ in the aesthetic and humanist *value* they attach to the literatures of "the East," but this is a difference of emphasis alone, both sharing the more important ground of the problem of assimilating them into the European universal library. (As we shall see later on, these distinct but related positions may be identified as "Orientalism" and "Anglicism," respectively.) Each of the above images and elaborations, to which I shall return at more length at various points in this book, is a rich and powerful invocation of "literature" (in a broad sense) as a world encompassing reality. Each was produced in a different language—German, English, Bangla, Spanish, Arabic, and Turkish, respectively—is distinct and different from the others, and emerges from and speaks to a very different historical context. But together they belong to the history of the emergence of a world of peoples, an understanding of the world as an ensemble of nations and civilizations, each in possession of its own distinct textual and expressive traditions. On the one hand, each of them seeks to capture a cosmopolitan or "one-world" reality; on the other, they all seem unable in the end to overcome entirely the pull of the local and the particular. This paradoxical manner of conceiving of human diversity is, properly speaking, European in origin, dating back at most to the mideighteenth century—that is, to the Industrial Revolution. But, as I shall argue at some length in subsequent chapters, such ideas have repeatedly proven their power and efficacy in the world by being absorbed into non-European societies undergoing dramatic transformation under direct or indirect colonial domination. It is, to say the least, ironic that it is on this modern *European* intellectual ground of a theory of literature as *national* institution that colonial intelligentsias have typically staked their claims to historical agency and return to national origins from the disruptions of the colonial process. Given this European genealogy, the nationalist claim to autonomy is clearly an exaggerated or even spurious one, reproducing the *form* of a mode of modern European thinking about culture and society, and therefore it is as sure a sign as any of the "cunning" of (colonial) reason, which itself provides the ground on which a certain kind of anticolonial imagination emerges and elaborates its historical and cultural claims.[2]

If the literary representation of the universal library may be said to be an image of literature as world encompassing reality, the concept of world literature, which has proven equally irresistible at decisive moments in the bourgeois era, is by the same token a systematization of the former. And more concretely, as B. Venkat Mani has noted, the possibility of world literature has been from the beginning closely linked with the social and cultural institution of the library and the historical processes it embodies, the library being an "agent" of world literature.[3] Whether conceived as a collection of works of translocal significance, as David Damrosch has suggested, or as an intellectual problem, way of thinking, or system of organization and cataloguing of works, as it were, rather than a body of writings as such, as Franco Moretti suggests, "world literature" seems to evoke the paradoxical nature of the universal library.[4] Michel Foucault famously described the universal museum and universal library of modern Europe as "heterotopias of infinitely accumulating time" that embodied "the idea of accumulating everything, of establishing a sort of general archive, the will to enclose in one place all times, all epochs, all forms, all tastes, the idea of constituting a place of all times that is itself outside of time."[5] But what is the relationship between this "will" to accumulate time itself and the history of European expansion worldwide, the expansion of the idea of Europe itself as that which contains the entire world? As the above formulations clearly reveal, the very assembling of the universal library seems to highlight some of the complexities of achieving the one world in this particular manner. Clearly, there is something paradoxical about the idea of the universal library, an idea that begins to consume itself in the very process of its elaboration. In its drive toward the universal, it seems inadvertently to heighten the presence and visibility of the particular. And for all its claims to inclusiveness, it cannot quite conceal the asymmetrical arrangement of power that structures it as an apparatus and a field. Who assembles the universal library, under what conditions, and to what purpose? What are its principles of selection, arrangement, and organization? Who, as Mani asks, has "borrowing privileges" from it, that is, who gets to use it and according to what rules, exactly?[6] What, if any, is its dominant language? To whom can it be said to belong? What is the relationship between the *universal* in "universal library" and the *world* in "world literature"?

The global cacophony of the early twenty-first century seems to generate different varieties of what we may call *one-world thinking*—diverse perspectives on contemporary economic, social, cultural, and political life that all nevertheless require imagining the world as a *continuous and traversable space*. This is now a pervasive discourse, informing a wide range of conflicting interests and practices including even forms of right-wing nativism in some cases. Given the ubiquity of such ways of thinking, could the claims being made in this book themselves be understood as an instance of such breezy one-world talk? In other words, in speaking of the one world, how do we not acquiesce in the ideological practices of those dominant sectors of society—including that ultimate abstraction and totality, *global* society—that have most widely produced and circulated this discourse? Navigating in and around this question and problem is one of the challenges taken up in this work. It is or at least ought to be fairly uncontroversial that such forms of imagining the horizon of the social in our extended historical moment, all the varieties of talk of the achieving of a "borderless world," are linked in various ways to the rise of the modern multinational corporation in the postwar era and the governmental, inter-governmental, financial, and commercial structures that have been instituted alongside it, forms that have been extended and intensified in the "neoliberal" post–Cold War era—the various institutional frameworks of the contemporary global capitalist system and world market, in short.

First used in a widely successful book by the Japanese corporate consultant Kenichi Ohmae in the early 1990s, the term "borderless world" was quickly transformed into a cliché—that is, an apparently transparent description of a world condition requiring no analysis of its agendas and interests—finding its way into an enormous body of writing ranging from management studies to the institutional discourse of "global health," academic humanities and social sciences, and even countercorporate activism by professionals in many fields such as medicine, law, engineering, architecture, and teaching.[7] The critical task in our present moment is to try to understand in every instance of the invocation of the borderless world—whatever conceptual or rhetorical form it might take—the precise nature of its links to structures of power across the world: these links range from the reflexive commitments of those media commentators or so-called experts who function as the house intellectuals of capitalism today— think Thomas Friedman or Niall Ferguson—to attempts to appropriate the image of the borderless world for radical politics at various sites across the world.

The financial crisis of 2008–2009 and subsequent recession—and in some countries and regions full-blown depression—were from the beginning a global event and have generated new forms of activism and protest, most notably the Occupy movement, whose methods and gestures have proven remarkably mobile across oceans and continents. On June 15, 2013, Turkish police retook by force Gezi Park in the Taksim area of central Istanbul and cleared it of the "occupiers" who had been protesting for seventeen days the wildly uncontrolled "development" pursued under the ten-year rule of the "moderate" Islamist but *radically* neoliberal Justice and Development Party (the AKP), which has, among other things, created a bubble economy in real estate amid the devastation of historic urban spaces in one of the most extraordinary historic cities in the world. It is worth noting the remarkable fact that among the structures in the park destroyed by the police, as in Zuccotti Park in downtown Manhattan and Syntagma Square in Athens at earlier moments in recent years, was the protestors' spontaneously assembled library. The assembling of a "people's library," as it has come to be called, has in fact been a distinct feature of the new politics of occupation and assembly across the world, a remarkable fact that surely it must be part of our task to try to understand.[8] What is the relationship between "world literature" and these practices of collecting and reading in New York, Athens,

Istanbul, and numerous other sites across the world whose existence is linked to the desire to defamiliarize the everyday structures and practices of neoliberal capitalism? This is neither a trivial nor a merely occasional question—it is, quite simply, one version of the broader question about the *politics* of world literature today as institution and as forms of writing, reading, teaching, valuation, and circulation, and I shall return to it near the end of the book. The people's library embodies the desire not just for different books—than those enshrined in national curricula or literary cultures or in globalized commercial publishing, for instance—but for different ways of reading, circulating, valuing, and evaluating them. As such, it constitutes an important site for thinking about the distinct politics of literature I am attempting to elaborate here.

We may pursue this question (of the politics of world literature) from a somewhat different angle as well. To speak of a borderless world is to suggest the superseding or, at the very least, diluting of the forms of sovereignty that have been institutionalized in the modern system of states perhaps "since the Peace of Westphalia," as the cliché goes.[9] The mere magnitude of such a possible historical development should lead us to be cautious about the casual use of such notions. Official and semiofficial ideologists of European unification, for instance, have routinely represented it as the overcoming of the post-Westphalian order in the continent, whereas in fact many of the concepts, practices, and logics associated with the modern state, such as notions of cultural or civilizational uniformity and the institution of territorial borders, have to a certain extent simply been enlarged and mapped onto the continent as a whole, a process most visible precisely in those border regions and countries, like Greece, where "Europe" comes in contact with its historically determined others. The institution of the nation-state border has indeed undergone a series of transformations in recent decades. But as Sandro Mezzadra and Brett Neilsen have argued in an important recent book, the result has in fact been a *proliferation* of borders rather than their disappearance.[10] And in neoliberal border regimes such as that of the European Union, some of the functions that have traditionally clustered at the nation-state border have come to be redistributed throughout social space. Every point in social space has become, for those who are visibly construed as aliens, a potential site of a border experience, while the ability to cross international borders continues to be distributed unequally among populations defined by class, race, ethnicity, religion, gender, or nationality and usually a shifting combination of these factors.

The fact is that as capital continues to enhance its ability to move and act ever more swiftly across the world, to behave as if it inhabits a borderless world, the conditions of the physical movement of populations, which is necessitated by the economic and political imbalances of contemporary capitalism and the needs of capital itself, become ever more differentiated and, for large numbers of human beings, ever more perilous. Can we really speak of "literature" as a single world-encompassing space without reference to these material and ideological features of the structures of mobility, and therefore also *immobility*, across the globe? We clearly cannot, because the mobility of literature is a social phenomenon, that is to say, part of the wider social phenomenon of mobility and movement as such in late capitalism. But the prevalent literary discussion seems to proceed nevertheless in the blissful serenity of the supposed perception that the age of the *worldwide* has indeed arrived. We are obliged to ask *at which locations in the world exactly* such perceptions of the worldwide acquire their aura of transparency. The international geography of academic conferences, literature festivals, literary prize competitions, and other similar practices of contemporary literature surely facilitates such "beyond borders" perceptions for those of us who participate in them in one way or another. What would it mean to consider these supposedly borderless literary experiences alongside the far more treacherous experience of borders for hundreds of millions of people worldwide? I shall return to the question of the border in our times more directly later in the book, but Chapters 1 and 2 set up the problematic, as I analyze the ways of thinking and writing that have historically played a role in the *cultural institution* of borders in the long era of nationalisms and nation-states, which is of course also the era of the rise of literature as a worldwide system or set of practices. These historically determinate forms of human mobility and immobility institutionalized in border regimes matter a great deal to the line of critical thinking about literature that I develop in this book. I shall seek to demonstrate here that *world literature has functioned from the very beginning as a border regime*, a system for the regulation of movement, rather than as a set of literary relations beyond or without borders. Put somewhat differently, we might say that the cultural sphere now generally identified as world literature, far from being a seamless and traversable space, has in fact been from the beginning a regime of *enforced* mobility and therefore of *immobility* as well.

To be concerned professionally with those cultural and social practices, and more specifically practices of writing, that are generally classified and recognized today as literature is of course to deal with mostly *elite* practices of various sorts in a rigorous sense. In the societies of the Global South, in particular, literary practices typically involve attempts at representation of social worlds from the location of elite segments of society and, in world literature, properly speaking, *globally* privileged segments of society. Given this social distance between the practitioners of literary discourse (including of course criticism as well) and the most deprived strata of society worldwide— from the slum dwellers of the world's megacities, deprived of the most basic benefits of modern urban civilization, to destitute farmers permanently on the edge of devastation from drought, land theft, and the vagaries of markets and prices—any attempt to "incorporate" such social groups and such life conditions in literary discourse is confronted with the irreducible question of the very possibility of representation across the "international division of labor."[11] The work of the critic under such conditions is to reveal the internal workings of such attempts at representation and the social locales (that is, the modes of "filiation" and "affiliation," in Edward Said's sense of these terms) from which they are made.[12] But we also know—as has been argued from a range of ideological positions—that the forms of written language or textuality that we call literature have the capacity to illuminate and help produce knowledge of various aspects of our individual and collective lives in the modern world even when immersed in the life of a small and exclusive class and its everyday milieu. We need think here only of Balzac, Austen, Multatuli, Soseki, Proust, Tagore, Lampedusa, or Qurratulain and the reading of their works by progressive and radical critics (from Marx onward) over the years. The ability to think "the world" itself, whether in literary-critical thinking or other discourses and practices, is hardly distributed evenly across the world, even though its cultivation is an important task and a necessity, given those very asymmetries and inequalities. Miguel Tamen has recently asked with reference to practitioners of the prevalent U.S. academic discussion of world literature, "do they ever get to the World section of their *New York Times?*"[13] The accusative trenchancy of this rhetorical query notwithstanding, there is a genuine question here about our ability to speak of "the one world" from the perch of the academy in the North Atlantic zone and about *what forms of attention precisely* to the world outside this zone are consequently called for. It is this question that I seek to explore in this book.

Forget English! is an examination of the variety of one-world talk that is world literature, and this term will refer to a number of related things in the course of the study: first of all, "world literature" is a *concept* that, I shall attempt to show, has a genealogy that leads to Enlightenment-era intellectual and literary practices; second, linked to the first sense, it marks a contemporary *field of study*, predominantly, though by no means exclusively, in the academic humanities in the North Atlantic countries, a field that has seen a stunning success since the beginning of the new millennium, disseminating its discourse widely throughout the worlds of teaching, research, writing, publishing, and reading; and third, and most broadly, it refers to these *practices and institutional frameworks*, which make possible and compelling the experience of literature as a worldwide reality.[14] The academic discipline of comparative literature arose gradually in the second half of the nineteenth century in Western Europe and North America on ground that had already been prepared by the discourse of world literature, a ground that is revealed, for instance, in the flourishing of literary histories in the period that attempted to take a general or "world" perspective, however limited their actual purview to the major European languages. And a renewed discourse of world literature today, embodied in anthologies, journals, and critical monographs and collections, seems on the verge of taking over completely the disciplinary space of comparative literature.[15] Throughout its history, world literature in each of the senses outlined above has functioned as a *plane of equivalence*, a set of categorical grids and networks that seek, first of all, to render legible *as literature* a vast and heterogeneous range of practices of writing from across the world and across millennia, so as to be able, second, to make them available for comparison, classification, and evaluation. World literature is therefore fundamentally a concept of exchange or, in other words, a concept of bourgeois society. Furthermore, the history of world literature is inseparable from the rise of English as global literary vernacular and is in fact to some extent *predicated* on the latter. At its core, therefore, this book is an attempt to expose and explore the relationship between English and its others, especially the languages of the Global South.

What are the rhetorical and epistemological conditions of possibility of the concept of world literature and whose interests does it serve? Does it make more sense to speak of world literature in the singular or the plural? Is world literature primarily a descriptive or normative concept, and in what way are the two aspects related to each other? What needs in bourgeois society and culture does the concept fulfill? What kinds of literary practice does it reference, envision, or produce? What possibilities does it create (or foreclose) for conceptualizing the universal and the particular? Is "world literature" best understood as system or as practice? What other forms of "world thinking" does world literature rely on or, alternatively, replace or suppress? What is its relationship in this current avatar to, for instance, the literature of Afro-Asian and Global South solidarity or to the literary cosmopolitanism of the Soviet cultural sphere? Linguistic (and therefore "cultural") plurality has historically been a pronounced feature of human life—so what is the fate of this aspect of human experience in globalization? Can humanism ever be monolingual? Is "world literature" an adequate rubric for asking questions such as these? If "Orientalism" is the cultural logic of the modern, bourgeois West in its outward orientation, what precisely is its relation to world literature, the concept of a single literary system or ensemble that, at least in theory, encompasses all the societies of the world? Is philology still the "method" for conceiving of world literature, as it was for an entire tradition of critical thought, including such disparate figures as Goethe, Erich Auerbach, and Edward Said?

And finally, under what conditions exactly—methodological, conceptual, and institutional—can the practices of world literature be revalued and refunctionalized for a radical critique of our world, or "the world made by capitalist globalization," as Pheng Cheah has recently put it.[16] This is the first constellation of questions, concerning the possibility and consequences of thinking of literature as a worldwide reality, with which this book is concerned.

Given the ubiquitous presence of English in the world today, it seems absurd to suggest that it either has been or ought to be—or, even more implausibly, *wants* to be—"forgotten." But if indeed English is now everywhere, then surely it is also not anywhere in particular, and ubiquity or universality entail their own form of invisibility: missing the forest for the trees, especially and precisely when you happen to be *inside* the forest. But "universality" is perhaps too strong a word for our purposes—after all, hundreds of millions of human beings across the world have still little or no access to English and speak, read, or write in one or more of thousands of different existing languages and dialects. It is incontestably the case that the number of languages spoken on the planet has continually shrunk in the modern era and continues to do so in our times and that English, broadly conceived, is often the beneficiary and the agent of such changes. But still—*universal?* And yet, if it is indeed true that there are more people in China with at least some formal instruction in English than there are people in the United States, as is often now said, you know that some great river has been crossed forever.

Coming to the terrain of literature per se, a seemingly simple phrase like "English as a language of literature" appears hardly so simple on closer view, concealing fraught scenarios of linguistic and literary acquisition, assimilation, and dissemination across decades and even centuries. It points us in at least three different directions, each of which offers a certain view of the landscapes through which the others pass: English as the language of original composition ("Anglophone literature"), English as the language of reading ("the Anglophone reader"), and English as medium of translation, evaluation, and adjudication in literary relations on a worldwide scale (that is, in "world literature"). This book is concerned with each of these aspects of what we might speak of as the *cultural system* of English.

"World Anglophone literature" is, in one or another of its variants, one of the ascendant cultural rubrics of our times. This is true as much in academic literary studies as in the wider world of literary publishing. But this rise of the Anglophone has often taken the form of a reification or even an apotheosis; that is, it has been treated as a transparently universal good, not accompanied by a critical self-examination about its own conditions of possibility. How does English become available in a given society for the first time as a language of literature? What is its social position and relation to its various "others"? Through what practices and mechanisms did it come into this position of global preeminence? Such questions, foreclosed in the prevalent discussion, will be confronted head-on in this book. Above all, it asks what it might mean to speak *in English*, the quintessential world-encompassing language, of literature as a world-encompassing reality. Hidden inside world literature is the dominance of globalized English—this is, at the broadest level, the argument that is presented here.

In post–Industrial Revolution colonialism, broadly understood, the language of the colonizer was a problematic and painful acquisition. As a range of anticolonial thinkers and more recent scholars of colonialism have demonstrated over the years, the emergence of a racialized (and agonized) colonial subject was profoundly linked to the colonial language. As Frantz Fanon argued in the early 1950s in his study of the psychology of colonial racism, *Black Skins, White Masks*, language was a privileged site of the work of power in colonized society. Every subject people had experienced "the death and burial of its local cultural originality" and thus found itself "face to face with the language of the civilizing nation." Through command of the French language, he noted, the "Negro of the Antilles," for instance, became "whiter," that is, closer to being a "real man" (*véritable homme*). But the fantasy of linguistic command was just as consistently shattered by the ever-elusive nature of the promised identification—he is merely "quasi-white": "He talks *like* a white man."[17] This ambiguous and ambivalent acquisition of the colonizer's language thus marked colonial subjectivity as an alienated condition, lived in between comfort zones and European and native forms of authority. In his later writings, immersed in the practice of the

Algerian Revolution, Fanon came to view the colonial language as a major site of revolutionary practice itself, which was engaged in the "work of exorcising the French language," exposing both its claim to being *logos* as well as the arbitrary nature of its signs.[18]

Fanon states explicitly that his intention is to "broaden the field of [his] description and through the Negro of the Antilles include every colonized man."[19] This is part of the radiating power of his analysis: making the historical experience of the societies of the Caribbean and, in his later work, Algeria and Africa more broadly exemplary of certain facets of the colonial process as such at a certain moment in its history. To a certain extent, I make similar methodological use in this book of the historical experience of societies in South Asia and the Middle East. But I depart in more significant ways from Fanon's formulation, which has become canonical for a whole swathe of theory and criticism in "postcolonial" and "transnational" studies in the countries of the North Atlantic, an alienated formation in a metropolitan language coming to be seen as the quintessence of the postcolonial condition. For I seek to demonstrate here, first, that the effectiveness of colonial rule extends also to the *ascription* of culture, tradition, and "originality" to the colonized, not simply to their destruction or denigration, and, second, that in neoliberal postcolonialism (to coin a phrase) the place of English (or, alternatively, French) in the relationship between dominant imperial centers and dominated peripheries takes both a much-expanded and dramatically different form compared to the colonial moment elaborated in Fanon's work. And this new worldwide situation of English ought to compel us to a reconsideration of the cultural processes of colonialism itself.

The question of a dominant world literary language is not just part of the subject matter of world literature studies; it has a more foundational relationship to the very concept itself. Auerbach—scholar of Latin and Romance literatures, German-Jewish émigré, one of the founders of comparative literary studies in the interwar and postwar periods, and the author of arguably the most important formulation of the idea of world literature—viewed Goethe's *Weltliteratur* as an attempt to think diversity and uniformity in the same instance. For Auerbach, it was clear that it was precisely the great concentration of human life in the modern era, its convergence and standardization, that had produced such concepts of human diversity as world literature. He argued that if humanity should "succeed in withstanding the shock of so mighty and rapid a process of concentration—for which the spiritual preparation has been poor [*innerlich so vorbereiteter Konzentrazionsproceß*]—then man will have to accustom himself to existence in a standardized world, to a single literary culture, and only a few literary languages, and perhaps even a single literary language." Such an outcome would mean, Auerbach pointed out, that "herewith the notion of *Weltliteratur* would be at once realized and destroyed."[20]

I shall return to Auerbach in some detail in Chapter 4, but suffice it here to say that this notion of a possible future is a "figure" in a precise sense, a rhetorical structure of exaggeration that nevertheless seeks to reveal an actual potentiality in the contemporary configuration of the world. Clearly, as an image of the future, it delineates a utopia and dystopia at the same time, a future toward which we could only take a contradictory stance of revulsion and anticipation: *anticipation* because of its promise of universal human communication—an overcoming of the post-Babel "confusion of tongues," at last!—and *revulsion* because of the loss and violence entailed in its emergence.[21] How close exactly we are to such a condition—one single major language of literary adjudication, translation, and even expression worldwide—is not possible to ascertain with absolute certainty, but from our present historical perspective, it seems fairly evident that if such an eventuality were ever to come to pass, that single "natural" language of world literature would be English—if we bracket off for the moment the question of whether contemporary literary English is one single language. There is no more worldwide a literature today than that in English. And even if it were to be argued, correctly, it seems to me, that we are very far indeed from a single dominant language of literary *composition*, we could nevertheless say that this one language is preeminent in the forms of mediation and adjudication that constitute world literature. It is English that seems to have usurped in our times the ancient Babel dream of universal comprehensibility and communication.

This book is an attempt to think critically (and therefore historically) about the potential worldwide situation of language and literature that is revealed in Auerbach's remarkably prophetic for-mulation of the concept of *Weltliteratur*, written in the 1950s, a bit over sixty years ago, when, to quote a sociolinguist, "any notion of English as a true world language was but a dim, shadowy, theoretical possibility."[22] It is a call for vigilance against ways of thinking that might naturalize and normalize this state of affairs and the forms of historical amnesia it rests on and facilitates in turn. Under the condi-tions of neoliberal capitalism, whenever English rises to dominance in a particular cultural and social sphere for the first time—the ap-pearance and global success of the Pakistani Anglophone novel in recent years, for instance, or that of its Indian predecessor a few de-cades ago—it seems at once to naturalize itself, erasing the scene of politics and power that marks its emergence. This retroactive ability of English in its contemporary "global" form to suspend its own pre-history should be of interest and concern to criticism and to human-istic study more broadly.

The "rise" of English to worldwide preeminence—including literary preeminence—is one of the most pronounced cultural and social developments of the modern era, with profound implications for, among other things, languages and cultures of writing on a world scale. It has been the language of two successive world empires—the territorial British Empire for 200 years from the middle of the eighteenth century and the (for the most part but not exclusively) nonterritorial imperial structures of U.S.-led global capitalism since the middle of the twentieth. However, this institutionalized *visibility* is only part of the story. It is an element in the social situation (and power) of English worldwide that it can assume an aura of univer-sality and transparency, including as language of theory and criti-cism, *disappearing* from view precisely as it assumes various mediating and officiating functions. Any critical account of literary relations on a world scale—that is, any account of world literature as such—must thus actively confront and attend to this functioning of English as *vanishing mediator*, rather than treat it passively as neutral or trans-parent medium, both as a world language of literary expression and as the undisputed language of global capitalism. In fact this role of English as mediator has its own history, from its beginnings in the very inception of world literature in the colonial era to its "globalized" form in our own times.

If English is now incontestably the lingua franca of neoliberal capitalism, the language, for instance, in which individuals in a wide range of professions and in various sectors of industry and finance can most reliably expect to be able to communicate with their counterparts from across the world, then we might say that this book is concerned with a subset of that global linguistic reality, namely, the situation of English as *global literary vernacular*—English not merely as a language of literary expression but as a cultural system with global reach, not simply a transparent medium but an assemblage and apparatus for the assimilation and domestication of diverse practices of writing (and life-worlds) on a world scale. In both these spheres of functioning, therefore—that is, both in its wider role as a global language and in the more specialized role as literary language—English is involved in exchange relations: relations, in other words, in which values are produced and exchanged, where historical particulars are made fungible and put in circulation. As Ronald Judy argued some years ago, this global situation of English on the threshold of the digital era is in a line of development from the politics of language in decolonization, even for former French colonies like Algeria and Tunisia.[23] And I fully share the concerns voiced by those critics who argue that contemporary practices of world literature in North America, given their reliance on translation from the world's languages into English, participate at the very least in a leveling out of linguistic particularities. Emily Apter, for instance, has warned against the emergence of a "translationally translatable monoculture"; Gayatri Spivak has described the situation as the "literatures of the world through English translations organized by the United States"; and Jonathan Arac has wondered whether, given the indisputable fact that writing composed in English is the most worldwide body of literature today, the world-encompassing ambition of world literature could really be at base a case of "Anglo-globalism."[24] But I argue here that the role of "English" in mediating world literary relations predates by centuries the age of globalization, properly speaking, namely, the role that the cultural system of English has played historically in the transformation of these very "other" linguistic spaces, especially those of the Global South, so that it is necessary to displace the question of the postcolonial national language from its fixed place in the politics of authenticity. And it is pertinent to ask whether the modes of production and dissemination of "theory" itself, especially Franco-American poststructuralist theory, constitute today a subset (and motor) of this monoculture.[25]

Subsequent chapters will thus examine the long prehistory of these more recent changes of the postwar era in the social situation of English as a world literary language. How historically has the cultural system of English played the role of absorbing and appropriating distant and diverse modes of life into the expanding bourgeois world? How exactly does it become available as a literary language for the first time to a society in which it does not originate? How may we describe the relationship between contemporary English in its global role as a language of literature and its various linguistic others worldwide? Is it a situation of hegemony, strictly speaking—a normalized and naturalized power—or a form of domination that is incomplete and contested, and if so, in what ways, exactly? What is the role played by English as cultural system in the great epochal shift we think of as the "modernization" of literatures written in those other languages? How are we to conceive of the prehistory of the contemporary "Anglophone" novel, which clearly plays a disproportionate role in the circuits of circulation and validation of world literature? Is it descended from non-Anglophone narrative traditions (in Asia or Africa, for instance) or from the eighteenth-century "Oriental tale" in Europe? What exactly is its relationship to the life-worlds that it claims to depict but that are not lived in English? Could the same be asked, at a different level of analysis, of the novel written in such languages as standardized Arabic, Hindi, or Urdu? What is the role of English in the creation of world literary publics through translation and other means? What role does it play in determining which forms of writing "make it"—and which do not—into world literature? What forms of (literary) mobility in the world does English represent? What does it mean that the discussion about world literature takes place disproportionately in the Western languages and above all in English? But *wherever English is or goes in the world, it is dogged by its various others*—this is the basic premise of the argument presented in this work, which it variously assumes, defends, or elaborates. In order to be understood as critical thinking, properly speaking, criticism in English thus bears toward *itself* the responsibility of "unflagging vigilance against any fraud it promotes," to quote Theodor Adorno on the responsibility of "the returning émigré" toward the language and world that are his or her own but from which he or she has been violently separated.[26] It is this vigilant and split relationship to English that this book seeks to cultivate—in English. It is of course hardly possible (let alone desirable) to literally "forget English" in our present conjuncture, but in this book, I insist on the necessity and possibility of thinking past, around, and *about* it. This is the second set of questions— concerning the global situation of literary English—that will concern us here.

If "English" is the ether that permeates the space of world literature, a third set of issues pertains to the *cultural logics* that world literature embodies and represents. I approach this problem by offering a historical argument, namely, that world literature had its origins in the structures of colonial power and in particular the revolution in knowledge practices and humanistic culture more broadly initiated by Orientalist philology in the late eighteenth and early nineteenth centuries, which developed in varying degrees of proximity to the colonial process. In historical terms, my main thesis is thus that *a genealogy of world literature leads to Orientalism*, a fact that the contemporary discussion appears by its very nature to be incapable of recognizing. More specifically, this genealogy leads to the classical phase of modern Orientalism in the late eighteenth and early nineteenth centuries, an enormous assemblage of projects and practices that was the ground for the emergence of the concept of world literature as for the literary and scholarly practices it originally referenced. Furthermore, the cultural and social logics which, since the appearance of Edward Said's landmark study, we have called Orientalism, *continue* to structure the practices of world literature, even when in transformed and updated forms that do not allow the continuities to be perceived immediately as such—hence the need for a genealogy, that is, a critical-historical examination of a certain constellation of ideas and practices in its accretions and transforma-tions over time.[27]

Orientalism (and world literature) are thus approached here as an articulated and effective imperial *system of cultural mapping*, which produced for the first time a conception of the world as an assem-blage of civilizational entities, each in possession of its own textual and/or expressive traditions. This "scene" of world literature's emer-gence in colonial capitalism was thus irreducibly a *political* one in a larger historical sense, and the contemporary practice of world lit-erature in all its senses under neoliberal global capitalism remains equally a politically fraught process—a politics of culture that it is the aim of genealogy to unmask and to make available for criticism and analysis. In other words, we might say that if the concept of world literature always contains within itself an attempt (or at least the desire) to bridge the social distance between the First and Third Worlds, between the centers of the world system and its peripheries, our name for the logic of this bridging is "Orientalism." I should note, however, that the method adopted here—the assembling of a wide and textured cultural archive and in fact the purposeful artic-ulation of distinct bodies of work and text—diverges from that which is conventionally associated with genealogy at the present moment, which often consists of the isolated manipulation of a single concept, sometimes with reference to centuries and even millennia, in the course of a few pages.[28] To this limited extent, it is closer to the method followed in *Orientalism* by Said himself, who, after defining Orientalism as "an exercise in cultural strength," had immediately cautioned that "it is better not to risk generalizations about so vague and yet so important a notion as cultural strength until a good deal of material has been analyzed first" (*O*, 40).

Despite the reputation of Said's book as a sort of foundational text for concern with cultural relations on a planetary scale, the specifics of that book's conceptual armature or the archive with which it en-gages do not seem to play a significant role in the present discussion and intensification of interest in the effort to comprehend literature as a planet-wide reality. This is certainly the case with Moretti's numerous and influential writings on the subject, although he was for many years a colleague of Said's, and even in Pascale Casanova's

World Republic of Letters, whose English translation was published in a series edited by Said. And the recent attempt by Theo D'haen to write an overall history of the concept of world literature from its nineteenth-century origins into our own times gives scant attention to the role of Orientalist practices in its emergence and subsequent development.[29] The fact that this is a somewhat elementary observation about these influential works does not make the facts any less striking. Such elisions imply that the discussion more or less forecloses an adequate account of the asymmetries and inequalities of the institutions and practices of world literature. As will be familiar to readers of Said's work, he describes Orientalism as a highly effective and "worldly" but *protean* object of knowledge, requiring dynamic and varying definitions that shift according to conceptual constellation and perspective. Here are some of his well-known formulations from the early pages of the book: "Orientalism is a style of thought based upon an ontological and epistemological distinction made between 'the Orient' and . . . 'the Occident'"; from the eighteenth century on, it "can be discussed and analyzed as the corporate institution for dealing with the Orient—dealing with it by making statements about it, authorizing views of it, describing it, by teaching it, settling it, ruling over it"; it "*is*, rather than expresses, a certain *will* or intention to understand, in some cases to control, manipulate, even to incorporate, what is a manifestly different (or alternative and novel) world"; it is "a system for citing works and authors" and "a library or archive of information commonly and, in some of its aspects, unanimously held"; and it is "a kind of free-floating mythology." What such diversity of definition and designation reveals, first of all, is the complex nature of the object named in the title of Said's study. He is keenly aware of the fact that "Orientalism" is a *composite* object, a suturing together of disparate practices, representations, works, motifs, "projects," institutions, and archives, whose very deliberate articulation in an act of intellectual imagination makes visible the larger underlying network of relations between them. What emerges from this range of definitions is a conception of a mode of *action* and effectiveness in the world, a will and an intention, furthermore, "that is by no means in direct, corresponding relationship with political power in the raw, but rather is produced and exists in an uneven exchange with various kinds of power." When I speak of Orientalism in this study, therefore, I refer, as does Said, to a particular "nexus of knowledge and power" or a type of knowledge in its worldly "career" (*O*, 2, 3, 13, 23, 41, 53, 27, 5).

The same year as the appearance of Said's *Orientalism* saw the publication of Bryan Turner's *Marx and the End of Orientalism*, a quiet little book that was unfortunately eclipsed by its bigger and more brash contemporary. But there are significant areas of overlap between them. Turner defined Orientalism as "a syndrome of beliefs, attitudes and theories which infects, not only the classical works of Islamic studies, but also extensive areas of geography, economics and sociology." It led, Turner argued, to the production of "internalist" theories of the history of Middle Eastern societies, viewing them as stagnant and unchanging due to a range of their internal features, from attenuated class structure to reliance on traditional forms of authority. The historical form of such theories was often a sort of reverse teleology—an initial efflorescence followed by decline. And this picture of Islamic civilization was drawn precisely in contrast to an ideal type of the Western societies at the center of the world capitalist system. Orientalist knowledge-claims were thus essentialist in two related ways, positing, on the one hand, a conception of "Islam" as a "coherent, homogeneous, global entity," and, on the other, a "decline thesis where Islam is seen as declining because of some flaw in its essence."[30] Furthermore, Turner argued, the Marxist tradition, and Marx himself, while trying to break out of the Orientalist "syndrome" and its many essentialisms often relied on and reproduced precisely these characteristic assumptions and conclusions. But Said, it seems to me, took the argument further, viewing Orientalism not merely as varieties or modes of *misperception* of "Oriental" realities but rather as knowledge practices embedded in the historical process of the *production* of those very realities. More broadly, we might therefore say that, historically speaking, "Orientalism" is the name of the *cultural logic of colonial rule* in the post–Industrial Revolution era, that is, the cultural logic of the bourgeois order in its outward or nondomestic orientation.

In establishing this usage, however, it is important at the outset to make one clarification. For scholars of the British Empire, the word

"Orientalist" has specific historical resonances in tension with "Anglicist"—as the names of the two sides in the great colonial debate about the nature and direction of British rule in India that lasted for several decades from the late eighteenth to the middle of the nineteenth centuries and ranged across an expanse of practices and institutions, including education, law, art and architecture, and urban planning.[31] The former referred to those administrators, ideologues, and ideas of colonial rule that advocated a "preservation" of native forms under British tutelage, while the latter signified those that called for the transformation and rationalization of at least segments of native society along bourgeois-European lines—their *Westernization*, in short. (*Anglicism* is thus simply the name for the project of Westernization as practiced within the British Empire.)[32] The text of Macaulay's with which I began this prologue is of course a leading and well-known expression of the Anglicist side of this debate. I shall argue at various points in this book, however, that Orientalism, despite its rhetoric of "preservation" of Asiatic forms, in this sense itself represented as much of a logic of sociocultural *transformation* (and in fact Westernization) as Anglicism did, requiring the *Orientalization*, as it were, of the social and cultural forms under its purview. Furthermore, Anglicist and Orientalist ideas and practices, properly speaking, overlapped considerably in ways that remain invisible to those historians who take their polemical self-definitions at face value.[33] It is not always understood that Said, in his powerful designation of Orientalism, whether deliberately or otherwise, collapsed these supposedly mutually antagonistic tendencies—a *productive* conflation, as it turns out, since it allows us to glimpse the colonial logic in its entirety, though not always in its internal complexity. In this book, I too collapse the two from time to time in line with the current usage but at relevant points will also elaborate the distinction between them in order to explicate their distinct work as elements or moments within the overarching and contradictory logic of sociocultural transformation under colonial rule.

At the present moment, at least in literary studies, attention to Orientalism seems to have reverted more or less exclusively to the form of cataloguing representations of this or that social collective in this or that body of Western literature. While I recognize the value of this form of scholarship, my contention is that the critique of Orientalism must ultimately lead us to the Orientalized spaces themselves. For "Orientalism" consists of those Western knowledge practices in the modern era whose emergence made possible for the first time the notion of a single world as a space populated by distinct civilizational complexes, each in possession of its own tradition, the unique expression of its own forms of national "genius." It is the name for the vast cultural apparatus in modern Western culture for the establishment of identitarian truth-claims around the world—an *imperial* task, par excellence. A precise aphoristic formulation of this question comes in one brief luminous sentence in Said's essay on the late works of Jean Genet: "Imperialism is the export of identity."[34] But it should be understood that this is a broad historical statement; the actual modalities of the varieties of Orientalisms in their social effects in the range of societies with which they are concerned vary a great deal from pace to place and time to time.[35] As Stathis Gourgouris has shown, even northern European philhellenism of the eighteenth and nineteenth centuries worked in this manner when directed at contemporary Greek society. It represents, he argues, a colonization of the realm of the *ideal* rather than of the real.[36]

It is symptomatic and significant, therefore, that when Said turns to thinking explicitly about the implied reader of his text, he can only describe a *dispersed* figure, split between different social locations worldwide. In addition to "students of literature and criticism," "contemporary students of the Orient," and the "general reader," Said writes, his critique of Orientalism is directed toward "readers in the so-called Third World": "For them this study proposes itself as a step toward an understanding not so much of Western politics and of the non-Western world in those politics as of the *strength* of Western cultural discourse, a strength too often mistaken as merely decorative or 'superstructural.' My hope is to illustrate the *formidable structure of cultural domination* and, specifically for formerly colonized peoples, *the dangers and temptations of employing this structure upon themselves or upon other*." Recalling Antonio Gramsci's assertion in the *Prison Notebooks* of the "imperative" to produce an "inventory" of the "infinity of traces" that the historical process has left on the critical subject itself, Said makes a remarkable confession: "Much of the personal investment in this study derives from my awareness of being an 'Oriental' as a child growing up in two British colonies. All of my education, in those colonies (Palestine and Egypt) and in the United States, has been Western, and yet that deep early awareness has persisted. In many ways my study of Orientalism has been an attempt to inventory the traces upon me, an Oriental subject, of the culture whose domination has been so powerful a factor in the life of all Orientals" (*O*, 24, 25). The Orientalized subject has a split "awareness" of itself, a divided consciousness of the self produced as other and, inversely, as the object of the historical will, intention, and "project" of an other. Thus, far from ignoring the possibility of historically autonomous action on the part of the colonized and far from viewing Orientalism as a totalizing and absolute system of representation from which there is no escape, as some readers have suggested over the years, Said's critique of Orientalism amounts to a *call* to precisely such action, an invitation to historical self-transformation in the very process of the "critical elaboration" of the self.

Said places the rise of modern Orientalism within the general process of secularization of Western culture in the early modern era. His account of this process is of some interest to us here:

> Modern Orientalism derives from secularizing elements in eighteenth-century European culture. . . . But if these interconnected elements represent a secularizing tendency, this is not to say that the old religious patterns of human history and destiny and "the existential paradigms" were simply removed. Far from it: they were reconstituted, redeployed, redistributed in the secular frameworks just enumerated. For anyone who studied the Orient a secular vocabulary in keeping with these frameworks was required. Yet if Orientalism provided the vocabulary, the conceptual repertoire, the techniques—for this is what, from the end of the eighteenth century on, Orientalism *did* and what Orientalism was—it also retained, as an undislodged current in its discourse, a reconstructed religious impulse, a naturalized supernaturalism. (*O*, 121)

Said's critique of Orientalism is thus in essence criticism of its, we might say, "naturalized supernaturalism," of its remapping of

humanity in terms of supposedly secular cultural logics whose Man-
ichean modalities with respect to human collectivities, and in particular those societies that are Christianity's traditional antagonists,
can only be understood as a "reconstructed religious impulse."[37] The
doctrines of Orientalism, its repertoire of authoritative representations of Oriental-Islamic societies, thus constitute "a secular post-
Enlightenment myth whose outlines are unmistakably Christian" (O,
115). It is in this sense that *Orientalism* may be said to offer an account of the cultural logic of (Western) bourgeois society in its global
or outward orientation, in its encounter with and reorganization of
human societies on a planetary scale. Against this, as it were, *false*
appearance of the secular in history and its attendant antagonisms—a
fundamentally localized (that is, Western) emergence that simultaneously carries the force of the universal in history—Said points not
so much to a utopian and distant future without those, as it were,
theological antagonisms as to the question and possibility in the historical present of "surviving the consequences" of these structures
and logics "humanly" (O, 45).

Said conceives of this anti-identitarian imperative as the classically
secular-critical task, concerned with the here and now, attentive to the
dense and ultimately inassimilable fabric of society. It is no accident
that "Secular Criticism" is the main conceptual essay of the first book
that follows *Orientalism* in Said's trajectory, for it may in some important ways be read as a methodological reflection backward on the
critical project of the latter. As I have argued elsewhere, the figure
of Auerbach exiled in Istanbul that provides a sort of running leit-
motif in that essay is an exemplary figure for secular criticism in
Said's terms precisely because, as a figure of displacement and dis-
possession, it marks a certain distance and fissure from the tran-
scendentalization of cultural authority, forms of reckoning cultural
community, transmission, and descent that are based, as it were, on
the "quasi-religious authority of being at home among one's people."[38]
The critique of imperialism (and of Orientalism more specifically)
is inseparable for Said from criticism of culture as transcendental-
ized authority, all those cultural forms, both the conventionally religious and the supposedly secular, whose appeal to authority is placed
outside the fabric of social interest and the possibility of historical

transformation. For instance, in comparing Macaulay's appropriation and dismissal of "the native literature of India and Arabia" in line with the logic of colonial rule and John Stuart Mill's exclusion of the colonized peoples from the space of "liberty" as such—these two iconic moments of liberal imperialist thought in the nineteenth century—Said notes,

> Both are related to the point I made earlier about Auerbach, that culture often has to do with an aggressive sense of nation, home, community, and belonging. . . . Macaulay's was an ethnocentric opinion with ascertainable results. He was speaking from a position of power where he could translate his opinions into the decision to make an entire subcontinent of natives submit to studying in a language not their own. . . . In turn this validated the culture to itself by providing a precedent, and a case, by which superiority and power are lodged both in a rhetoric of belonging, or being "at home," so to speak, and in a rhetoric of administration: the two become interchangeable.[39]

Secular criticism is thus a radically historical practice, opposed in concrete and detailed ways to metaphysical grounding and authorization of culture, both secular and religious, constantly unearthing its social filiations and affiliations and identifying the "human" costs of failing to subject to such criticism the process of critical thinking itself.

This elemental aspect of Said's project is either lost on those of his current readers who have found their way to the emerging orthodoxy of the "postsecular" or political-theological in the humanistic disciplines and yet cannot quite do without Said's understanding of imperialism in its cultural and epistemological dimensions, or it is actively disdained for its investment in the secular imagination and in criticism itself.[40] Taking up this concern once again, I am interested here in the significance of historical Orientalism for the fabrication, in non-Western societies in the course of the nineteenth and twentieth centuries, of forms of cultural authority tied to the claim to authenticity of (religious, cultural, and national) "tradition"—*turāth*, *rivāyat*, or *paramparā* in some of the languages that will concern us here—and thus, given the links between such forms of authority and the *majoritarian* state in the modern era, for the emergence of the kinds of social fissure that have often accompanied such transitions. Both religious and secular traditions in this sense in the modern era—the Arab tradition and Islamic orthodoxy, for instance, or Indian civilization and Hinduism—are products of the Orientalist conjuncture and, far from excluding the religious, the secular cultural complexes have themselves been produced by their anchoring in religious elements configured in majoritarian terms.

If *Orientalism*, despite its wide reputation, remains still a strangely misunderstood and underexplored book, this is possibly because readers in the literary-critical disciplines are generally still not trained to be at ease in at least some of the "Orientalist" archives with which it engages, and those readers who are professionally assigned the mastery of those archives in the division of labor in the humanities sometimes respond defensively to its relentless (and occasionally overreaching) criticism of their disciplinary methods and procedures. The entire problematic of whether European writers and scholars engaged in the representation of non-European realities were exercising their power over those life-worlds or engaged in genuine attempts to overcome the limits of their own cultures or societies— whether they were humanists or racists, to put it somewhat bluntly, in terms of a supposed binary that does not quite hold—preoccupies even so perspicacious a historical scholar and reader of literature as Srinivas Aravamudan, who argues, against what he takes to be Said's position, that the writings of what he felicitously calls Enlightenment Orientalism were "not just bent on the domination of the other but also aimed at mutual understanding across cultural differences."[41] Who in their right mind could really argue to the contrary? Certainly not Said, though the problem may in part be due to the rhetorical register of parts of the argument in *Orientalism*, where Said seeks to trace his larger theme of power and knowledge at the level of individual writers and their mind-sets or even intentionality, leaving itself vulnerable to such a reading if read in isolation. But why should we read such passages in isolation from the rest of the book or from the enormous body of Said's other writings that clearly point away from such a possible reading? At one level, in fact, Said is concerned precisely with demonstrating in what (different) ways exactly Western Islamophilia and Islamophobia constitute distinct but related varieties of Orientalism. In other words, when a late eighteenth- or early nineteenth-century European writer turns to "India"— available to him or her first and foremost as a newly canonized textual corpus—for a stock of motifs and images, explicitly with the hope of overcoming the limitations or provinciality of hitherto existing European ideas about literature, culture, religion, or antiquity, he or she is still engaged in an exercise that is fundamentally European in nature, that is, *embedded* in a strong sense in the centers of the emergent world system and concerning its peripheries.

The *material* effects of these textual practices on those other societies—they are material because they are social and political— some of which I explore in this book, are fundamentally asymmetrical and unimaginable in reverse. As Said pointed out, for instance, with decisive implications, 'Abd al-Rahman al-Jabarti's *'Ajā'ib al-āthār fi al-tarājim wa al-akhbār* (a mostly untranslatable title in rhymed prose that may be rendered very roughly in English as "Marvelous Traces of Discourse and Events"), a chronicle of life in Egypt that provides a contemporary Egyptian account of life during the Napoleonic invasion of 1798, could not possibly have the same material presence in the world as the massive compendium *Description de l'Égypte*, compiled by the team of scholars who had worked under the auspices of the military invasion.[42] Intentionality is not irrelevant to this mode of cultural and social analysis, but it is far from being the exclusive or even dominant mode of determining the "worldly" reality, as Said calls it, of cultural practices, including textual ones. This is what Said references as "contrapuntality," the imperative to excavate the material inequalities of texts as events in the world and the asymmetry of cultural transactions, not some happy-go-lucky concert of the world's peoples and civilizations. In fact, contrapuntality is in one sense precisely a critique of this (European) view of the world as an assemblage of supposedly equal peoples, nations, or civilizations, produced and developed in exactly the decades (and more broadly centuries) of an ever-accelerating conquest of these very societies and civilizations and their rendering into—in Marx's words, from writings on colonial India to which I shall turn in some detail in Chapter 1—a "heap of ruins."[43] The entire globally dispersed twentieth-century project of "decolonizing the mind," in the felicitous phrase of Ngũgĩ wa Thiong'o, is based on a clear-sighted recognition of this historical reality.[44]

It has become de rigueur in books concerning world literature—even those that are critical of its claims—to perform ostentatiously the global crisscrossing that the concept itself seems to call for, producing almost a distinct style of writing, typified by the stringing together of the names of (say) a dozen different writers from several countries repeatedly into as many paragraphs as possible. I proceed somewhat differently here, providing a critical historiography, first, of the concept itself and, second, of its applications and consequences with respect to one region of the world and its languages and literatures. This emphasis in the book is on the archive of literature either from or concerned with the Indian subcontinent and, more precisely, its northern region. The varieties of Orientalism that will concern me are therefore primarily Indological—mainly British but also French and German—and "classical" (that is, concerning Sanskrit) as well as "vernacular" (especially concerning Urdu and Hindi); but the framework brought to its study is a comparative one, and whenever possible and necessary, I also address questions that pertain to Persian, Arabic, and even Turkish Orientalisms and literatures. I seek to elucidate how "India" has been implicated in the mutual entanglement of Orientalism and world literature but also, more crucially, how it can also be a site for a *critique* of this entanglement. How exactly are we to conceive of Orientalism as the genealogical origin of world literature? What is the relationship in this regard between Orientalism as a scholarly activity and as imaginative literature? If Orientalisms of all varieties can be understood as generating discourses of authenticity, as I have argued earlier, what precisely is their relationship to nationalist claims to authenticity over and against the historical disruptions of the colonial process? This is the third group of questions, concerning Orientalism as the cultural logic of bourgeois modernity in its outward orientation, that will concern us in this book. But more broadly I hope to demonstrate what consequences follow for our critical practice if we explicitly link the question of Orientalism to that of world literature, a linkage required by the history of these two formations themselves.

It will therefore be clear, I hope, that the book seeks to present a *comparatist* approach to the history and contemporary worldwide situation of English as a literary and cultural system and its role in the emergence and functioning of world literary relations. But by no means is it meant to provide an exhaustive account of even the skeletal structure of literary relations on a "world" scale, let alone the sinew and muscle that make them whole. This is an argument about one distinct line of development from emergent cultural practices in eighteenth-century Europe, a line of development that is embedded in the social life of English as a language of literature, Orientalist scholarship, colonial and postcolonial pedagogy, and imperial administration and power. "English" is clearly a single thread in a much-larger historical weave, and I have no doubt that from other linguistic, literary, and historical locations—say, the Slavic sphere in the early Soviet decades, the discourse of literary modernity in Meiji and Taisho Japan, the emergence of a globalized literary French in our own times, or even the distinctly German trajectory of the concept and its dissemination through the world of publishing and therefore of reading practices—the pattern might look substantially different.[45] This multiplicity is in fact the very point of my argument here, as the plural nouns in the subtitle of the book are meant to indicate: the discourse of world literature, even in its most triumphalist "one-world" moments, reveals the multiplicity and particularity of its purportedly unitary object and relies on a range of Orientalist notions and practices for the arrangement and comprehension of its textual materials. But it is also my conviction that the pattern I describe here is a central and significant one, first of all because it is not entirely without influence on these other cultural configurations but also because it is a prototypical case, *exemplifying* some of the decisive structures, asymmetries, and routes and modes of cultural transmission in the modern world in the colonial and postcolonial eras.

The problem of Orientalism as I have sought to redefine it here is the crucial missing link in preeminent contemporary accounts of world literary relations, even those that are broadly sociological in their conceptual orientation. In Damrosch's work, the role of the Orientalists is typically viewed as a neutral process of the discovery and insertion of non-European textual exampla in the (European) sphere of world literature, rather than as the politically charged process of acquisition and assimilation that I take it to be. In the case of Casanova and Moretti, the elision could be laid at the feet of world-systems theory itself, which both authors rely on in their works. World-systems theory has been criticized by humanists for its deterministic economism, its inability to attend to the specific sociocultural logics that institute the inequalities between "centers" and "peripheries," to the reality of antisystemic pressures and projects, and to the fact that no social system, no matter how comprehensive, can consume and exhaust the forms of social and cultural life, let alone all possibilities of thought and imagination. Although these criticisms are at least partially correct, they miss the point with regard to the humanists' task in this connection—the possibility (and usefulness) of a critical engagement with the center-periphery model that would make it more responsive to these problems, the application of a humanistic supplement to its rigidly economistic forms.[46] The model is for us an unavoidable one, making visible at the very least the systemic *aspects* of relations of inequality on a world scale, and I myself rely on it to a great extent in this book. And whereas the recent discussion appears to reveal a certain strain, if not outright hostility, between those who employ a "center-periphery" conceptual framework and those more reliant on "empire-colony," I see the tension between these rival frameworks as a *productive* one and based within their somewhat different relationships to the historical as such. The former model represents a certain abstraction from the historical process of the constitution of empires and their colonies, which allows, among other things, a broadening of its field of application, incorporating, as it does, postcolonial relations as well. But this does not mean that the latter polarity is itself not the result of abstraction from the historical process. On the contrary, it very much marks a conceptual abstraction but one that grants to the historically particular a certain visibility rather than subsuming it entirely into the language of generality by making any specific particular more or less equivalent to all other similarly situated particulars. Throughout this book, I therefore alternate between these usages, using each one to modify and enrich the perspectives made possible by the other.

The problem with Moretti's and Casanova's use of the center-periphery model is its wholesale and largely uncritical and positivistic "application."[47] This means that each of them fails to understand the nature of the very social and cultural processes that assign societies, languages, and practices of writing either to the center or to the periphery. Precisely how literary traditions or intelligentsias acquire the one status or the other in the world literary system—or that of "semi-periphery" somewhere in between the two—is a question that remains foreclosed in their works. In Moretti, the question seems to be avoided by simply mapping the world literary system onto the world-system as such in Immanuel Wallerstein's original sense, as its superstructural aspect, so that centers and peripheries in either, it seems to be assumed, more or less correspond with each other.[48] And Casanova, attempting to avoid this strong economism, can go no further than a vague notion of the "autonomy" of the former from the latter. Their respective works are salutary in having emphasized *inequality* as the primary structural principle of world literary space rather than *difference*, which has been the dominant preoccupation in the discussion of world literature since the late eighteenth century, including in Goethe's late-in-life elaboration of the idea of *Weltliteratur.* But they give us no account whatsoever of the exact nature of these forms of inequality and the sociocultural logics through which they have historically been instituted, logics for the institution of inequality that *incorporate* notions and practices of "difference" and proceed precisely through them. It is these logics that I refer to collectively as Orientalism, or, rather, Orientalism-Anglicism, in this book. But beyond this failure to understand the mutual imbrication of inequality and difference, Moretti and Casanova also share an evisceration of an entire other dimension of the idea of world literature from its inception: namely, its normative force and its links to a historical and teleological conception of humanity that views the world as historical and intersubjective horizon rather than simply as a certain extent of geographical space populated by objects—either by literary genres that circulate between centers and

peripheries (Moretti) or by centers that adjudicate the literary productions of the peripheries (Casanova), as we shall see in more detail
in subsequent chapters.[49]

In his fine study of the Latin American novel in a global frame,
Mariano Siskind has made a distinction that is useful for our purposes here, distinguishing "the globalization of the novel" from "the
novelization of the global." The former refers to the worldwide spread
of the novel as a genre in the course of the nineteenth and twentieth
centuries from its origins in a handful of languages in the western
European countries, while the latter signifies the very treatment of
"the global" within this globalizing form: the first points to the systemic (and, for Siskind, more or less invariant) processes of the universalization of the bourgeoisie and the preeminent place of the novel
form within that historical process, while the second indicates the
varieties of strategies used by individuals and groups of writers to
bend the form to their local needs as members of an emergent
bourgeoisie. The first points to an externalist approach to the novel,
whereas the second points to an internalist one. To this extent,
Siskind seems to be following the structure for novel studies established by Moretti in his two-volume compendium and collective study
of the novel across the world.[50] I shall return in a later chapter to
evaluate the merits of Siskind's argument about the novel as a "universal" form. But two related problems with his argument are worth
outlining here in order to further define the line of argument I am
elaborating. The cultural relationship between emergent bourgeoisies in the world's peripheral regions and the bourgeoisies of the
world centers, Siskind argues, is marked by a *desire* for modernity
on the part of the former, which takes for them the form of emula-
tion of the latter. This claim, which he makes with respect to the
Latin American intelligentsia in the nineteenth century, could be extended, with minimal modulation, to many other regions of the colonial world, including the ones that will concern us here. But Siskind
goes further and argues that consequently "the operation of universalization that constitutes the discursive basis for the globality of
the novel should not be understood as an instance of the periphery's
cultural subordination to the core. . . . That is, in the nineteenth
and early twentieth century the representation of the particularity

of bourgeois European culture and its institutions as universal was an enterprise shared by intellectuals and practitioners both at the center and at the margins of a global discursive field that sanctioned the universality of the novel-form."[51] At various points in this book, I shall proceed precisely on the premise that the expressed desire for bourgeois modernity among colonial intelligentsias is a sign not of the absence of (colonial or imperial) domination or subjugation but rather precisely of such relations of inequality. The very use of the term "globalization" for eighteenth- and nineteenth-century historical realities leads to a circularity of argument in Siskind's work: once that earlier historical process is given the name "globalization," its differences from the processes in our own times become occluded. It obviates the historical specificity of colonial relations within a somewhat ahistorical model of centers and peripheries. At the very least, then, we might say that the concept of world literature is always marked by an attempt to conceive of the universalization of certain aspects of modern bourgeois culture and society. In fact it appears to be *forced* to confront this issue even when it seems like its particular deployment in any given context might be intended to avoid it.

In Chapter 1, I begin by laying out the conceptual and historical groundwork for the study as a whole. The main historical premise here is that what we call modern Orientalism is merely the cultural system that for the first time articulated a concept of the world as an assemblage of "nations" with distinct expressive traditions, above all "literary" ones. Orientalism thus played a crucial role in the emergence of the cultural logics of the modern bourgeois world, an element of European *self*-making, first of all. But as Raymond Schwab observed a long time ago, the philological revolution also sought to make the world *whole* for the first time, and it is this specific *modality* of making the world whole that will concern us here.[52] At the center of this worldwide enterprise was of course the British Empire, arguably the most linguistically diverse imperial formation in the history of the world. The very birth of modern philology, and of the comparative method as such at the center of the modern humanities, was directly linked in a myriad of ways to this complex historical conjuncture, as a wide range of scholarship has demonstrated over the years. I seek to demonstrate here in concrete historical terms that world literature was from the beginning an eminently Orientalist idea, made possible by the new philological and institutional practices that made up the world of modern Orientalism. Its emergence was contingent not only on the dissemination of the textual materials made available for the first time by the Orientalists' translational labors but also on the canonizing of Orientalist procedures and concepts of cultural difference as such. In the first section of this chapter ("Historicism and Orientalism: Reading the World"), I seek to demonstrate that such Orientalist ideas were inseparable in their emergence from the forms of philosophical historicism that are contemporary with them, and I discuss these links in some detail through the writings (and influence) of Johann Gottfried Herder, William Jones, Wilhelm Schlegel, and Goethe. Decades before Goethe's first use of the term, Herder and Jones had laid its basis in their respective theories of the mutual relations between the languages and cultures of the Old World, and in Schlegel's work, as Michel Foucault observed in *The Order of Things*, the modern Indological paradigm achieved its settled form at the center of the philological humanities.[53] And in the second section ("A Heap of Ruins: Colonialism, Capitalism, World Literature"), I demonstrate that world literature was from its inception a concept and a practice, in a strong sense, of bourgeois society, that is to say, a concept of exchange, and that this fact was first understood by Marx and Engels in the *Communist Manifesto*, less than two decades after Goethe's coining of the term. They viewed it as part and parcel of the bourgeoisie's continuous attempt to create a "world market," which entailed (and continues to entail) the almost continuous and massive destruction of lived social and cultural forms across the world's diverse societies. I seek here to restore Marx to the contemporary discussion of world literature, from which he seems to be often missing, even in the work of Casanova and Moretti, each of whom represents a variant of a sociological approach to the question. Every occasion of the achieving of a "world" status by a local practice of writing must be understood as an element within a new phase in the history of the development of the "world market." (I reserve Auerbach's remarkable intervention in the history of the concept of world literature, and the use made of it by Said, for separate and fuller treatment in Chapter 4.)

In Chapter 2, I turn to the process I call the *institution of Indian literature*. The primary argument developed in the first part of this chapter ("Calcutta Orientalism, Phase I: Europe's Age of *Śākuntala*") is that the conditions for the development of the concept and the practices of world literature were first established in the new Orientalist philology that began to appear in the 1770s and especially the Indology that emerged as part of the work of the colonial state in Calcutta in that decade—what I am calling *Calcutta Orientalism*. This revolution in humanistic knowledge affected European culture profoundly, a second ("Oriental") renaissance in the West, as Schwab called it a long time ago, but more importantly, from my perspective in this book, contributed to a slow but cumulatively massive *Orientalizing* of culture in the colonized society itself. I examine the first emergence of the idea of a unique Indian civilization in this corpus, its dissemination throughout the European literary sphere, and its eventual installation in Indian society itself as the core cultural belief of the new, English-educated middle-class that emerged in different parts of India in the course of the nineteenth century. It is at the core of my argument that Orientalist theories of cultural difference are grounded in *a notion of indigeneity as the condition of culture*—a chronotope, properly speaking, of deep habitation in time—and that therefore *nationalism is a fundamentally Orientalist cultural impulse*. To take just one small example from the twentieth century, without the institution of this structure of knowledge, which was the result of the long work of Orientalism in the course of the nineteenth century, some of whose elements will concern us here, the structure of the historical narrative presented in so canonical a work of nationalist thought as Jawaharlal Nehru's *Discovery of India* (1946), in which the nationalist consciousness and imagination emerge at the end of a long arc of development out of Indic-civilizational roots, is unthinkable. I trace some of the variety of ways in which practices of indigeneity came to be installed in Indian society in the nineteenth century, instituting the canonization of ancient Sanskritic culture as the unique civilization of the subcontinent, the possibility of historical descent from which became the test of indigeneity in contemporary society for diverse social groups, cultural practices, and social imaginaries. This in my view is the full arc of the historical dialectic of Orientalism and/as world literature in its relation to culture and society in the subcontinent.

The institution of "Indian literature," that is, the single event of its emergence and insertion into the space of world literature, was thus a deeply fraught event, leading to social and cultural cleavages whose effects are still with us today. If these Orientalist practices were first developed in the Sanskritic preoccupations of the "first phase" of Calcutta Orientalism, the second, namely, the colonial project of the standardization of the "vernacular" languages, especially from 1800 onward, established them in a wider cultural terrain. My focus in the second section of the chapter ("Calcutta Orientalism, Phase II: What Is the 'Language of Hindoostan'?") is therefore on the question of the now-split vernacular of North India, namely, Hindi-Urdu—identical at the level of spoken language but now in many ways distinct in terms of "higher" vocabulary and literary practices (and of course in orthographic terms). I chart the effects of indigenization as an Orientalist practice on this linguistic-literary field and examine the transformation of the pluralist logic of this cultural space as it entered the (colonial) "world republic of letters" and was submitted to its logic of indigenization. This indigenizing logic of linguistic differentiation provided the cultural basis for the ultimate differentiation and standardization of two distinct political identities along religious lines in North India and infiltrated the cultural politics even of those regions, like Punjab and Bengal, that were, strictly speaking, outside this linguistic zone. This politics of linguistic and literary indigenization is a distinct element in the larger historical process that culminated in the religio-political partition of India in 1947 and is thus at the same time an important element in the history of the worldwide institution of world literature. In the third and final section of this chapter ("Literary History and the Beginnings of Colonial Time"), I argue that literary modernity, properly speaking, in (colonized) societies like India subject to Orientalist practices may be said to begin not so much with the emergence of such characteristically modern genres as the novel, as is often suggested or even just assumed, but rather with the acquisition of a canonical *literary history* by a premodern corpus of writing. I demonstrate the way in which the (modern) linguistic split in the linguistic and literary field of the northern Indian vernacular was actualized by the canonization of two distinct (and rival) literary histories for its corpus of writing.

In Chapter 3, we come to the situation of English as a "global" literary language in the postcolonial era and the structure of its relations to its various "others" worldwide, in particular the so-called vernacular languages of the Global South. I examine this relationship both in general terms and within a variety of modes of Anglophone writing itself. In the first section of this chapter ("A World of English"), I analyze the modes of domination of English as literary language and cultural system, which now constitute the preeminent ground of adjudication and assimilation of diverse bodies and practices of writing into world literature. Using South Asia once again as my main archive, I argue that the relationship of English to the Indian vernaculars in our own time replicates and updates the cultural logic of the colonial state at the threshold of the Anglicization of segments of the elites in Indian society in the mid-nineteenth century. In the second part of the chapter ("'Out of the Garrets of Bloomsbury': The Anglophone Novel from Anand to Aslam"), I trace the persistence of the Orientalist versus Anglicist debate of the early colonial state in debates in our own times about the Anglophone novel and its apparent role in world literature as India's "representative" literary form. The chapter presents a critical theory of this form, the Anglophone novel in and from the subcontinent, in relation to its vernacular linguistic environment, from the 1930s to our contemporary moment. Taking Mulk Raj Anand's *Untouchable*, which is situated historically at the culmination of the colonial process and the threshold of decolonization, as the starting point for my analysis, I analyze the tensions that constitute the Anglophone novel as a form. Taking Salman Rushdie's works as emblematic of the "boom" in Indo-English fiction, I then analyze the ways in which these later novels stage their own relationship to the vernaculars—"subaltern" speech forms, for instance, or vernacular literary cultures, such as that of Urdu. Signs of these literary and cultural others of English often appear within these novels packaged as the vehicle for the pleasures of the form itself. Finally, I turn to the contemporary emergence of an Anglophone novel practice in Pakistan that is being widely hailed as the arrival of a new literature not only for Pakistan but for South Asia as a whole—such writers as Nadeem Aslam, Kamila Shamsie, and Muhammad Hanif. The tension between English and the vernacular—voice and imagination—is renewed and reinscribed in a handful of these works through an engagement with Urdu and its social worlds. Hovering above these works, I argue, is the question of the possibility of a distinct "Pakistani" historical experience and its representation in "epic" form. And in the final section of the chapter ("The Ghazal among the Nations"), I turn to Anglophone poetry, namely, the translingual (and transnational) poetic practice of Agha Shahid Ali, self-described "Kashmiri-American," one of whose most remarkable experiments has been the transposition of Urdu poetic forms and rhythms into writing in English. All these Anglophone authors—variously validated in the contemporary space of world literature—are immersed in the question of the nationalizing (that is, *partitioning*) of society, culture, literature, and social imaginaries in the subcontinent in the twentieth century and thus offer us resources for thinking about the historical arc of the dialectic of indigenization and alienization whose philological archive I analyzed earlier.

In Chapter 4, the focus turns once again to the concept of world literature itself to examine its refashioning in the work of Auerbach and the engagement with it by Said, bringing to my reading of Auerbach the genealogy of world literature I have developed in earlier chapters. Much of the argument here takes the form of a close engagement with Auerbach's landmark essay "Philology and *Weltliteratur*," which I situate in its historical moment, the Euro-Atlantic aftermath of war, genocide, and imperial decline. In the first section of the chapter ("The One World and the End of World Literature"), I examine the dialectic of the universal and the particular that Auerbach attributes to the concept and with which he engages in a productive manner. The figure of the philologist in Auerbach's essay is, I further argue, a figure for the cosmopolitan European subject in the transition to the postcolonial world, attempting to refashion its cultural authority in the wake of these momentous historical transformations. I read this figure alongside that of the ethnographer in

Claude Lévi-Strauss's *Tristes Tropiques*, a contemporary work that shares with Auerbach's essay the European pathos of the emerging one world.[54] The philologist and the ethnographer in these works are figures for the humanist European subject and for the European subject as humanist, produced in distinct disciplinary formations but sharing this ground of the reconstitution of the European subject put under stress by historical developments—above all, decolonization as a world historical event. And in the second section of the chapter ("A World of Philology"), I examine Auerbach's (and following him, Said's) *exilic* rethinking of the philology of world literature. Auerbach's innovation in the history of elaborations of this concept is the decoupling of modern philology—his "method" for the study of world literature—from the organicist forms of historicism in which it had been born in the late eighteenth century and its rearticulation with the exilic imagination (and exilic experience) in the twentieth. He accomplishes this in part by counterposing Vichian historicism to the Herderian, and it is this rearticulation of philology that Said takes as his own starting point in his engagement with Auerbach's work. Said's critique of the Orientalist dimension of modern philological practice, with its ties to the imperial process, which had remained unmarked and therefore unexamined in Auerbach's writing, completes the transition. Said rewrites Auerbach's high-modernist motif of (European) exile as the affective and cognitive orientation of the criticism of culture and society and their relation to the structures of domination in the contemporary world.

I began this prologue with various instances in modern literature of representations of the universal library as figures of world literature. I conclude now with a concrete embodiment of this figure by turning to an institution in a city that, as in the colonial nineteenth century, is once again one of the financial centers of the world economy. As Mani has noted, much as "literature codes the world in verbal and aural signs and promotes representation—aesthetic, epistemic, political—libraries present themselves as prolific, substantial, and expansive 'texts' that rely on the collective knowledge about the world." Housed in its "new" building in the London neighborhood of St. Pancras, the British Library presents itself as one such text, encoding the multilayered historical processes of its origin and development, the "historical contingencies that condition accumulation and classification, circulation and distribution, patronage and accession, orderly organization and disorderly contention."[55] It has largely silenced early critics of its design since opening to the public in 1997, the critics having famously included Charles, the endlessly waiting heir to the throne and amateur critic of modern architecture, who derided the design as reminiscent of both a train station and a secret police academy. The broad consensus since it became the functioning home of the United Kingdom's "national" library is that whatever it may lack in its exterior design, it more than makes up for in its interior, a warm and inviting set of spaces conducive to research and writing. Visitors enter the building from the large street-level plaza, which is dominated by the Scottish-Italian artist Eduardo Paolozzi's bronze *Newton*, a giant mechanical, nuts-and-bolts man, seated and leaning over, in the manner of Isaac Newton in William Blake's well-known print, engrossed in making measurements with a mathematical instrument on the ground at his bare feet. (In the print, it is on an unrolled length of parchment that seems to be an extension of the mathematician's body.) Paolozzi thus makes reference in his sculpture to each side of the "two cultures" of knowledge—science and mathematics as well as the arts and humanities, and Enlightenment as well as Romanticism. On entering the building through the main doors, visitors find themselves in a cavernous hall that is several stories high, with windows, balconies, and overhangs at various levels overlooking the entrance space from various directions. Toward the back of this enormous space is a dimly lit, rectangular glass tower that rises in the middle of the building, emerging seemingly from below street level and rising up into its upper reaches. On one floor, the tower is surrounded by a railing that can be approached by visitors for a closer look at the tower's contents. It is full of books—old books, including many impressively large volumes, most bound in morocco leather, the spines beautifully tooled in gilt.

The collection known since 1973 as the British Library—which is, by most measures, the largest library in the world—came into formal existence through a series of donations to the British Museum in the early years of its existence in the late eighteenth century.[56] This included the handing over by King George II in 1757 of the so-called Old Royal Library of the English sovereigns, whose contents were absorbed into the museum's general collections. But a second royal "gift to the nation" by George IV in 1823 of the roughly 60,000 books and 19,000 pamphlets of the so-called King's Library came to acquire a special status in the museum in Great Russell Street in Bloomsbury, eventually acquiring a new gallery for its storage and display (now known as the Enlightenment Gallery). The collection donated by George IV had been built largely by his father, "mad" King George III, as befitting the monarch of an emergent modern empire and is considered by the institution of which it is now part as "one of the most significant collections of the Enlightenment," containing many of the earliest printed books, the collection as a whole ranging from the mid-fifteenth century to the early nineteenth.[57] There is something endearing about this gesture, which speaks of domestic dramas—one imagines the son, having been relegated for nearly a decade to the role of regent, belatedly inheriting the throne in his late fifties and sweeping the house clean of the possessions of his deranged and demanding parent. The books in the glass tower in St. Pancras are the contents of the mad King George's library. As an architectural element, the tower thus makes a powerful statement about the historical continuity in British life from the monarchical order to a bourgeois and democratic one—from "Royal" to "British" or "National" institutions. It seems to commemorate the slow transformation of an absolutist monarchy into a modern bourgeois nation-state anchored to its past through a constitutionally constrained monarch and suggests that in this "gift" from the king to the people, in this transformation of the private collection of the king into a public institution, the cultural patrimony of the modern nation was born.

Situated on an upper level and toward the back of the British Library building is what is now called the Asian and African Studies Reading Room. Here, scholars can consult, along with other materials, the vast collections of what used to be the India Office—and before its creation, the East India Company—the institutions through which Britain's Indian possessions were governed over the centuries, first on behalf of the board of directors of the company and, after its dissolution following the brutal suppression of the Great Rebellion of 1857, known to colonial historiography as the Sepoy Mutiny, the ministers of the Crown. The entire central archive of the British administration of India is available for scholars to peruse in this reading room. But besides these official records, printed books, maps, photographs, personal papers, and other materials, the India Office collections include a large number of manuscripts "in the Oriental languages," as the catalogue description has it, including precious volumes in Sanskrit, Persian, Arabic, and a number of the vernacular languages of the subcontinent. In many cases, these are the only known copies of the works in question, and they were acquired at various times throughout the life of the East India Company and its successor. As briefly described in a small bibliographic pamphlet titled *Urdu Language Collections in the British Library*, available to readers in the reading room, the manuscripts "were acquired from various sources but before the early twentieth century the majority came from the libraries of Indian princes and retired servants of the East India Company and the India Office." The manuscript holdings, we are told, are "rich and varied, with many rare items of literary or artistic merit. [They contain] some of the earliest Urdu manuscripts extant today, a large number of autograph or otherwise distinct items, and several fine examples of calligraphy and illumination. Poetry forms the backbone of the collection, especially genres favored by early and medieval Urdu poets."[58]

Of the eight "special collections" known to contain manuscripts in Urdu, the first to be listed is called the Delhi Collection, and its description, of admirable brevity, reads as follows: "Consisting primarily of Arabic and Persian works, the collection represents about three-fourths of what remained, in 1858, of the royal library of the Mughal Emperors. . . . In 1859, the Government of India purchased the remnants of the royal library for just under 15,000 rupees at a sale organized by the Delhi Prize Agents. In 1867, 1,120 volumes, the less valuable of the manuscripts, were sold. The remainder, approximately 3,710 volumes, were transferred to the India Office [in London] in 1876. These include 144 items in Urdu."[59] "Delhi Prize Agents" is one of those euphemisms that are ubiquitous to the culture of British imperialism, like "District Collector" for the official tasked with extracting agricultural revenues from a population of cultivators in a rural administrative district. It refers to the individuals appointed by the army to give some semblance of order and bureaucratic efficiency to the unhindered universal looting by British soldiers of all ranks throughout the city after its recapture in September 1857 from the Indian rebels who had held it for much of the summer during the Great Rebellion. Individual British officers made their fortunes in the immediate aftermath of victory, but the prize agents, who had entered the defeated city in the footsteps of the victorious soldiers, continued their "work," meticulously recorded, into the 1860s. The "Delhi Prize" is a recurring subject of the discussions among officials in India and in London during these years that are preserved in the Parliamentary Papers, but it is only one such rubric, similar designations ("Lucknow Prize," "Jhansi Prize," et cetera) being utilized to indicate the loot acquired in other centers of rebellion throughout the affected areas of North India.[60] Every colonial war or campaign in India won by the colonizers (and numerous "scientific" expeditions) produced such loot, including some more famous objects, such as the notorious Koh-i-noor diamond, now set in a Maltese cross in the so-called Queen Mother's crown among the crown jewels on display in the Tower of London, and the throne of Maharaja Ranjit Singh, on display at the Victoria and Albert Museum, both acquired in the defeat of the "last major indigenous power in the subcontinent," the Sikh kingdom, in 1849.[61] Not to put too fine a point on it, then, the Delhi Collection of manuscripts in the British Library consists of the remnants of "the royal library of the Mughal Emperors" that was taken from the fort in Delhi in the aftermath of the summer-long siege of the city, in the midst of the massacres, demolitions, banishments, and other forms of collective punishment that reduced it to a ghost town in the matter of a few months.

Why have I chosen to conclude my introductory remarks about the project developed in this book, which concerns the feasibility of the contemporary concept of world literature, with this little "reading" of the disparate contents of the British Library? It is a tale about the visibility and invisibility of the different components of the national library of the United Kingdom and, more broadly, about the extremely asymmetrical and unequal formation of the archive in the modern world. I have read it admittedly as a parable of sorts, but what kind of parable, exactly? Why should we care about the fate of *any* king's possessions? And what, if anything, does it tell us about the contemporary compulsion, institution, promise, and failure that is world literature? At one level, this is a story about the extraction of value—symbolic and cultural as well as material—by the colonial powers from their conquered and administrated territories. It seems to highlight the powers of absorption of the "good European library" in the era of European expansionism that was so powerfully evoked by Macaulay twenty years before the Indian rebellion in a bureaucratic debate about the future of education in Britain's Asian colony—powers that have social, political, military, and even epistemological dimensions. But it foregrounds other kinds of asymmetry in the world as well. No impressive architectural structure is ever likely to house *this* king's library in the land where it originated. Governments in both India and Pakistan have demanded the restitution of the Queen's gaudy diamond—a claim needing to be publicly rejected as recently as February 2013 by a sitting British prime minister on a visit to India—but so far as I know there is no record of any state in the subcontinent showing any interest in the restitution of the Mughal library.[62] This lack of interest in the former royal library of the Mughal rulers of India is no doubt a small detail in the life of the elites that ascended in 1947 to the helm of the state that had been fashioned by colonial power—by dividing it into two (and, later, three) states—but it is not a trivial one and speaks volumes about their intellectual, political, and social instincts and capabilities.

We might make a few initial observations concerning this situation. First, it reflects the tawdry and thoughtless consumerism of the ruling classes in the subcontinent and the region more broadly in the era of neoliberalism, elites that typically desire shopping malls, not libraries. (The Indian ruling class of the Nehruvian era represents the most obvious counterpoint to this contemporary situation.) It is a desire that can overpower even religious piety of the most conservative sort, as evident in the hideous shopping-mall-hotel-condominium complex, including a grotesquely enlarged and kitsch facsimile of the (already kitsch) Big Ben clock tower, with the expression "Allahu akbar" inscribed above the huge clock face, that now looms over the Kaaba shrine in Mecca. It was built—by the Binladen construction and real estate conglomerate—after the demolition of a historic hilltop Ottoman citadel that had itself been built for the protection of the shrine, which was repeatedly threatened by, among others, Wahhabi iconoclasts, in the eighteenth and nineteenth centuries.[63] The Abraj al-Bait tower complex, which includes a twenty-story-high shopping mall, is reportedly only the first of its kind, and more are in the planning. It is thus possible that the Saudis may in effect be secularizing the sacred geography of Mecca and the surrounding region in ways that recall the fate of formerly sacred spaces of pilgrimage sites in the advanced capitalist world, such as Santiago de Compostella in northwestern Spain, surrounding it with the paraphernalia of well-heeled tourism. This would be historically ironical if we follow Americo Castro in his understanding of the apostolic cult itself as Iberian Christendom's response to the orientation of the dominant "caste" in the peninsula—that is, Muslims—toward the Hejaz and more precisely the shrine in Mecca.[64] From Istanbul to New Delhi and beyond—by way, we might say, of Dubai—the shopping mall may be the characteristic modern architectural structure of our times in the region, marking the arrival at a certain form of late modernity.

More pertinent to our present concerns, however, is the fact that a narrative of historical continuity of the sort promoted by the glass tower in the British Library does not seem to be possible in the postcolonial subcontinent, even in India, whose "national" culture can of course marshal powerful chronotopes of antiquity, as we shall see in subsequent chapters. The historical experience of being colonized—that is, the transition to capitalism and bourgeois modernity under the conditions of colonial subjugation—introduces historical disruptions that cannot be subsumed in a narrative of continuous historical development, as is possible in metropolitan societies—hence the specific forms that the crisis of authenticity (the desire for a return and restoration to an origin) takes in postcolonial societies. But in South Asia there is an additional complexity as well: the "Mughal" (and, more broadly, "Muslim") can only function at the limits of these "Indian" chronotopes that posit an *Indic* core as the ever-present origin, thereby appearing as modes of interruption of the national historical narrative. When, for instance, Nehru, in his famous speech at the moment of independence from colonial rule, spoke of the present as that rare historical moment in which "the soul of a nation, long suppressed, finds utterance," the historical temporality inherent in that statement was far from an unambiguous one, quite independently of the speaker's intentions. More precisely, we might say that the statement marks the *indecision* in nationalist culture regarding the length of the interregnum in national life—whether it corresponds to the 200 years of British rule or to the millennium since the arrival of Islam in the subcontinent.

And the "national" nature of Pakistani state narratives is of course always in question, made incoherent by the fact, as Rushdie put it memorably three decades ago, that "Indian centuries lay just beneath the surface of Pakistani Standard Time."[65] From Aziz Ahmed's *Studies in Islamic Culture in the Indian Environment* to Aitzaz Ahsan's *The Indus Saga*, defense of the view of Pakistan as the logical culmination of some underlying process of millennial historical development in the subcontinent—a distinct Muslim collective life from the very beginning, in the case of the former, and the civilization of the Indus riverine system reclaiming its independence from the plains of North India, in the latter—has typically involved an unembarrassed disregard for long-established and even incontrovertible historical facts.[66] On the one hand, the Indic as a secular concept of culture tied to the (Indian) nation-state—the concept of the latter is anchored in that of the former—works to conceal its own religio-political (that is, modern) markings. And, on the other, Pakistani nationalism, which seeks to replicate the procedure of the (Indic) national, fails necessarily in this project precisely because, as the nationalism of a minority marked by religious difference, it cannot quite suppress its religious markings. *Literature*—that is, the modes of writing, reading, teaching, circulation, and historicization that conform to the now-global category of literature—has played a distinct and unique role in the historical process that has installed these complexities and contradictions in the social and cultural lives of the societies of the subcontinent.

This "reading" of the structure of the British Library, the universal library par excellence in our times, as a sort of parable in brick, steel, glass, and mortar about sociocultural realities on a global scale is not meant as a morality tale and should not be confused with an attempt to "justify and defend the innocence which confronted modern Western colonialism"—a form of sentimental thinking that has become popular over the past several decades among sectors of the Indian national intelligentsia.[67] The "document of civilization" that was the "royal library of the Mughal Emperors" was itself also patently a "document of barbarism," that is, a distillation and concretion of distinct forms of historical violence and the exploitation of human beings. It would be absurd to attribute a historical innocence to it in its moment of encounter with the Euro-colonial bourgeois order, as it would be meaningless to attempt to "justify and defend" its right to exist. And this individual act of plunder is of course merely one, and a latecomer at that, in a whole series of events that repeatedly destroyed and reshuffled the contents of major collections in the subcontinent and its neighboring regions over the course of the previous several centuries.[68]

The multiple resonances of this cultural "transaction" or event, whose history is both embodied and hidden away in the British Library, must be sought in the vastly different fates of these two libraries in the transition to the modern world, in the historically significant but unremarked absorption of the one by the other. It reveals for us something crucial about aspects of the constructing of this world itself. "World literature" came into being (only) when the cultural system of the modern bourgeois West had appropriated and assimilated—that is, "discovered," absorbed, recalibrated, rearranged, revaluated, reclassified, reconstellated, compared, translated, historicized, standardized, disseminated, and, in short, *fundamentally transformed*—the widely diverse and diffuse writing practices and traditions of the societies and civilizations of the "East," which extended in the Euro-Occidental imagination from the Atlantic shore of North Africa to the littoral of the Sea of Japan. So the organization of the disparate contents of the United Kingdom's universal library makes clear the fuller resonance of the statement that "the whole native literature of India and Arabia" could be subsumed into "a single shelf of a good European library." And the seizing of "prize" from a premodern social economy and its being put into circulation in a capitalist world economy is thus not merely an effective *image* for this epochal shift in the relations between the North Atlantic "center" of the world system and its various peripheries in the "East." We should view it as a *concept* for this historical process of appropriation that is immanent to that process itself, developed and used internally by its various actors.

Hamra Abbas's remarkable four-panel artwork, *All Rights Reserved* (2006), an image from which is used for the cover of this book, is a distillation of these issues at the intersection of culture and possession, knowledge and appropriation, and the histories of imperialism and nationalism. The image is based on a detail from an illustration in a famous Mughal manuscript of the Padshahnama (Pādśāhnāmeh, 1656–1657), a Persian-language history of a portion of the reign of Shah Jahan (r. 1628–1658), which is the personal property of the English monarchs as part of the so-called Royal Library housed at Windsor. The stunning double-page image in the original depicts the wedding procession of Dara Shikoh, the great scholar, prince, and martyr for an ecumenical vision of religion and governance in the subcontinent, whose succession of his father was usurped by his younger half brother, Aurangzeb, whose subsequent rule is associated with religious orthodoxy and the consolidation of sharia and who has consequently served as the bête noire of nationalist and progressive thinkers and commentators at least since the middle of the mid-nineteenth century.[69] The detail itself shows a number of figures, probably servants and even slaves, carrying tribute and gifts for the King on the occasion of his son's wedding. The piece is remarkable for its detail of depiction of the subaltern retainer class of the Mughal imperial context, including racially and regionally recognizable faces, from Persian and Turkic ones to a *ḥabaśī* ("Abyssinian," that is, black African).

The illuminated manuscript was "acquired" in the late eighteenth century in Lucknow, from the library of the princely rulers of Avadh (usually transcribed as "Oudh" in colonial times) and presented as a personal gift to George III by John Shore (Lord Teignmouth),

Governor-General of the company's possessions, a close friend of William Jones, and the author of the first "memoir" of Jones's life compiled from his letters and other writings.[70] The title of Abbas's work is taken from the catalogue of a rare exhibition of the manuscript, and the detail we are concerned with here is itself on the cover of the catalogue.[71] Her technique is basically to change the image enough to be able to use it without violating the Royal Collection Trust's proprietorial rights. She has whited out the trays of tribute that the servants are carrying on their heads and reproduced them in an identical placement on another panel of the work. All these layers of density in the history of this manuscript are resonant in Abbas's work, from the contemporary artwork's relationship to precolonial art, its misplaced tribute, we might say—she was trained in the so-called neo-miniature practice developed at the National College of Art (NCA) in Lahore—to the unavoidable detour through the (institutional as well as conceptual) networks of the "Orienalist" historical configuration. In other words, the work is a sort of brooding (but also sharply sardonic) reflection on cultural possession, (mis)appropriation, reclamation, and translation—all in the context of the global neoliberal "intellectual property" regime and its descent from the colonial world.[72] The legal claim to possession mimicked in the title of the work—"All Rights Reserved"—becomes a metaphor for a wider cultural predicament: postcolonial aesthetic practice cannot imagine its own history as a linear one but rather one characterized by distance, detours, and displacements.

Forget English! is a study of this larger process of assimilation and its consequences for the structure of relations between different languages, traditions, literatures, intelligentsias, and reading publics on a world scale and seeks to make a number of interventions. It enters the ongoing discussion about the globalization of literary relations from a sharply critical angle, discovering in the contemporary world structures and relations whose genealogy takes us to the national, linguistic, continental, civilizational, and racial definitions, asymmetries, hierarchies, and inequalities of the colonial era. It insists in particular on the need to consider the social and cultural situation of the languages of the Global South at a range of locations in world society, from subnational ones to the global horizon itself. In most of the societies of the South, English is never spoken (or written) out of hearing (or writing) range of its various others, a basic perception that this book takes seriously as the starting point for an understanding of the role of English as a world literary language, including as a language of criticism. And it demonstrates that "world literature" itself has always signified a system of unequal relations between a handful of Western languages—above all English—and these languages of the South. But an unmediated and uncritical notion of the "vernacular" or particular—and this is perhaps the politically most consequential argument presented in this book—has never been able to mount an adequate critique of the "cosmopolitan," global, or universal, since, far from being a space of unmediated autonomy, it has itself been constituted through the processes of the latter. Neither side of this debate about literature and culture as a worldwide reality seems capable of dismantling the essentialism through which it views the cultural products of the societies of the global periphery. A politics of language, literature, and culture affiliated with the struggle for survival and autonomy of postcolonial societies must therefore configure differently the relationship of the cosmopolitan and the vernacular, the universal and the particular, in order to facilitate ways of thinking about culture and society that do not simply replicate the extant antinomies of power on a world scale, and it is to such a politics that this book seeks to make a small contribution.

It is not an accident, therefore, that the title of this book takes an imperative form. "Forget English!" is the imperative for Anglophone criticism to take seriously and examine critically its own historical situation as a discourse in a *particular* language and cultural system, relying on the latter's historical rise and *worldly* success, which includes the ability to provide the conditions of legibility of diverse and heterogeneous practices of writing in numerous languages as (world) literature. English as a language of literary and cultural criticism exercises no less a dominance today than it does as a language of imaginative literature, and it has become, among other things, for instance, the means of circulation of Continental "theory" worldwide. Whereas English was once the vehicle for a distinctly Anglo-Saxon tradition of critical thinking—from Matthew Arnold, T. S.

Eliot, and the *Scrutiny* writers to Northrup Frye or the U.S. Agrar-
ians and New Criticism—it now distributes globally a mode of
thinking, namely, "theory," that claims to come from nowhere in
particular. It is indeed in this manner that post-1970s Continental
theory and its American modulations (and especially deconstruction)
have typically been disseminated in the literary spheres of such languages as Arabic, Hindi, and Urdu in recent years—as the most
advanced and in fact universal approach to the reading of literature.
As both an intellectual-critical and pedagogical exercise, therefore,
"world literature" can only mean taking such a critical and *skeptical*
attitude toward the modalities and the possibility of achieving the
one (literary) world, the possibility of assembling the universal library. If, on the one hand, I urge world literature studies to take
seriously the colonial origins of the very concept and practices they
take as their object of study, on the other, I hope to question the more
or less tacit nationalism of many contemporary attempts to cham-
pion the cultural products of the colonial and postcolonial world
against the dominance of European and more broadly Western cultures and practices. In sum, therefore, this book attempts to open
up the current discussion about world literature to a number of larger
questions of social theory—from the constitution of nation-state sovereignty, its social and cultural logics, and its ties to the colonial
order to the nature of the global imperium in late capitalism.

Let me end here on a note that is both personal and methodological in nature. This book is concerned with the possibility of humanistic knowledge of social and cultural forms in the Global
South—the "Urdu ghazal" or "Anglophone novel," for instance—the
societies outside the traditional circuit of the European and more
broadly Western humanities or, more accurately speaking, placed in
various ways at the margins of their intellectual universe: constituted
as objects of knowledge for Orientalism, anthropology, or comparative literature. In other words, I am interested here in the possibilities
of knowledge across the imperial divide and the international division of labor. I view this as simultaneously a theoretical and historical question, that is, as a line of conceptual analysis necessitated by
the historical formation of the modern humanities in relationship
with the geopolitical structures of power of the modern world in

both the colonial and postcolonial eras. My own training was inter-disciplinary, in two separate humanistic disciplines, namely, literary studies and anthropology (both the British/social and American/cultural varieties), with an added dose of Islamic-Arab area studies. As is now well understood, each of these disciplines contains a distinct Western practice for the understanding of non-Western social and cultural realities, each organized around a concept of culture and each with its own distinct notions of social, cultural, or linguistic difference and particularity.

The practices and ideas associated with anthropology and literary studies are very much part of my intellectual makeup, but I have come to view myself as situated at a certain angle to each of them. Each appears to me, as a knowledge practice, to be marked in its own distinct way by problems and shortcomings in its attempt to bridge the social distance between its own world and that of its objects. To some extent in my work, I have therefore used the location of each as a basis for the examination of the methods and possibilities, as well as limitations, of the other. Anthropology, in its insistence on an experiential encounter with the social life-world that is the object of research, should be a corrective for postcolonial or transnational literary studies in the Anglophone North Atlantic, which too often consist of mastering a now largely settled canon of two dozen or so novelists, mostly of English, which is added to with the first books of bright young things from time to time. No detailed knowledge of the languages, history, politics, and conflicts of the countries or regions in question appears to be necessary in order to claim "expertise," not even knowledge of the concrete and material situation of English in those societies. On the other hand, the emphasis on textuality, that is, the insistence on the codified and mediated nature of all social and cultural experience, and therefore the insistence on the necessity of *reading* and interpretation, is a challenge to the traditional positivistic anthropological predilection for, as it were, "just the facts, ma'am," to quote Sargent Joe Friday, an early fictional icon of the city where I live. This positivism seems to have survived in some of the supposedly most "advanced" forms of anthropological thinking today, even as they draw on the so-called antifoundation-alist aura of French poststructuralist theory. The criticism of extant practices in literary studies around the concept of world literature that is offered in these pages draws, in a self-critical way, on this double intellectual and disciplinary legacy.

I am aware of running the risk that what I have to say in this book might be misconstrued as the (heavily footnoted) flashing of a middle finger at existing practices in the discipline of literary studies and the ways in which it conceives of the contemporary literary world. Dear Reader, avoid that temptation. There is no polemical intent here, just an *attempt* to think critically about our concepts and categories or "the way we think now" about the world in which we live.

1

Where in the World Is
World Literature?

EVEN AS "WORLD LITERATURE" becomes part of the intellectual vocabulary of a wider public sphere beyond academic humanities circles, at least in the Anglophone North Atlantic, it is sometimes difficult to see it as much more than an arcane preoccupation of students of literature, of little interest even to scholars in the other humanistic disciplines, from art history to anthropology. This is at least in part due to developments in the literary field itself, which has seen a resurgence of specialization and seems less and less to engage questions and ways of thinking that have bridged disciplinary boundaries in recent years. More concretely, in the current revival of the concept of world literature, something of considerable importance appears to be largely missing: namely, the question of Orientalism. While the authority of Edward Said's *Orientalism* has become more or less incontrovertible for broad sectors of the critical humanities, the book also seems to be treated as a work firmly situated in the past, whose historical achievement may be appreciated but whose methods, archives, and larger stakes have been largely superseded by the emergent realities of our world. I do not think that it would be an exaggeration to say that the present interest in literary relations as a planet-wide reality bypasses the question of Orientalism's "worldly" efficacy almost entirely. It may actually be the case that, despite the massive pedagogical consequences of Said's book over the past few decades, people trained as critics and scholars of literature are nevertheless still not comfortable in engaging with the Orientalist and area studies archives. The modern discourse of world literature thus pays scant attention to the very historical process that is its condition of possibility, namely, the assimilation of vastly dispersed and heterogeneous writing practices and traditions into the space of "literature." This process of assimilation is an *ongoing* one, repeated constantly in the very forms of circulation that constitute world literature. It is the origins and historical unfolding of this process that I shall explore in this chapter and Chapter 2.

Historicism and Orientalism: Reading the World

We might begin to address this problem with a discussion of Pascale Casanova's widely cited *World Republic of Letters*, a work that has generated a broad discussion since its translation into English, which presents an argument about the emergence of international literary space in Europe in the early modern era and its expansion across the continent and beyond over the past four centuries. The overall armature of the book rests on the identification of three key moments in the development of this international literary space and seems to follow fairly closely the chronology established by Benedict Anderson in *Imagined Communities*.[1] The first, its moment of origin so to speak, is the extended and uneven process of vernacularization in the emerging European states from the fourteenth to the seventeenth centuries. The next turning point and period of massive expansion comes, Casanova argues, again following Anderson's periodization, in the "philological-lexigraphic revolution" starting in the late eighteenth century and the widely dispersed invention of national cultures—languages, literatures, varieties of *völkisch* traditions—that ensued. Casanova argues that the new practice of literature to emerge in the late eighteenth and early nineteenth centuries, linked to a new conception of language and its relationship to its community of speakers, is an element within, and a modality of, "the first enlargement of literary space to include the continent of Europe as a whole." The third and, for Casanova, ongoing period in the expansion of this world literary space is linked to the historical "event" of decolonization in the post–World War II era, "marking the entry into international competition of contestants who until then had been prevented from taking part."[2]

My point of entry into this formulation is what I take to be its most consequential misconception: for Casanova, non-Western literary cultures make their first effective appearance in world literary space in the era of decolonization in the middle of the twentieth century. Casanova thus fails to comprehend the real nature of the expansion and rearrangement of this until then largely European space in the course of the philological revolution. It is through the philological knowledge revolution—the "discovery" of the classical languages of the East, the invention of the linguistic family tree whose basic form is still with us today, the translation and absorption into the Western languages of more and more works from Persian, Arabic, and the Indian languages, among many others—that non-Western textual traditions made their first wholescale entry *as literature*, sacred and secular, into the international literary space that had emerged in early modern times in Europe as a structure of rivalries between the emerging vernacular traditions, transforming the scope and structure of that space forever. This moment, which Casanova reads almost entirely through Johann Gottfried Herder, is mistaken by her for a redrawing of the internal cultural map of Europe, rather than a reorganization that is planetary in scope, in the sense that this emerging constellation of philological knowledge, perhaps best known to us now from Said's reading of it in *Orientalism*, posits nothing less than the textual cultures and languages of the entire world as its object in the final instance. Moreover, this assimilation of "Oriental" writing practices proceeded by *classicizing* works from antiquity, that is, by arranging and establishing them as the core canon and original tradition of a civilization, well before turning to contemporary writers and forms of writing. The modalities of the former process of classicization established the rules and regulations for the later assimilation of contemporary writing. We should note, however, that the world as an assemblage of cultural units or entities was, more accurately speaking, divided in metropolitan knowledge practices in the imperial era between "primitive" societies and ancient "civilizations." As Suzanne Marchand, for instance, has shown in her important critical history of Oriental studies in Germany, the emergent disciplines in the humanities in Germany in the nineteenth century were divided between those concerned with so-called *Naturvölker* and *Kulturvölker,* respectively.[3] (And many societies once regarded in the imperial world system as the former now of course produce major literatures of the sort once attributed exclusively to the latter.) This disciplinary division of labor between anthropology and Orientalism, however, each with its canonical concepts and methods for the study of its own segment of "the rest" of humanity, did not preclude frequent overlap and cooperation between them. In a broader sense, therefore, we might say that metropolitan aesthetic discourses about the world's colonial peripheries retain an element of the anthropological, always in a mutually determining tension with the concept of the expressive traditions and practices of European civilization.

Casanova's is a misreading of the scope even of Herder's work, for his various attempts to generate ways of thinking about the "education of mankind," even while voicing skepticism about the proliferation of this frame of thought among his European contemporaries, must themselves be viewed as part of the larger German and European Orientalist enterprise. Herder not only relied on the work of professional Orientalist scholars and travelers for his historical syntheses but ought himself to be considered as such, not simply because, as Marchand has argued, of his significant writing on what he called Hebrew poetry (and since "the Orient" in German culture was largely biblical-Hebraic well into the 1770s) but also because of his pioneering importance in igniting the German interest in ancient India, on which he wrote extensively from the 1880s on.[4] More broadly speaking, philosophical historicism of the sort associated with Herder cannot be understood without examining its relation to the properly Orientalist ideas of cultural difference, such as those elaborated by William Jones in both the "Islamicate" and "Indic" phases of his work, to which I turn shortly, and the reverse is also the case: the Orientalist enterprise, too often examined as a free-standing discourse and set of practices, needs to be reexamined as part of larger cultural and intellectual configurations at the threshold of the modern West. Orientalism was not merely the conduit for bringing non-Western cultural exempla to a European reading public (already) trained in historicism—though it was also that. More importantly, it was in fact the *ground* on which such ideas could be elaborated, tested, and contested.

As is well known, Herder began in his writings of the 1770s, including the *Treatise on the Origin of Language* (written during December 1770, published in 1772), to mark a break with conceptions of the origin of language that had been dominant in the eighteenth century and that viewed the origin and development of language as such as part of the history of humanity—we need only think here of the well-known works of such eighteenth-century predecessors of Herder's as Jean-Jacques Rousseau and Étienne Bonnot de Condillac, both cited in Herder's work. The *Treatise* is composed explicitly as a refutation of the theory of the origin of language evinced in Rousseau's own *Discourse on the Origin of Inequality* (1754). Herder refuted, on the one hand, the widely held contemporary ideas about the necessarily divine nature of the creation of human speech but also, on the other, Rousseau's postulation of a state of nature in which "man" had no need of speech. With reference to the latter, Herder spoke contemptuously of "that phantom of his, natural man" and argued that the capacity for reflection and reasoning, the quality that distinguishes man from the animals, was not dissociable from language and that if "reason was not possible to man without language, . . . then the invention of the latter is to man as natural, as old, as original, as characteristic as the use of the former."[5] Herder thus sought to remove the question of the nature of human language and the possibilities of knowledge from the rhetorical structure of speculative-historical narratives of the "education of mankind" and made it available to the possibility of historical investigation. Already in section 2 of the *Treatise*, Herder speaks of the separate evolution of distinct languages, some, like Hebrew, giving us clues about the "original" forms of human speech. But in a series of subsequent writings—such as *Yet Another Philosophy of History for the Education of Mankind* (*Auch eine Philosophie der Geschichte zur Bildung der Menschheit*, 1774) and the widely encompassing *Ideas for a Philosophy of the History of Mankind* (*Ideen zur Philosophie der Geschichte der Menschheit*, 1784–1791)—he argued more systematically that human intelligence always took historical form and could only be exercised in language, in particular languages at particular times and, to a great extent, in particular places. Herder rejected the modes of contemporary thinking associated with the sweeping developmentalist schema that placed enlightened modernity at the pinnacle of mankind's civilizational evolution, arguing instead that no system of beliefs and values could be the basis for making judgments about another. Each human collective was to be seen as an organic whole, embodying its own unique "genius" and spirit—its *Volksgeist*—that could only be understood and judged on its own terms, by entering into the viewpoint of its native members.

The consequences over the next century, even merely in Euro-American culture, of the rise and acceptance of these ideas about the boundedness of thought in language are legion and too well known to require rehearsing here in detail. They range from the emergence of secular methodologies of interpretation of the scriptures to romantic notions about the imagination and history and even the forms of cultural relativism that are foundational to both British and American anthropology in the early twentieth century—Bronislaw Malinowski and Franz Boas, the modern codifiers of these respective traditions, had each received the heritage of Herderian historicism as part of their intellectual formation in Germany.[6] But Herder, unlike his teacher Johann Georg Hamann—the other leading figure of (and predecessor in) what, in a number of works, Isaiah Berlin has identified as the "counter-Enlightenment"—insisted at the same time on being able to speak of *Humanität* in general, to be encountered in the *diversity* rather than similarity of human forms, a *potential and ideal* rather than something "ready made."[7] Herder's reputation as progenitor of German nationalism and the even more damning judgment of his being the source and inspiration for Nazi raciology are questions of some complexity. It would be wrong to see in Herder a fully formed and radical German nationalism, as later critics have sometimes done, to say nothing of those in the national-socialist era who considered themselves his acolytes.[8] His strong historicism implies that no one people or way of life can claim superiority over any other, let alone use it for its own ends, and his concept of *Humanität* is precisely that of an irreducible concert of peoples. On the other hand, as Sarah Lawall has noted, "Herder's stress on empathy *(Einfühlung)* and experience, his insistence on the discreteness

and plurality of national and ethnic characters, and his belief in
the metaphorical quality or intentionality of perceptions, keep his
world history from being the mere workings of a perfectly balanced
neoclassical machine."[9] It is instructive in this regard that when
German idealism took its most precipitous plunge into nationalism
three decades later (and half a decade after Herder's death) in French-
occupied Berlin, in the form of Johann Gottlieb Fichte's *Addresses
to the German Nation*, in which the German appears as the "original
man," the term *Humanität* itself was rejected as dead and incompre-
hensible to native speakers of German and alien to their collective
wisdom, to be replaced with the supposedly authentic Germanic
compound *Menschenfreundlichkeit*. (Being a loan-translation, however, this term can no more pass the test of indigenousness than
could the word it was meant to replace.)[10] But it is also the case that
Herder provides the most detailed and early elaboration of what I
call *nation-thinking*, those emergent discursive strategies and modes
of writing that made it possible for the first time to conceive of human
societies in more or less secular national-cultural terms.[11] It is therefore not incorrect to view Herder as a progenitor of the romantic
and organic national concept as such, whose notion of language and
culture is so deterministic as to spill over into the territory theorized
decades later in Germany, France, and elsewhere in Europe as bio-
logical race.

Yet Another Philosophy is a broadside against the dominant tendencies of the modern age, often adopting an ironic, mocking, and even
sarcastic tone about what Herder considers the artificiality and pre-
tentiousness of the philosophes' insistent appeal to universal reason.
This "enlightened" propagation of a relentless pursuit of abstract
reason—and Herder's most frequently appearing antagonist is
Voltaire—makes of human life a hollow shell, ignoring the realm of
"feeling" that is at the heart of the social bond between human beings at all levels of society, from the family to the nation: "The eternal
foundation for the education of mankind in all ages: *wisdom* instead
of science, *piety* instead of wisdom, the love of *parents, spouses, children* instead of pleasantries and debauchery. *Life well-ordered, the rule
of divine right by a dynasty*—the model for all civil order and its institutions—in all this mankind takes the *simplest* but also the *most*

profound delight." This original core of feeling and attachment, more-over, "has no equal at all in our philosophical, cold, European world."[12] Furthermore, Herder criticizes the philosophes as historians for judging past eras of history—that is, *other societies*—on the basis of the values and supposed accomplishments of their own, which means that they fail to grasp the core, the specific preoccupations and accom-plishments, and the unique sources of felicity and communal well-being of the peoples under consideration:

> Even the image of happiness changes with every condition and location (for what is it ever but the *sum* of "*the satisfaction of desire, the fulfillment of purpose,* and the gentle overcoming of needs," all of which are shaped by *land, time,* and *place?*). Basically, then, all *comparison* becomes *futile.* As soon as the inner *meaning* of happiness, the *inclination* has changed; as soon as external *op-portunities* and *needs develop* and *solidify* the *other* meaning—who could compare the *different* satisfaction of *different* meanings in *different* worlds? . . . Every nation has its *center* of happiness *within itself,* as every ball has its center of gravity.[13]

Any generation or era in history can moreover only build on what it has received from earlier ones. But the philosophers' self-orientation leads them to a blindness to the myriad particulars that make up the life of a people and produces a relentless universalism that can only ever find others lacking the attributes of enlightened culture and so-ciety. As a corollary of this screed against the Enlightenment forms of universalism and cosmopolitanism, which can only produce a "me-chanical" view of life, Herder launches a defense of particular, local, historically established, and communal ways of life, such as in the ancient Germanic world—organic "*communities of brothers living beside one another.*" Ancient and time-tested means of inculcating virtue—all the myriad forms of education that human societies have developed over the ages in accordance with their values and "center of gravity"—are being abandoned for a universal and superficial "*re-finement to mannered pleasantries.*" Whereas once "wisdom was al-ways narrowly *national* and therefore reached deeper and attracted more strongly, . . . how *widely* it casts its rays now! Where is what

Voltaire writes not read? The *whole world* is well-nigh glowing with *Voltaire's lucidity!*"[14] But there is a fundamental tension in Herder's work, these radically particularist ideas about language, religion, literature, mythology, and ritual coexisting uneasily with the "education of mankind" narrative frame common to Enlightenment thinkers. The story of mankind's education or formation begins in the "Oriental world" (that is, the world of the Old Testament) and proceeds through Egypt, Greece, Rome, early Christianity, and the Middle Ages, culminating in the Renaissance. The tension is revealed in the note of irony present in the title itself: *yet* another philosophy of history for the education of mankind.

The French are of course at the core of Herder's critique, for the culture of the French Enlightenment is for him inherently a colo-nizing one: within Europe, there has come to be a universal fashion for French culture and ways of thinking: "the rulers of Europe are speaking French already, and soon we will *all* be doing so." Given the abstract, mechanical, rootless, and hence superficial nature of their culture and thinking, the French are mere "*apes of humanity*, of *genius*, of *good humor*, of *virtue*—and precisely because they are nothing more, and are themselves aped so easily, *they are such for all of Europe*." But the destructiveness is being visited on a world scale, and all the European powers—England, France, Holland, Spain, and the Catholic Church ("the Jesuits")—caught up in the fever for civi-lizing the "savages," are playing their part: "*Where* are there no European colonies, and where *will* there not *be* any? The fonder sav-ages grow everywhere of our liquor and luxury, the more *ready* they also become for our conversion! Everywhere they are brought closer to *our culture*, by liquor and luxury especially, and before long— God willing!—all human beings will be *as we* are: *good, strong, happy men!*"[15] Herder thus expresses here that strain of conservative eighteenth-century thought, which includes Edmund Burke, that viewed the world-scale violence of empire building as a logical ex-tension and practical application of liberal-Enlightenment ways of thinking.[16] But here we may also glimpse the fundamental paradox of counter-Enlightenment critique, that while trumpeting its par-ticularism it stages its riposte to the universalism of Enlightenment thought and defense of particular life-ways as a *universal critique* of

Enlightenment and on the basis of the *universal public* that it takes to be the latter's distinct (and questionable) achievement.

For Herder, the purest, highest, and most spontaneous expression of the spirit (or *Volksgeist*) of an organic community is its poetic tradition. And needless to say, this is a "bardic" conception of poetry—to borrow a term from Katie Trumpener—in rejection of the dominant neoclassicism of the time and its promotion by learned societies, academies of letters, and the like, to say nothing of "enlightened" absolutist rulers like Prussia's Frederick the Great, Voltaire's intellectual and literary protégé but also worldly patron and friend.[17] "Poetry," Herder writes, "is a Proteus among peoples; it changes its form in accordance with a people's language, morals, habits, temperament, climate, and even their accent." Furthermore, the creative vitality of a people can only be given adequate form in its own language: "We cannot blame a nation for loving *its* poets above all others and not wanting to abandon them for foreign ones. The poets of a nation are, after all, *its* poets. They have thought in *its* language; they have used their imaginations within *its* context; they have felt the needs of the nation within which they were raised, and to those needs they have addressed themselves. Why should not a nation, therefore, empathize with *its own* poets, for a nation and its poets are tightly interconnected by a bond of language, thoughts, needs, and feelings."[18] These original, primitive, and natural forms of poetic expression are the shared heritage of humanity in which the core of human existence comes through—hence Herder's (proto-romantic) "affection for autonomous, unself-conscious, natural poetry," as Marchand has noted, and hence his emphasis on the earliest and supposedly unadulterated cultural forms of every ancient civilization.[19] This is the case, for instance, with his monumental work on the "spirit of Hebrew poetry," written in the form of a dialogue, which is an attempt to reconcile the Christian notion of the "truth" and originality of the scriptures with the new philological and secular conception of poetry, departing from the work of the Anglican Bishop Lowth, whose lectures on the subject published in 1753 had long become the canonical approach to the poetry of the Hebrew Bible.[20] For Herder, the Old Testament is to be understood as "true" not in a literal sense but because it expresses the collective spirit and wisdom of the ancient

Israelites, God's chosen people in their own time—thus making possible a secular reading of it for its "mythical" contents. And in his extensive writings on ancient India especially in the last decade or so of his life, Herder put in jeopardy even the belief in the universality of the Judeo-Christian revelations, refusing to judge Indian religiosity on the latter's terms.[21]

Such a concept of cultural and historical difference, therefore, could hardly have been concerned primarily with the uniqueness of the traditions of the French and the Germans, as Casanova has suggested. It concerns the question of human diversity on a world scale. It is certainly the case that "competition" with the French intelligentsia and its symbolic capital in the European republic of letters is the *context* proper to understanding the emergence of Herderian historicism. Herder and his fellow travelers of *Sturm und Drang* (Storm and Stress) in the 1770s, including the young Goethe, elaborated an idea of the unique creative genius of peoples precisely as members of an emergent German intelligentsia chafing against the "universal" symbolic force of French letters. It revealed the ideological impulse of a weak emergent bourgeoisie, without a unitary state, let alone an empire, condemned to watching the Industrial Revolution from afar. And we could also say that Goethe's late-in-life dissemination of the idea of *Weltliteratur* was motivated at one level by the sense that German literature was at an inherent disadvantage with respect to the English or the French in not being backed by a powerful state and its institutions. But this does not preclude, at another level of intercultural relations, a shared interest (with the French or British) in the absorption and systematization of the writing practices and traditions of Europe's various others—Orientalism, in short. Modern Orientalism emerged from the very beginning as a continent-wide network and system of relays. And colonial raison d'état, narrowly conceived, of individual imperial states did play an important role from one context to another, but not as the overarching principle of its intellectual and "scientific" development. To view the history of Orientalism in Germany as fundamentally different from that in France or Britain because of the absence or at best lateness of imperial experience in the German case, as Marchand has done, is to have misunderstood this multiple, but simultaneously singular and pan-European, nature of Orientalisms in the eighteenth and nineteenth centuries.

In Chapter 2, I shall turn to William Jones's "discovery" of Sanskrit after arriving in India in 1783 as a judge of the Supreme Court at Calcutta—a cultural "event" with far-reaching consequences for the intellectual developments that are of concern in this book and that was in fact received and consumed as an event throughout the European literary sphere into the mid-nineteenth century. But it is important here to examine closely some of Jones's earlier work, in particular the two essays—"On the Poetry of the Eastern Nations" and "On the Arts, Commonly Called Imitative"—appended to his first collection of verse, *Poems, Consisting Chiefly of Translations from the Asiatick Languages* (1772).[22] M. H. Abrams, in his classic study of the emergence of Romantic poetics and criticism, singles out Jones as one of the very rare writers among his contemporaries who "deliberately set out to revise the bases of the neo-classic theory of poetry" and points to the second of these essays as the first statement of the emergent "expressive" theory of poetic composition that was to find its fruition in the work of the English and German Romantics. Jones was "the first writer in England," Abrams notes, to fuse various dispersed contemporary lines of thinking concerning poetic language—"the ideas drawn from Longinus, the old doctrine of poetic inspiration, recent theories of the emotional and imaginative origin of poetry, and a major emphasis on the lyric form and on the supposedly primitive and spontaneous poetry of the Oriental nations"—into an explicit and systematic account of the "original" nature of poetry.[23] Abrams overstates the case for Jones's break with "neo-classic" norms, however, as part of Jones's concern in the book as a whole appears to be to introduce his readers to the possibility that Oriental verse could live up to the ancients' "standard of true taste," and he is anxious to insist that "It must not be supposed, from my zeal for the literature of *Asia*, that I mean to place it in competition with the beautiful productions of the *Greeks* and *Romans*."[24] On the other hand, despite Abrams's reference to Jones's interest in "Oriental" traditions of verse, Abrams mentions only the second of Jones's two essays in speaking of his role in the emergence of the new poetics and thus underplays the impact of the Oriental poetic traditions in Jones's revisionist project: "In 1772 he published a volume of translations and 'imitations' of Arabic, Indian, and Persian poems to which he added an important 'Essay on the Arts called Imitative.'"[25] (Abrams is also forgetting the place of Turkish in Jones's schema.) When the two essays are read together, as they are clearly meant to be, they reveal a more complex picture of the cultural transactions that constitute the moment and become available to us for a more expansive understanding of the range of historicist ideas and of the diffusion of "lyric" sensibilities, practices, and theories across the world over the following century.

The second, more general essay (on "imitation" in poetry) begins by identifying a profound and widespread error in aesthetic thinking in the eighteenth century that for Jones has classical roots:

> It is the fate of those maxims, which have been thrown out by very eminent writers, to be received implicitly by most of their followers, and to be repeated a thousand times, for no other reason, than because they once dropped from the pen of superior genius: one of these is the assertion of *Aristotle*, that *all poetry consists in imitation*, which has been so frequently echoed from author to author, that it would seem a kind of arrogance to controvert it; for almost all the philosophers and criticks, who have written upon the subject of *poetry*, *music*, and *painting*, how little soever they may agree in some points, seem of one mind in considering them as arts merely imitative.

Noting that "in some *Mahometan* nations" this is patently not the case and "no kind of *imitation* seems to be much admired," Jones goes on to argue for the origins of poetry in "strong, and animated expression of human passions, of *joy* and *grief, love* and *hate, admiration* and *anger.*" "Genuine" poetry is thus no more than "some vehement passion" expressed "in just cadence, and with proper accents" and *"pure and original musick,"* simply that same poetic composition "expressed in a musical voice, (that is, in sounds accompanied with their Harmonicks)" and "sung in due time and measure." True poetry (and also true music and painting) produce in the reader (or listener or beholder) "a kind of rapturous delight . . . not by imitating the works of nature, but by assuming her power, and causing the same effect upon the imagination, which her charms produce to the senses." The nature of poetry is thus to *give expression to genuine feeling*, since "the passions, which were given by nature, never spoke in an unnatural form" and a "man, who is really joyful or afflicted, cannot be said to *imitate* joy or affliction." Though his overall purpose is to define "what poetry *ought to be*," Jones writes, he has had to begin "by describing what it really was among the *Hebrews*, the *Greeks* and *Romans*, the *Arabs* and *Persians*."[26] The essay on the poetic practices of the "Eastern nations" thus provides the ground for the elaboration of the broader ideas about poetry and expressiveness, with a view to their lessons for poetry and poetics in the European languages.

Jones begins this essay, the first of the two, with a description of the physical geography of "*Arabia* [or] that part of it, which we call the *Happy*, and which the *Asiaticks* know by the name of *Yemen*," and of its influence on the "manners" of its inhabitants, since "the genius of every nation is not a little affected by their climate." It is a utopian account, in the well-known and recognizable European traditions of the valorization of the primitive: "no nation at this day can vie with the Arabians in the delightfulness of their climate, and the simplicity of their manners." And since "whatever is *delightful to the senses* produces the *Beautiful* when it is described, where can we find so much beauty as in the Eastern poems, which turn chiefly upon the loveliest objects in nature?" Furthermore, "we must not believe that the *Arabian* poetry can please only by its descriptions of *beauty*; since the gloomy and terrible objects, which produce the *sublime*, when they are aptly described, are no where more common than in the *Desert* and *Stony Arabia's* [sic]." Given the importance of the oasis and the verdant valley in Arabian life, therefore, "it is a maxim among them that the three most charming objects in nature are, *a green meadow, a clear rivulet*, and *a beautiful woman*." And as the Arabians are "such admirers of *beauty*, and as they enjoy such ease and leisure," it is not surprising to see them "naturally be susceptible of *that passion*, which is the true spring and force of agreeable poetry; and we find, indeed, that *love* has a greater share in their poems than any other passion." The prophet Muhammad—referred to in this same passage as "the impostor"—being "well acquainted with [this] maxim of his countrymen," thus "described the pleasures of heaven to them under the allegory of *cool fountains, green bowers*, and *black-eyed girls*, as the word *Houri* literally signifies in *Arabick*; and in the chapter of the *Morning*, towards the end of his *Alcoran*, he mentions a garden, called *Irem*, which is no less celebrated by the *Asiatick* poets than that of the *Hesperides* by the *Greeks*." Moreover, the natives of Arabia enjoy the singular advantage over the inhabitants of most other countries that "they preserve to this day the manners and customs of their ancestors, who, by their own account, were settled in the province of *Yemen* above three thousand years ago."[27]

A similar correspondence between geographical environment and poetic imagery may be seen, Jones asserts, in the case of the Persians, who adopted the conventions of Arabic poetry with the arrival among them of the religion of Muhammad. But they adapted it to their own more settled and urban social environment, the desert and tribal imagery of Arabic poetry thus undergoing an inflection appropriate to this milieu: "The remarkable calmness of the summer nights, and the wonderful splendour of the moon and stars in that country, often tempt the *Persians* to sleep on the tops of their houses, which are generally flat, where they cannot but observe the figures of the constellations, and the various appearances of the heavens; and this may in some measure account for the perpetual allusions of their poets, and rhetoricians, to the beauty of the heavenly bodies." This softening of the physical conditions of life (compared to the Arabs) thus also means "that *softness*, and *love of pleasure*, that *indolence*, and *effeminacy*, which have made them an easy prey to all the Western and northern swarms, that have from time to time invaded them," but "this delicacy of their lives and sentiments has insensibly affected their language, and rendered it the softest, as it is one of the richest, in the world." Western readers of their poetry will fail to appreciate its beauty and richness if they do not attend to its historical and geographical particularity: "We are apt to censure the oriental style for being so full of metaphors taken from the sun and moon; this is ascribed by some to the bad taste of the *Asiaticks*; *the works of the Persians*, says M. De Voltaire, *are like the titles of their kings, in which the sun and moon are often introduced:* but they do not reflect that every nation has a set of images, and expressions, peculiar to itself, which arise from the difference of its climate, manners, and history."[28] And finally, from Persia the poetic culture traveled, again on the back, as it were, of Islam, first to the Turkic-speaking peoples of Central Asia and then to India, to be refashioned yet again according to the conditions and needs of these places and peoples. Needless to say, then, the India in this essay, briefly touched on near the end, is largely Indo-Persian and Indo-Muslim—an association that changed dramatically after Jones's arrival in Calcutta, when, as Maryam Khan has shown, the Muslim in India began to appear more clearly in his writing as a mobile and detachable—that is, nonindigenous—element.[29]

Thus, Jones's text is a key and early moment in what, in a series of works, Virginia Jackson and Yopie Prins have called the "history of lyric reading," the gradual expansion of the reach of "lyric" norms of expression—often contradictory and unsusceptible to definition—to encompass our sense of the poetic as such.[30] This gradual transformation is one of the more marked literary developments of the modern era in the Western tradition. But this change in habits of reading and writing is in fact an intercultural and *worldwide* process, though it is important to stress that these transformations have been far from either linear or symmetrical in their unfolding. Certainly, the lyricization of poetry in the West has had effects in other parts of the world, producing all kinds of new tensions and reconstellations in poetic reading and writing practices in many different traditions, especially in the so-called peripheries of the modern world literary system. But in fact the historical trajectory is a more complex one, for the prehistory of "lyric reading" in the West leads back to the constellation I have been discussing in this chapter—the Orientalist "discovery" of the "ancient" poetic traditions of the "Eastern nations." Jones's book of 1772 (the poems as well as the essays), like Herder's study of the poetic style of the ancient Hebrews (1782), is thus an exemplary text of the pre-Romantic conjuncture, in which entire bodies of "Oriental" verse begin to be conceived of, on the one hand, as the unique and spontaneous expression of the spirit, mind, or psyche of a distinct people and, on the other, as marked by a spontaneity and authenticity of "expression." The question of the Oriental or Asiatic lyric is thus an unavoidable one for a consideration of the early practices and concepts of world literature.

At the center of Jones's rethinking of poetics at the threshold of the modern era is the genre of the ghazal. When he speaks of Asiatic poetic forms, especially from the Persians onward in his scheme of historical transmission, he is essentially speaking of this one poetic genre in particular. Although he does not name the genre in the essays I have discussed here, almost every one of his poetic examples from Arabic, Persian, and Turkish lies within the space signified by it. At the center of the ghazal, thematically speaking, is the problematic of *love* or, perhaps more accurately, of *desire and devotion*, which gets within the form a somewhat conventionalized but at the same time highly complex treatment. It is marked by a personal and intimate mode of address, highlighting such affective states and sensibilities as intensified desire for union with the beloved, the rigors and disciplines of love, and indefinitely delayed union. Etymologically, the word is derived from the Arabic verbal root *gha-za-la*, which means to spin (something) and, by metaphorical extension, to court or woo, to speak words of love (to a woman), to flirt. (*Ghazal* shares this root with the English *gazelle*, a link and a resonance to which I return in Chapter 3.) The conventional historical account traces the origins of the form to the Arabic *qaṣīda* in the sixth to seventh centuries and more specifically its opening section, the *naṣīb*, which is typically addressed to a beloved. It is in Persian in Abbasid times that it first becomes the free-standing form with the meter and rhyme schemes that we recognize today as such and through Persian is introduced into more or less every literary language of the wider Islamicate world. The ghazal has historically been practiced from Spain to Bengal, at the very least, making it one of the most widely practiced poetic forms of the Old World. And from Goethe and Federico García Lorca to J. S. Merwyn and Adrienne Rich, poets in the modern West over the past two centuries have engaged in writing practices that they themselves have conceived of as the composition of ghazals.

The ghazal has thus proven to be a remarkably resilient transnational and translingual form. As the editors of a recent critical an-

thology on the genre have suggested, this extraordinary dissemination, adaptation, and translation over the centuries mark the ghazal
as one of the most widely practiced and disseminated forms in world
literature.[31] In light of my larger argument here, however, this proposition needs to be reformulated in the form of a question: how may
we rethink "world literature" itself to make it responsive to this form's
complex history? In South Asia, the ghazal has historically been at
the epicenter of the crisis of modernity—I return to this question in
some detail in Chapter 2—that is, it has been an exemplary site for
the elaboration of the contradictions of the nationalization of language and literature and the insertion of this nationalized literary
space into world literature, the process that I am calling *the institution of Indian literature*. The genre had entered the Indian languages
at a relatively late stage, continuing to be associated with composition in Persian, producing a distinct and recognizable "Indian style"
(sabk-e hindī) in late medieval and early modern Persian literature.[32]
In the vernacular of North India, that is, Hindi-Urdu, the ghazal
contains within itself an entire social universe in a mediated and styl-
ized form, populated by such stock figures as the disconsolate lover/
speaker, the distant beloved, the rival for the beloved's attention and
affections, and the moral scold, the figure of social and religious orthodoxy. In a series of social, formal, and linguistic realignments in
the early eighteenth century, the ghazal in the vernacular became
linked to the Persianate "feudal" elites of the declining Mughal Empire. Any attempt to write a literary history of the form thus needs
to confront the question of how, with such social origins, it could
have been gradually transformed into one of the most disseminated
poetic forms in modern times in any version of the language of North
India. But it is to say the least ironic that when a critical practice
emerged in Urdu under the impact of colonial rule in the late nineteenth century—the colonial-reformist poetics of the so-called *na'ī
rauśnī* (the new light) movement associated with Aligarh University, figures like Muhammad Husain Azad, to whom I return in
Chapter 2—it produced a utilitarian critique of the lyric traditions
of Urdu and Persianate culture more broadly, the very "Oriental"
corpus of the lyric that, a century earlier, Orientalists like Jones and
his avid Romantic readers had utilized in their attempt to "revive"

poetry in the modern West. To be more precise, this critique consisted of both romantic and utilitarian elements, articulating ideas about authenticity of expression with those concerning social usefulness.

Writing of the lyric as a distinctly modern form, Theodor Adorno wrote, famously, that "the Chinese, Japanese, and Arabic lyric" and "manifestations in earlier periods [presumably in Europe] of the specifically lyric spirit familiar to us are only isolated flashes. . . . They do not establish a form."[33] He seems not only ignorant of the poetic cultures of Asia and the Near East that he is referencing here, which is to be expected, but also unaware of the complex history of the very categories he is deploying: he merely expresses, rather than exploring critically, the fundamental ambiguity of the modern experience of lyric. For "lyric" sensibility emerged in Europe at the threshold of modernity in the encounter with "Oriental" verse and, having taken over the universe of poetic expression in the West, became a benchmark and a test for "Oriental" writing traditions themselves, erasing in the process all memory of its intercultural origins. These transactions are surely part of any genealogy of the lyric, that is, any critical-historical account of how "lyric" has come to be conceived of as such in modern literature.

Although in a general sense it would be correct to regard many aspects of Jones's work as allied with the "neoclassical" side in the eighteenth-century intellectual landscape, what emerges in these two essays of Jones's published in 1772 is thus a theory of "national" poetic genius and its relation to the "climate, manners, and history" of a people that overlaps in significant ways with such a pre-Romantic work of Herder's *Yet Another Philosophy* of 1774. What Herder and Jones offer in these works are early versions of the *chronotope of the indigenous*—that is, spatiotemporal figures of habitation (in a place) in deep time—that became canonical for humanistic knowledge in the nineteenth century and whose effects in one colonized society I explore more fully in Chapter 2. To put it more broadly but also more succinctly, then, the emergence of philosophical historicism cannot be separated out from the entire Orientalist enterprise as it underwent a massive transformation and expansion in the 1770s and 1780s, making available the hitherto unknown literary exempla of far-flung and ancient bodies of writing, codified as the unique traditions of distinct civilizations, interpreted through emergent ideas about historical and cultural particularity. More precisely, this early codification of Orientalist knowledge, to which, as we have seen, Herder himself made a significant contribution, is the very *ground* on which the new ideas of cultural difference came to be elaborated, tested, contested, and defended. In Herder's late works themselves, which bring him closer to the Romantics, properly speaking, these two strands of contemporary European thought—Orientalism and philosophical historicism—are finally fused together, no longer visible as distinct elements, and this fusion becomes the ground of Romantic thought and its contributions to the so-called Oriental Renaissance, such as, for instance, in Friedrich von Schlegel's *On the Language and Wisdom of the Indians* (*Über die Sprache und Weisheit der Indier,* 1808). Said's entire effort in *Orientalism* was (at one level) to argue for the centrality of Orientalism, as cultural logic and enterprise, to the emergence of modern European culture, to Europe's self-making, and against those dominant conventions of intellectual and literary history that treat the entire colonial process as extraneous or at best marginal to the main lines of modern European development. But Said himself unwittingly (and mistakenly) reverts to this convention when he treats the emergence of "historicism" as distinct from and logically and causally prior to modern Orientalism as one of the four historical "elements" that made the latter possible.[34]

Returning once again to the use Casanova makes of Herder to mark the second stage of her developmental schema, we may now note that her nearly exclusive focus on Herder's writings of the early 1770s, which predate the infusion into the European intellectual-literary sphere of the properly Orientalist ideas of linguistic and cultural diversity, allows her to formulate the argument about the transformation of (European) world literary space without reference to the gestalt shift in knowledge and culture made possible by the assimilation of the Oriental exempla that became increasingly available to European reading publics in large numbers for the first time gradually from that very decade onward. She views even Goethe's use of the term in the late 1820s, as I have already noted, entirely in terms of the entry of German literature into the European republic of letters and consequent competition with the more established French literary culture, entirely without reference to Goethe's long history of involvement with Oriental literary matters.[35] Casanova follows a common historiographic convention when she speaks (correctly) of a "Herder effect" in the then more "peripheral" parts of Europe, from Poland and Hungary to the Balkans, providing a charter for intelligentsias and elites in smaller and variously dominated societies to proclaim their cultural independence by the elaboration of a native *national* literature in their *own* language.[36] But in fact this "effect" of historicist-Orientalist thinking is visible in the formation of the system of nation-states *on a world scale* in the nineteenth and twentieth centuries. More broadly, then, Casanova fails to recognize the fundamental difference and disjuncture between the modalities of the first and second stages of her historical schema— intra-European "competitive" vernacularization, in the first instance, and a *colonial* absorption and transformation, in the second—and inserts them instead within a narrative of continuous expansion of world literary space. As I shall show in Chapter 4, Casanova essentially makes the same mistake as Erich Auerbach in singling out and foregrounding philosophical historicism in this manner while making Orientalism disappear from view altogether.

And with respect to the after-lives of historical-particularist positions associated with figures like Herder, we might go even further and say that wherever and whenever in the nineteenth and twentieth centuries Enlightenment is challenged with counter-Enlightenment, universalism with particularism, cosmopolitanism with nativism, and positivism with vitalism—and, more broadly, whenever a "nation" is understood in the first instance as an organic unity of the people quite independently of the presence or absence of a unified state—the heritage of these intellectual and cultural orientations is in some fashion in play. Historicist ideas thus hover over the nineteenth century not only in Europe (and, by extension, America) but in every society inducted by force in one fashion or another into the intra-European imperial system. Even in places such as India, in which English-language and/or Western-style vernacular education began to be introduced very fitfully in the first half of the nineteenth century, these ideas linking peoplehood to place, language, and literature were introduced to native students through the writings not only of the Indologists, properly speaking, but also such British Germanophiles as Thomas Carlyle, whose early essay "The State of German Literature," which launched his career as a writer, not only excoriated the provincialism of the British charge of "enthusiasm" against German culture but made explicit the imperative for all peoples to produce a "national" literature that could represent their way of life and mentality to the larger world: "A country which has no national literature, or a literature too insignificant to force its way abroad, must always be, to its neighbours, at least in every important spiritual respect, an unknown and misestimated country."[37] To "force its way abroad"—that is, to enter the space of world literature—is thus an inherent feature of every properly *national* literature. "World" and "nation" are in a determinate relationship of mutual reinforcement here, rather than simply one of contradiction or negation.

To put it somewhat differently but also more precisely, while the historicist-Orientalist ways of thinking canonized an emphasis on the variety of ways of being human, they did so in order to establish the *same* manner of being different: the *ultima ratio* of the Herder effect, already to be glimpsed from time to time in Herder's own writings, is a "spiritual" map of the world consisting of individual and distinct ("national") peoples, each *similarly* different from all the others, even if not always *equally* different. (I shall return to this question in more detail in Chapter 4 with reference to Auerbach's work.) What is perhaps more important to the purpose at hand, however, is that the counterpoint to the forms of Enlightenment universalism ("the Herder effect") can only be understood as an inescapable element of the dialectic of Enlightenment itself—hence the illusory element in any *strong* claim to authenticity on the part of nativist cultural projects in the colonial and postcolonial world.

The concept of *Weltliteratur* that emerged in Goethe's writings in the late 1820s was largely Herderian in orientation—if we understand by "Herderian" the nexus of philosophical historicism and Orientalism that I have been charting here. Although Goethe clearly meant by *Weltliteratur* an organized exchange of a higher "spiritual" nature between writers, artists and intellectuals committed to universal

Humanität, the concept as it emerged in his writings and developed over the course of the nineteenth century was nevertheless tied to philological practices that depend on a notion of an organic link between a people and its language and place, its *literature* understood as the natural and unmediated *expression* of its unique character and genius. In other words, Goethe's concept leaned against the vast Romantic-*völkisch* cultural edifice in the early nineteenth century—the collections of folk-songs and folk-stories, dictionaries and grammars, philological treatises, Orientalist translations, and literary histories of national cultures that proliferated in the period and defined its cultural ambience—that had itself been built on the foundations that Herder had laid and which in turn it had helped to shore up. Authentic national literatures rose out of those primitive *Volk* cultures, and world literature was a space and a mode of intercultural communication among especially the literati of different nations whose goal was the translating and transmitting of these national creative products into a more universal sphere of cultural exchange. Goethe of course conceived of *Weltliteratur* in relation to more material forms of exchange, a cultural space that would mirror (and would hasten) the coming closer of the world's disparate places as a result of both commercial and military developments and inventions. As Fritz Strich noted in his famous study, *Goethe and World Literature*, Goethe hoped that "world literature would make an active contribution to expanding trade and commerce, and that on the other hand the ever-increasing speed and ease of intercourse would facilitate the formation of a world literature."[38] But the very concept of such communication assumes the particularity and discrete nature of the entities that are to be put into intercourse, namely, national-ethnic or civilizational intelligentsias and sociocultural formations. *This* is the genealogical origin of the principles of organization of world literary space, which enforce the *same* manner of being distinct or different. In Chapter 4, I turn to Auerbach's rethinking of *Weltliteratur* in the aftermath of the Second World War, which may be understood, as Paul Bové has shown, as a reorientation of the concept from a distinctly Herderian to a Vichian historicism, abandoning the organic conception of language and society associated with the former that had remained dominant in nineteenth-century philology.[39] I shall argue further that this turn from one version of eighteenth-century historicism to the other marks the distinctly *exilic* nature of Auerbach's project, famously announced in the call, adopted from the medieval Franco-German mystic Hugh of St. Victor and repeatedly cited by Said, to treat "the entire world as a foreign land." *Mimesis* itself is in fact at one level a repudiation of Herderian *Volksgeist* as analytical method not only in its explicitly pan-European cosmopolitanism but also in the differentiation of European civilization itself at its very origin into distinct (and, to an extent, antagonistic) Hebraic and Hellenic elements.

As I have argued at some length, it is a rather obvious and (it seems to me) incontrovertible historical fact that the deep encounter between English and the main Western languages and the languages of the global periphery as media of literary expression did not take place for the first time in the postcolonial era, let alone in the supposedly transnational transactions of the period of high globalization, but at the dawn of the modern era itself; and this encounter fundamentally transformed both cultural formations involved in it but especially the latter. But this fact either has not been rigorously treated in the contemporary critical discussion about transnational literary relations or, more commonly, has been missing entirely. And this empirical failing has conceptual consequences, for instance, in Casanova's work: because this initial charting of non-Western traditions of writing on the emerging map of the literary world in the Orientalist conjuncture is suppressed or cannot be perceived, such figures as Kateb Yacine, V. S. Naipaul, and Salman Rushdie come to provide the exemplary types of non-Western writer (as they all do for Casanova); the psychology of *assimilation* into metropolitan languages and cultures and such models of cultural change as creolization and *métissage* consequently become the privileged mode of understanding literary practices linked to life-worlds outside the metropolis; and the far more complex and elusive tensions and contradictions involved in the emergence of the modern non-Western literatures disappear from view altogether. In fact, as we have seen, this process of assimilation took place on the ground of *antiquity* and the positing of a lost Golden Age against which all indigenous forms of the modern would by definition be found wanting.

The effects of the reorganization of culture and knowledge in the course of the philological revolution were far reaching, not just for the European intelligentsia but for those very colonized and semi-colonized societies, and more specifically the textual traditions, that were now brought under the purview of these new knowledge practices. In order to comprehend the structure of literary relations that is now a planet-wide reality, we need to grasp the role that philological Orientalism played in producing and establishing a method and a system for classifying and evaluating diverse forms of textuality, now all processed and codified uniformly as *literature*. As Vinay Dharwadker has argued in a pioneering essay, the forms taken by "British and European representations of literary India . . . lie not so much in the 'nature' of the Indian materials as in the intellectual contexts of European literary thought." [40] The (now universal) category of literature itself, with its particular Latinate etymology and genealogy, marks this process of assimilation of diverse cultures of writing, a process only partially concealed by the use of such vernacular terms as *adab* (in Arabic, Persian, Urdu, and Turkish, among others) and *sāhitya* (in Hindi and a number of the Indian vernaculars) to signify the new literariness.

This, I want to suggest, is the suppressed element in the concept of world literature from its inception, namely, the far-reaching refashioning of a range of societies around the world in the new phase of colonial expansion that accompanied and followed from the Industrial Revolution. By the time Goethe reignited and disseminated the term in the last years of his life—his first reported use of it on January 31, 1827, is in the context of his having recently read a "Chinese novel"—it represents a *retrospective* look, with the global shifts in the structures of "literary" knowledge it is intended to reference having already been a long-established reality, including of course in the life of the poet himself, whose writing practice, as is well known, was deeply affected by his reading of a German translation of Jones's *Śākuntala* in 1791—well before his better-known encounter with the verse of Hafez in the second decade of the next century. Philosophical historicism and Orientalism are the double intellectual legacy that both make this new concept possible and to which it points in turn. And by the time the term is resurrected by Marx and Engels more than a decade after the publication of the *Conversations with Eck-*

ermann, which had reported its earliest use by Goethe, it is relatively speaking an old story indeed, appearing within a historical account of the rise and growth of the bourgeoisie as a global social force.[41]

A Heap of Ruins: Colonialism, Capitalism, World Literature

Marx and Engels's famous remark about world literature, much invoked in contemporary discussion but not often closely examined, comes in the long first section of the *Communist Manifesto*, "Bourgeois and Proletarians." The relevant passage is as follows: "In place of the old local and national seclusion and self-sufficiency, we have intercourse in every direction, universal inter-dependence of nations. And as in material, so also in intellectual production. The intellectual creations of individual nations become common property. National one-sidedness and narrow-mindedness become more and more impossible, and from the numerous national and local literatures, there arises a world literature." These remarks are made as part of the well-known discussion of the creation of the "world-market" by the bourgeoisie and the consequent "cosmopolitan character" it has given to "production and consumption in every country." This need for a "constantly expanding market for its products" is not an accidental one but rather dictated by the very nature of production in bourgeois society, which "cannot exist without constantly revolutionizing the instruments of production, and thereby the relations of production, and with them the whole relations of society." This compulsion inherent to its mode of production "chases the bourgeoisie over the whole surface of the globe. It must nestle everywhere, settle everywhere, establish connections everywhere." The varied processes of colonial expansion—military conquest, forms of tributary rule, seizing of agricultural revenues, destruction of native industries, bureaucratic governance, racial apartheid, brutal exploitation, notions and practices of the civilizing mission—are thus inherent to the logic of capital itself:

> The bourgeoisie, by the rapid improvement of all instruments of production, by the immensely facilitated means of communication, draws all, even the most barbarian, nations into civilization.

The cheap prices of its commodities are the heavy artillery with which it batters down all Chinese walls, with which it forces the barbarians' intensely obstinate hatred of foreigners to capitulate. It compels all nations, on pain of extinction, to adopt the bourgeois mode of production; it compels them to introduce so-called civilization [*sogennante Civilisation*] into their midst, i.e., to become bourgeois themselves. In one word, it creates a world after its own image. . . . Just as it has made the country dependent on the towns, so it has made barbarian and semi-barbarian countries dependent on the civilized ones, nations of peasants [*Bauernvölker*] on nations of bourgeois [*Bourgeoisvölkern*], the East on the West.[42]

The ease with which such categories of a colonialist nature as barbarian and semibarbarian circulate in this passage might make readers wary of its authors' conception of the relationship between capitalism and colonialism. But the overall effect of the passage is of course to the contrary, namely, a *dismantling* of the colonial categories of barbarism and civilization, the latter exposed for what it truly is: "so-called civilization," no more and no less than the bourgeois mode of production, that is, an emergent and expansionist system for the extraction of surplus value on a world scale. And Marx and Engels are clear that colonization represents an application on a worldwide scale of structures that had initially been established within domestic national spaces by making the country "dependent" on the city, that is, by transforming the relationship of city and country to that of center and periphery. The colonial periphery is thus in a way the global countryside of the imperial metropolitan countries.

One implication of the line of argument in this passage is that the concept of colonialism appears as internal to the concept of capital as such. This is not an appropriate occasion for a comprehensive survey of Marx's views concerning European colonialism and its relationship to the historical rise of the bourgeois mode of production, but we might at least recall that, writing in the fourth notebook of the *Grundrisse* a decade later, Marx notes unambiguously that the "tendency to create the *world market* is directly given in the concept of capital itself. Every limit appears as a barrier to be overcome."[43] But what kind of concept is it exactly, and what is its significance for our discussion here? As Ranajit Guha has shown in his remarkable book *Dominance without Hegemony*, there are in fact two versions of an argument about colonialism and capital in Marx's writings— "weak" and "strong" ones, we might say—the former, in postulating the "universalizing tendency of capital," views it as an irresistibly absorptive force "tearing down all the barriers which hem in the development of the forces of production, the expansion of needs, the all-sided development of production, and the exploitation and exchange of natural and mental forces."[44] If read in isolation, Guha notes, this observation "would make [Marx] indistinguishable from any of the myriad nineteenth-century liberals who saw nothing but the positive side of capital in an age when it was growing from strength to strength and there seemed to be no limit to its expansion and capacity to transform nature and society."[45] But Marx goes further, Guha observes, to distinguish between the overcoming of "barriers" *ideally* from their overcoming in *reality:* "Since every such barrier contradicts its [i.e., capital's] character, its production moves in contradictions which are constantly overcome but just as constantly posited. Furthermore. [*sic*] The universality towards which it irresistibly strives encounters barriers in its own nature, which will, at a certain stage of its development, allow it to be recognized as being itself the greatest barrier to this tendency, and hence will drive towards its own suspension."[46] The language of Guha's reading of this passage in Marx is a little less than unequivocal on this point, but "ideal" and "reality" in Marx's passage do not correspond, respectively, with a *concept* (of capital), on the one hand, and, on the other, empirical or "merely given" *social reality;* rather, both the "ideal" and the "reality" referenced here are *internal to the concept of capital itself* that Marx is elaborating. The forms of historical difference that mark the colony as a site of bourgeois modernity thus represent for Guha (and, in his view, for Marx) an *internal limit* of capital, not an external barrier to be overcome (or not) in practice. Following this line of thought a bit further, we might say that Guha's concept of the division of colonial space into "elite" and "subaltern" domains—a form of social inequality that is qualitatively different from the class structure of capital in the advanced metropolitan zones—is an attempt to formally express this relation between capital and colonialism, between the sociology of capital in the metropolis and that in the colony.

Thus, Frantz Fanon's famous statement that "Marxist analysis should always be slightly stretched [*légèrement distendu*] every time we have to do with the colonial problem" is not the sort of departure from Marx that it is sometimes taken to be but rather a making explicit and effective of certain possibilities in Marx's own writings. Fanon's argument that the "originality of the colonial context is that economic reality, inequality, and the immense difference of ways of life never come to mask the human realities"—or, to put it more precisely, that under colonial conditions the commodity form cannot quite accomplish a fetishization of capitalist social relations of exploitation and expropriation into a relation of free exchange—is perhaps not much more than an attempt to take seriously statements such as this one in the final chapter of the first volume of *Capital:* "The same interest which, in the mother country, compels the sycophant of capital, the political economist, to declare that the capitalist mode of production is theoretically its own opposite, this same interest, in the colonies, drives him 'to make a clean breast of it,' and to proclaim aloud the antagonism between the two modes of production." Political economy, Marx further argues in the same passage—he has in mind E. G. Wakefield, author of colonization schemes in Australia, New Zealand, and Canada and a historian and theorist of colonial settlement—has thus discovered not "something new *about* the colonies, but *in* the colonies, the truth about capitalist relations in the mother country." [47] In "The Future Results of the British Rule in India" (1853), one of the series of journalistic dispatches about Indian debates and conditions and Britain's imperial adventures more broadly that Marx wrote for the *New York Daily Tribune* in 1853 and then again in 1857–1858, he reiterates this insight: "The profound hypocrisy and inherent barbarism of bourgeois civilization lies unveiled before our eyes, turning from its homes, where it assumes respectable forms, to the colonies, where it goes naked." [48]

Marx's writings on colonialism have been subject to wide discussion in recent years, and a fuller survey of this secondary literature is clearly beyond the scope of this book. They have also, in my view, been often misrepresented or misunderstood, both by those, including Said, who have too easily dismissed their relevance for contemporary discussion due to their alleged proximity to colonial ways of thinking (Said's "Orientalism") and by those, like Aijaz Ahmed or Gilbert Achcar, whose basic instinct seems to be to defend them against "postcolonial" heterodoxy.[49] Bryan Turner's study of Marxism and Orientalism, which appeared the same year as Said's book, is a much less sentimental and more objective analysis of the strengths and weaknesses of various strands of Marxist thinking in this regard.[50] But it is quite clear to me at this point that Said's treatment of Marx as simply and fully another "Orientalist," on the somewhat flimsy basis of Marx's quoting of Goethe's *Westöstlicher Diwan* (West-Easterly Divan, 1819) in one instance and on his view of British colonialism as the "unconscious tool of history" in bringing about historical progress in Asia, is not only erroneous but unfortunate as well, since it leads to the charge, clearly incorrect in my view, that Said is an "essentialist" himself with a monolithic view of the West and gives succor to those in Arab society, namely, the "ultra-nationalists or the religious fundamentalists," as Achcar has recently argued, who discredit the role of Marxism in the struggle against imperialism, denigrating it as an import from the West. This uncharacteristically ham-handed reading on Said's part may indeed have been due to a lack of in-depth familiarity with a range of Marx's major works, as Achcar suggests, but to attribute to him an "essentialism" of Orient and Occident, as Achcar and others have done, betrays a lack of understanding of *his* broader corpus in turn, for at the core of his project is a thoroughgoing anti-identitarianism, as I have argued earlier.[51] In the afterword to a later edition of *Orientalism*, Said repudiated such descriptions of his work and argued, "*Orientalism* can only be read as a defense of Islam by suppressing half of my argument," at whose core was the view that the "construction of identity is bound up with the disposition of power and powerlessness in each society." Furthermore, "what appears in the West to be the emergence, return to, or resurgence of Islam is in fact a struggle in Islamic societies over the definition of Islam. No one person, authority, or institution has total control over that definition; hence,

of course, the contest."[52] But Said's critics' view of Marx (on colonialism) as well is often strangely one-sided and schematic. For
Achcar, since Marx had, as is well known, already broken free of philosophical idealism, albeit in stages (as explained by Louis Althusser), he
has escaped once and for all from essentialism, which is a fundamentally idealist tendency. As such, Marx therefore has nothing
whatsoever to do with "Orientalism." But the very terms of this
debate—whether Marx is for or against British colonialism in Asia and
whether he is able to sustain a stance of humanitarian "sympathy"
toward the suffering of Britain's Asiatic subjects at the destruction of
their ancient and hereditary means of subsistence and ways of life—
obscures what else is of value in these writings. In fact, they have
much of contemporary interest for those who, in the real tradition
of anti-imperial radicalisms in the twentieth century, have sought to
develop *experimental* ways of thinking about the structures of dominance, persistent inequities, and possibilities for freedom on a world
scale.

Marx seems to be engaged throughout his India writings in an attempt (and struggle) to develop a new historiographical language
that is neither triumphalist about the so-called accomplishments of
British capitalism in primitive and barbarous Asia nor reliant on
the clichés of "those who believe in a golden age of Hindustan," as he
puts it contemptuously in "The British Rule in India" (1853).[53] We
might call the first of these tendencies "Anglicist" and the second
"Orientalist," in the nineteenth-century British-imperial sense of
these terms. But this struggle in Marx's India dispatches to get beyond the colonial debate does not always end in success. Some versions of the argument about Asiatic or Oriental "despotism" in fact
represent an *amalgam* of Anglicist and Orientalist ideas in placing
society in precolonial Asia outside the possibility of historical transformation: "English interference having placed the spinner in Lan-
cashire and the weaver in Bengal, or sweeping away both Hindu
spinner and weaver, dissolved these small semi-barbarian, semi-
civilized communities, by blowing up their economical basis, and
thus produced the greatest, and, to speak the truth, the only *social*
revolution ever heard of in Asia." But Marx also views the threatened
"village system" of India as a moral economy and seems aware that

while (in his view) "England had broken down the entire framework of Indian society," no "symptoms of reconstitution" had yet appeared. Furthermore, in a turn that ought to be decisive for our understanding of the complexity of his position, Marx suggests a way of thinking about the *subjective and psychic* content of colonial experience: "This loss of his old world, with no gain of a new one, imparts *a particular kind of melancholy* to the present misery of the Hindu, and separates Hindustan, ruled by Britain, from all its ancient traditions, and from the whole of its past history."[54] This brief statement is remarkable for what can only be called its *anticipation* of a range of crucial and inescapable motifs and issues in colonial and postcolonial societies that have been the site of fierce contention into our own times—crisis of tradition, alienation from historically received forms, an exilic relation to that which nevertheless appears to be one's own, the inability to mourn properly that which is both present and gone. An adequate and progressive response to these historical circumstances, the passage seems to imply, does not require ignoring their reality, as some (and only some) forms of Marxist thinking in recent decades have sometimes implied. For all the recurring lapses into Anglicist or Orientalist (or both) ways of thinking about India's present and past in these writings by Marx, they are notable for the ways in which they resonate with the renewal of anti-imperial thinking in our own times.

How exactly may we then read the brief reference to world literature in the *Manifesto* in light of this understanding of Marx's conception of the colonial itself as epistemological structure and structure of feeling as well as an economic or politico-military one? It is clear that for Marx and Engels world literature is a practice (and concept) of bourgeois society, impossible to imagine as anything but a product of the Western European bourgeoisie's drive to create a world market. As such, it is inseparable from the work of destruction that has left native societies, as Marx noted five years later, in a "heap of ruins."[55] For Marx and Engels, world literature is thus the site of a contradiction and a struggle, both complicit in the emergence of a world market and pointing toward a distinctly *human* emancipation, the possibility of the overcoming of "national one-sidedness and narrow-mindedness" and the inauguration of human "communication" on a world scale. So, as with most practices and institutions of bourgeois society, here too Marx's method calls for a dialectical orientation toward the simultaneously creative and destructive nature of the bourgeoisie as a world historical force.

In "The Future Results of the British Rule in India," Marx notes the creation of a new social class in India, an unintended result of British policies, like the introduction of the railways and other modern means of communication and transportation. This too is a line of argument with profound contemporary significance. I shall quote the passage in full:

> From the Indian natives, reluctantly and sparingly educated at Calcutta, under English superintendence, a fresh class is springing up, endowed with requirements for government and imbued with European science. . . . I know that the English millocracy intend to endow India with railways with the exclusive view of extracting at diminished expenses the cotton and other raw materials for their manufactures. But when you have once introduced machinery into the locomotion of a country, which possesses iron and coals, you are unable to withhold it from its fabrication. You cannot maintain a net of railways over an immense country without introducing all those industrial processes necessary to meet the immediate and current wants of railway locomotion, and out of which there must grow the application of machinery to those branches of industry not immediately connected with railways. The railway system will therefore become, in India, truly the forerunner of modern industry. This is the more certain as the Hindus are allowed by the British authorities themselves to possess particular aptitude for accommodating themselves to entirely new labour, and acquiring the requisite knowledge of industry. . . . The Indians will not reap the fruits of the new elements of society scattered among them by the bourgeoisie, till in Great Britain itself the now ruling classes shall have been supplanted by the industrial proletariat, or till the Hindus themselves shall have grown strong enough to throw off the English yoke altogether. . . . [Their] country has been the source of our languages, our religions,

and [they] represent the type of the ancient German in the Jat
and the type of the ancient Greek in the Brahmin.[56]

We should note first of all that the seemingly transparent use of
"Hindus" in this passage (and elsewhere in the India writings) to
designate the entire population of the subcontinent is precisely
speaking an Orientalist convention, unimaginable without the entire work of the indigenization and Sanskritization of language and
culture undertaken by European scholars, colonial officials, writers,
and teachers over the previous six or seven decades. Second (and more
importantly), the role of unintended agent of the overthrow of the
bourgeoisie in the metropolis that was assigned in the *Manifesto* to
the working class, in the colonies is envisioned for the new *middle* class
to emerge under the conditions of colonial rule. The tension between
"native" and "proletarian" as concepts of social analysis that is sometimes viewed as an unfortunate feature of postcolonial thinking in
our times is thus present in Marx's own colonial writings. And the
derivative problem, whether anticolonial nationalist elites were a
progressive force deserving of the support of communists worldwide,
was to follow Marxist theory well into the twentieth century. It is to
be seen, for instance, in the famous debate on the so-called national
and colonial question in 1920 at the Second World Congress of
the Communist International between Vladimir Lenin and M. N.
Roy, the Indian communist in Mexican exile. The debate turned
on the question of whether communists should ally themselves with
"bourgeois democratic" parties and movements in anticolonial situations, a question that Roy, in a critique of Lenin's "draft theses,"
answered in the negative.[57]

Furthermore, Marx provides here in broad historical overview a
technologically determinist account of colonial governance and its
questioning by a new native elite—many decades before the rise of
any such movement in India, we might add—that became canonical
for subsequent Marxist and more broadly socialist accounts of colonial history. It was sometimes taken to absurd extremes in nationalist culture itself, such as the hopeful intimation toward the end
of Mulk Raj Anand's *Untouchable* (1935), arguably the first major
Anglophone novel written by an Indian, to which I shall return in

Chapter 3, that the coming of flush-toilet technology would put an end to the degrading and oppressive caste practice of untouchability. Although Marx is concerned here largely with the newly introduced forms of technology and their requisite forms of skills and social relations more broadly, his invocation of education—the natives "reluctantly and sparingly educated at Calcutta, under English superintendence" understood as the potential historical agents of a revolution in social relations—might open up a supplementary line of argument, more attentive to the forms of historical consciousness unique to this "fresh class" (Marx's phrase) and necessary for its reproduction.

I shall return to this matter at more length in Chapter 2, but suffice it here to say that the *Anglicist* project of the "Western" education of native elites was at the same time the means of transmission to them of *Orientalist* knowledge, fully formed procedures for the conceiving of certain forms of Sanskrit textuality as the basis for the *Indic* civilization of the subcontinent. Far from being mutually exclusive ideological formations, Anglicist and Orientalist ideas and practices *coexisted* productively in the cultural and educational institutions inaugurated by colonial power. With a view to a larger historical and geographical canvas, then, we might say that Orientalism in Said's idiosyncratic sense of the word—and, in terms of our reading of the Indian governance debate, Orientalism-Anglicism—is the cultural logic of bourgeois society in its outward, expansionist orientation; it is *the cultural logic of the bourgeois transformation of societies on a world scale*. (Said, in his single-minded attempt to rescue the notion of empire from "vulgar" economism, stops short of fully drawing out this conception.) The Orientalists' conventional notion of the "Golden Age" is thus the canonical concept of nationalism as well. And world literature, that is, the (bourgeois) understanding and experience of the world as an assemblage of "literary" or expressive traditions, whose very ground of possibility was the Orientalist knowledge revolution, thus functioned as the means for the insertion of the new "national" class of natives into the bourgeois world system. We may therefore indeed speak of world literature as a "cosmopolitan" concept, as Marx and Engels do, but this cannot be allowed to occlude the fact that it is *also* a particularistic or historicist one.

It is the effects of these shifts in knowledge and culture on the colonized societies, then, which constitute the objects, properly speaking, of the Orientalists' endeavors, that I am concerned with recovering here. None of the currently influential accounts of world literature, even those that draw on historical-materialist or generally sociological ways of thinking, seem concerned with such a historical reconstruction, a critical-historical understanding of the social life of world literature and the meanings and energies it carries over into the present from the past. The resurgence of world literature in our times—in academic discourse, in the practices of literary publishing, and in reading habits in the Global North and elite sectors of society worldwide—is in a strong sense a post-1989 development, which has appeared against the background of the larger neoliberal attempt to monopolize all possibilities of the international into the global life of capital. This mode of appearance of the literatures of the Global South in the literary sphere of the North is thus linked to the disappearance of those varieties of internationalism that had sought in various ways to bypass the circuits of interaction, transmission, and exchange of the emergent global bourgeois order in the postwar and early postcolonial decades in the interest of the decolonizing societies of the South. The most common general name for this alternative is Bandung, diffuse and dispersed, but also interconnected, attempts worldwide to reimagine the life of humanity from the perspective of peoples just emerging from the racialized denigration of colonial subjugation, which produced remarkable intellectual and artistic collaborations and conversations across the world, institutionalized in international conferences, exhibitions, publishing ventures, periodicals such as *Lotus*, *Marg*, and *Moyen Orient*, and numerous other forms.[58] And behind Bandung, both chronologically and in terms of antisystemic affinities, is that other history of imagining and practicing a literary international that emerged in the Soviet Union specifically as an alternative to the global reach of Euro-American modernism, given first programmatic elaboration by Andrei Zhdanov, Karl Radek, and others at the first Congress of Soviet Writers in 1934.[59]

A fuller engagement with the social and cultural imaginary of Bandung internationalism must await another occasion, but its historic disappearance in the post–Cold War era is very much an element in the triumphalist "We are the world" tone so clearly discernible in the self-staging of world literature in our times.[60] In many ways, the rubric "postcolonial literature" as used in the Global North now serves as a means of domesticating those radical energies—and not just linguistic or cultural differences—into the space of (bourgeois) world literature as varieties of local practice—as Indian, African, or Middle Eastern literary practices, for instance. And English as global literary vernacular facilitates and intensifies this disappearance of those alternative practices of the international that were conducted and institutionalized in the shade of Bandung just a few decades ago. The modes of circulation of Anglophone world literature today, including as (supposedly "neutral") medium of translation, thus serve to *naturalize* this specific version of the international or global, which is predicated on, and helps to reproduce, reading publics oblivious to the possibility of historical alternatives in the past or the present, even and especially in the Global South. My argument here rests on a view of English as a language of translation that does not fully correspond to either side of the quarrel between protagonists of the efficacy of translation and those who emphasize the stubbornly ineffable and untranslatable in language.

Emily Apter's *Against World Literature: On the Politics of Untranslatability* has perhaps already become the standard representative of the latter position, while on the other side could be ranged any number of scholars in translation studies, above all Lawrence Venuti.[61] It will I hope already be clear that I share Apter's "reservations about tendencies in World Literature toward reflexive endorsement of cultural equivalence and substitutability, or toward the celebration of nationally and ethnically branded 'differences' that have been niche-marketed as commercialized 'identities.'" Against these tendencies, Apter has proposed what she calls "a counter-move, [invoking] untranslatability as a deflationary gesture toward the expansionism and gargantuan scale of world-literary endeavors." The Untranslatable, furthermore, is to be understood as in Barbara Cassin's *Vocabulaire européen des philosophies: Dictionnaire des intraduisibles*, "not as pure difference . . . but as a linguistic form of creative failure with homeopathic uses."[62] One such homeopathic remedy on offer—that is to say, one such cure achieved by exacerbating the malady—is the purging of the language (of philosophy or literature) of its ethnonational claims and determinations. It is hard to imagine a principled opposition to this goal, one that seems to be shared across the intellectual and political spectrum today, all the way from Derrida's conception of (linguistic) origin as "prosthesis" to varieties of Marxist internationalism, by way of more or less Arendtian understandings of the nation-state's capacities for producing forms of statelessness and uprooting.[63] The question for us concerns how that purging might be achieved and what exactly the history of the ailment is or its etiology. Homeopathy is in some ways an apt metaphor for this process but my conception of it is more fully dialectical in nature, each element of the contradiction becoming the site of a (partial and located) critique of the other. And I view translation itself as a social process that cannot be fully comprehended exclusively as a problem in rhetoric or semiotics and am most interested, as I have already noted with reference to Jones and his generation, in its historical particularities as an Orientalist practice.

As for the relationship between the rise of English in particular contexts and its consequences for possibilities of world imagination, a case study of sorts is provided by contemporary Pakistan, where a middle-class Anglophone reading public has taken shape very rapidly in recent years alongside the development of local Anglophone fiction, the latter being an unprecedented development in Pakistani literary history. However, while this public has no trouble whatsoever seeing these writers along a Karachi–London or Karachi–New York literary axis, as writers with access to such outlets as *Granta* and the *Guardian*, it has in effect no knowledge whatsoever of *Lotus*, the literary journal of the Afro-Asian Writers Association that was edited from Cairo and then Beirut in the 1960s to 1980s and, near the end of his life, by Faiz Ahmed Faiz, the supposed "national" poet of Pakistan, who wrote mostly in Urdu. The Lenin Peace Prize, also utterly forgotten today in countries where it was once considered a notable and prestigious recognition, always included international writers among its multiple awardees each year and was conceived explicitly as an alternative to (and amalgam of) the Nobel Prizes for peace and for literature. (Over the decades, these included such figures as Bertolt Brecht, Louis Aragon, Anna Seghers, Mahmoud Darwish, and Faiz Ahmed Faiz.) As for all the major theories of world literature current today in the core societies of the world system, which are therefore also gaining prestige in many sectors of the global periphery, it is symptomatic that in essence they give an account of world literature as a concept, practice, or structure of the (Euro-American) bourgeois world, without any reference to these concrete historical alternatives and contestations throughout much of the twentieth century. And the critique of neoliberal ideology and practice more broadly in these times must fail in its self-assigned task if it simply relies on these neoliberal structures—such as the forms of domination of English as supposedly neutral medium—and does not confront them with a critical-historical understanding of their emergence under colonial conditions and their reproduction and transformations in postcolonial times.

Whether we view world literature as a conceptual organization or problem for research, as Franco Moretti has suggested, or, as David Damrosch has argued, as a body of literary works, namely, those that circulate "beyond their culture of origin, either in translation or in their original language," we cannot ignore the global relations of force that historically the concept has put in play and simultaneously hidden from view.[64] And this tension—way of thinking or reading versus form(s) of writing—is in fact internal to and as old as the concept itself. So a *critical* study of world literature must take us to this other terrain, the scene of its most efficacious results in the colonial and now postcolonial worlds. Moretti works with the premise that "the literature around us is now unmistakably a planetary system," consisting "of hundreds of languages and literatures." This figure of multiplication and excess is a recurring one in the discourse around world literature, for instance, in Auerbach's influential essay "Philologie der Weltliteratur" (1952). Moretti responds to this excess by absolving the reader from "just reading more texts" and argues that "world literature is not an object, it's a *problem*, and a problem that asks for a new critical method."[65] Moretti has been criticized—rightly, it seems to me—for recommending what he calls *distant reading*, a sort of global collaboration in which the theorist—located where, exactly, and writing in which language?—synthesizes the raw materials provided to him or her by a variety of "local" experts of the various vernacular literary traditions into an account of, for instance, the dissemination of the novel as a global form. In an amusing turn of phrase, Mariano Siskind has accurately placed the latter, the empirical fieldworkers in the peripheries, on "the ground floor" of world literature and the "*über*-comparatists" and synthesizers of the empirical material on an "upper level."[66] (In response to widespread critique of this notion of distant reading, Moretti seems to have doubled down recently, republishing several of the relevant essays in a volume with this title, *Distant Reading*.) In addition to leveling out the particularities of language and work, this conception seems to assume that "local" literary-historical accounts can be taken to be authentic elaborations of national or regional literary cultures, as opposed to, say, contested and contentious ones that are implicated not only in social relations and conflicts, broadly speaking, but in the very practices of world literature in specific ways. Furthermore, it seems vulnerable to the charge that it leaves intact the Western literary cultures in their normative structural role, the latter providing the forms of development against which all literary languages have to measure themselves.

But this last criticism perhaps goes too far, although Moretti himself may have contributed to this characterization of his work. The critics are responding to what we might call the weak version of Moretti's argument in the essay, the mechanistic account of diffusionist versus organicist modes of cultural transformation and insistence on systematicity and iron necessity—all the loose talk of a "law of literary evolution." Alongside this is another strand, however, that cannot quite be accommodated with the first one, a stronger version of the argument that seems alert to the historical and contingent nature of such historical developments as the emergence of "the Indian novel" and the literary-institutional as well as textual-formal "cracks" (Moretti is quoting Jale Parla here) that such historical encounters produce. Repeatedly in "Conjectures on World Literature," Moretti steps back from his own tendency of equating novelistic "form" with the metropolis and contents or "materials" with the peripheries. Instead, he proposes a tripartite division in the dissemination of the novel: foreign form–local materials–local form. The

"Anglo-French core," Moretti further writes, may have "tried to make [the world literary system] uniform, but it could never fully erase the reality of difference." In fact, "those independent paths that are usually taken to be the rule of the rise of the novel (the Spanish, the French, and especially the British case)—*well, they're not the rule at all, they're the exception.*"[67]

In other words, it seems to me that, despite appearances and Moretti's own seemingly strenuous efforts to the contrary, the terms of his argument should not be seen as an unequivocal reversion to a positivistic conception of world literature and are useful for those who wish to produce an account of the structural inequalities in world literary space while at the same time investing in a counter-imagination of literary relations without recourse to a permanent and overdetermining center. In fact, the argument I have been elaborating here concerning the modes of ascription of "peripheral" status to bodies of writing in their very insertion into world literary relations ascribes *greater* powers to the center than is the case in Moretti's account, since in my view the very modes of conceiving of vernacularity and indigeneity are products of the colonial process. But I view these powers themselves as historical processes, that is, as subject to change and contestation, inscribed and reinscribed in institutions and writing practices of various sorts, rather than as the modalities of the "law of literary evolution." These powers of domination produce system-*effects* and are experienced as *pressures* at a range of locations across the social, cultural, literary, and linguistic fields. Both these analytical orientations—attentiveness to the systemic aspects of "cultural" inequality as well as to its shifting and conjunctural nature—are or ought to be necessary elements of critical practice directed at "world literature."

And finally, taking seriously these scenarios of *domination* that emerged in the era of the birth of modern Orientalism will require some fairly dramatic revisioning of the model of national *competition* proposed by Casanova for what she calls the world republic of letters. The *metaphor* of the literary marketplace is in fact endemic to attempts to conceive of literature in international terms and seems to appear whenever a tradition of writing comes into articulation with bourgeois world literary space—for instance, in so "peripheral" a text as Muhammad Husain Azad's *Āb-e ḥayāt* (The Waters of Life, 1880), which is conventionally referred to as the first literary history of the Urdu poetic tradition written by an Indian and to which I shall return at some length in Chapter 2. Goethe himself used the metaphor of the market, as we have seen, but it comes into its own in Casanova's book, a metaphor that never quite comes to acquire conceptual force and is in itself no guarantee of a critical understanding of literary relations on a world scale.[68] In the end, we might note of Casanova not that she is too Paris-centric in her account of the world republic of letters—a common objection directed at her argument—but rather that she betrays an *inadequate* understanding of "Paris" itself as a world literary center, since it was, already by the 1820s and for much of the nineteenth century, the center of European Orientalism broadly speaking, and Indology in particular, synthesizing the materials continually provided by the British Empire to the European literary sphere.

The ongoing discussion about world literature has thus been both hugely encompassing and strangely timid: it seems unaware of the enormous role played by literature as institution in the emergence of the hierarchies that structure relations between societies in the modern world. The integration of widely dispersed, varied, and heterogeneous sociocultural formations into a global ensemble has taken place, especially at the most decisive periods in this historical process, disproportionately on and through this terrain. The concept and practices of world literature, far from representing the superseding of national forms of identification of language, literature, and culture, emerged for the first time precisely alongside the forms of thinking in the contemporary Western world that I have referred to as nation-thinking—namely, those emergent modes of thinking in the West that are associated with the nationalization of social and cultural life and point toward the nation-state as the institutional horizon of culture and society. For any attempt at a critical understanding of our present moment, the larger task is to comprehend the precise nature of this extended literary-philological moment, in which often-overlapping bodies of writing came to acquire, through a process of historicization, distinct personalities as "literature" along national lines.

The institution of literature, which has not received scholarly attention in colonial studies comparable to such practices of the colonial state as the census and ethnography, has its most decisive historical significance in the role it played in the formation of the new bourgeois, colonial-national intelligentsias who saw their historical task as the vernacularization of language and culture—a conceit of return to the language of "the people" that in fact consisted of unprecedented innovations whose actualization even in elite segments of society required a strenuous pedagogy.[69] These "national" traditions were formed through the destruction of varied and sometimes ancient cultures of reading, writing, and performing—developments that continue to pose challenges to literary cultures in the Global South into our own times. Shifting the conceptual registers somewhat, we might therefore say more precisely that the emergence and modes of functioning of world literature, as the space of interaction between and articulation of the "national" or regional literatures, are elements in the much-wider historical process of the emergence of the modern, bourgeois state and its dissemination worldwide, under colonial and semicolonial conditions, as the normative state-form of the modern era.

2

Orientalism and the Institution of Indian Literature

THE ROLE OF THE new Orientalist studies and associated literary practices in the emergence of intellectual and literary cultures of a Romantic bent in the West in the late eighteenth and early nineteenth centuries, and in the emergence of literature as such in the Romantic and modern sense, is not a developed subject of investigation today; but this has not always been the case, and in fact the role can hardly be overestimated. The influence is by no means limited to those famous (and numerous) European works—from *Vathek* to *Kubla Khan*, *Lalla Rookh*, the *West-östlicher Divan*, *Confessions of an English Opium Eater*, *Don Juan*, and beyond—that explicitly adopt Oriental themes, locales, or forms as their own but may be equated with the emergence of an entire cultural horizon, which Raymond Schwab, following Schlegel, famously conceived of as nothing less than a second ("Oriental") Renaissance in the West.[1] The arrival in Europe and into the European languages of works originating in the classical languages of Asia and the Middle East had far-reaching effects on generations of writers throughout the West. Starting in the mid-1780s, Sanskrit works were added to the Persian and Arabic, soon superseding both in their ability to cause a "mania" among literary publics across Europe.

Schwab, whose *La renaissance orientale* (1950) remains to date the most detailed mapping of the emergence and development of this cultural horizon from the late eighteenth to the late nineteenth centuries, went so far as to view the rise of Romanticism as little more than the extended "literary repercussions" of the Orientalist knowledge revolution.[2] This understanding of the origins of Romanticism in the Orientalist conjuncture, routinely expressed by many of the writers themselves and restated at key moments in the history of Romanticism studies, by such figures as Schwab and M. H. Abrams, is with few exceptions largely ignored in the discipline in our own times. In this chapter, I turn to this period, the long nineteenth century, in order to trace a series of sociocultural interactions between new philological practices, different bodies of verse and prose narrative literature, and literary history as a genre across a social landscape that connects the European literary sphere with the activities of the colonial state in India and emergent public spheres in the vernacular languages of that country.

Calcutta Orientalism, Phase I: Europe's "Age of *Śākuntala*"

William Jones, whose enormous influence in the nineteenth century on several generations of writers and intellectuals on several continents does not get the attention today in literary studies that it deserves, played an almost unique role in the early development of modern Orientalism of both the Persian-Arabic and Sanskrit-Indic varieties.[3] Jones's influential texts include, as we have seen, his "imitations" from classical Arabic, Persian, and Turkish poetry, most famous among them a ghazal of Hafez, followed in the 1770s and early 1780s with a Persian grammar and the *Histoire de Nader Chah*, a translation into French of a contemporary Persian history of the marauding eighteenth-century Iranian ruler, a translation of the pre-Islamic Arabic poems known collectively as the *Mu'allaqāt*, and then of course a range of works as the leading figure of the new Sanskrit studies to emerge from Calcutta after his arrival there in 1784. *Asiatick Researches*, the chief organ of the Calcutta Orientalists, launched by Jones in 1788, was republished and translated repeatedly back in Europe, its diverse contents further disseminated through numerous reprints and summaries in the popular press, and became the vehicle of their soaring celebrity. As Edward Said put it memorably in his essay on Schwab, the "job of displacements was apportioned to the great capitals: Calcutta provided, London distributed, Paris filtered and generalized."[4] A wide range of writers in Europe and America, most famously perhaps Goethe, absorbed both these Orientalist waves, if not always in the chronological order of their unfolding.

In Germany, the so-called Indo-mania of the 1790s was triggered by Georg Forster's German translation (1791), from Jones's English (1789), of the first millennium CE dramatic text attributed to Kalidas (Kālīdāsa), *Abhijñānaśākuntala* (or *Śākuntala* for short). This icon of the new knowledge found its way into the work of Herder, Goethe, Schlegel, and Novalis, among numerous others, leading Schwab to refer to the entire age as a "*Śākuntala* era."[5] Herder's own somewhat impressionistic view of India was turned into a sustained and more serious engagement largely as a result of the encounter with *Śākuntala*, about which he wrote repeatedly for the rest of his life, including a preface published in 1803.[6] He became one of the leading proponents of the Indian "spirit" in Germany, looking in ancient India for evidence, first, of a primordial monotheistic revelation and, later, for a vitalistic pantheism, bringing Indian sources into his responses to the famous *Pantheismusstreit* (Pantheism controversy) of the 1780s between Friedrich Heinrich Jacobi, Moses Mendelssohn, Immanuel Kant, and others.[7] And it was to this work that Herder turned in his attempt to break free of the authoritative Aristotelian view of drama refashioned for the times in Gotthold Ephraim Lessing's influential dramaturgical writings.[8] But, as with Jones in this regard, the effort to break free of the authority of classical norms is a less-than-unequivocal one, Herder's very defense of Indian aesthetic works as reflective of universal values and norms taking the form, as I have already noted, of their comparison to classical ones. In a detailed historical and textual study of the *Śākuntala* phenomenon, Dorothy Matilda Figueira notes that it "was received with such critical acclaim by its nineteenth-century European audience that it engendered in the century following Jones' translation no fewer than forty-six translations in twelve different languages."[9] Jones's translation helped to establish a new paradigm for "Oriental" translation with a stability of relationship to an "original" text or textual tradition, unlike not only Antoine Galland's *Les mille et une nuits* (1704) and Anquetil

Duperron's *Zend Avesta* (1771), a selection of the Zoroastrian scriptures that was widely referenced by Herder in own writings, but even Nathaniel Brassey Halhed's *A Code of Gentoo Laws* (1776), the most influential digest of "Hindu" law available to Europeans until Jones's translation of the *Mānavadharmaśāstra* (published as *Institutes of Hindu Law, or the Ordinances of Menu*, 1794) but whose "original" is likely to have been a written translation in Persian of an oral account given by a pundit in Bengali.[10] With his translation of *Śakuntala*, therefore, Jones helped to establish Oriental translation as a distinct mode of action in and on the colonial world, an asymmetrical mode of cultural transmission either linked in direct ways to the exigencies of colonial governance or at the very least reliant upon the conceptual systems and institutional frameworks put in place by the colonial state and the international imperial system. But as a mode of cultural transmission Oriental translation worked in two distinct but related ways: bringing the newly codified exempla of Oriental thought and imagination, that is, a "textualized India," to the various intellectual and aesthetic debates and projects internal to the European sphere, to European self-making, while at the same time codifying an image of the Oriental society in question—"the fixing of colonized cultures"—that, precisely through its circulation in the European literary sphere, became available to native intelligentsias in the process of their embourgeoisement and modernization.[11]

The fabrication of Kalidas as the "Indian Shakespeare," which took place first of all in Germany, marks perhaps the first assimilation of Sanskrit textual materials to the new category of literature and was to become instrumental in the nineteenth century in the repatriation, so to speak, of *Śakuntala* to the emerging colonial-nationalist intelligentsia in India as "their" greatest contribution to world literature.[12] An unelaborated notion, if not always an explicitly formulated concept, of world literature itself became a feature of nationalist culture from the late nineteenth century onward, as the stage for the reconciliation of all that is specifically Indian with universal and human values as such. Rabindranath Tagore is perhaps the exemplary figure of this negotiation, elaborating precisely such moves in "World Literature" (*Biśwasāhitya*), a well-known lecture first delivered in 1907.[13] And when Tagore extolled the greatness of the Sanskrit work, comparing it to *The Tempest*, he did so explicitly on the authority of Goethe.[14] In fact, since the appearance of *Śakuntala* in the Orientalist canon, it has been a cornerstone of that powerful and persistent modern narrative concerning the Orientalists' great "gift" to the Indian people of their own past and tradition—a narrative featured not merely in the official historiography of Orientalism into our own times but also in a wide range of nationalist writing in India itself, including, most famously perhaps, Jawaharlal Nehru's *The Discovery of India* (1946): "To Jones and to the many other European scholars India owes a deep debt of gratitude for the rediscovery of her past literature."[15] And the early role played by Germany in this process should help us understand Orientalism itself as a pan-European system of relays that cannot be reduced to an unmediated logic of colonial raison d'état, a position that Said's critics have sometimes incorrectly attributed to him.[16]

Empire was from the beginning a matter of translation and translation itself an anxious scene of fidelity and betrayal, as Bernard Cohn argued long ago with reference to Thomas Roe, James I's emissary to the Mughal court, who represents the beginnings of official English presence in the subcontinent.[17] And the precise historical context for the birth of the new Orientalist practice of translation in Calcutta was no less clearly political in an immediate sense, namely, the ascendancy of British rule in India in the second half of the eighteenth century and the conquest of Bengal in particular. With the victory in the Battle of Plassey in 1757, the British found themselves for the first time in possession of a large contiguous territory populated by an expanse of agriculturalists and, having seized the revenues of Bengal in 1765, felt the need for systematic knowledge of Indian society, whose economic dimension was described over forty years ago by Ranajit Guha in his *A Rule of Property for Bengal*, a pioneering study of knowledge forms and their role in the transformation of colonized societies.[18] On being appointed as the first governor-general of India, Warren Hastings, whom Edmund Burke was to help impeach over two decades later, began to create the first official and institutional context for the new Indological studies to emerge. Hastings is the first great patron and facilitator of this new philology emerging from Calcutta, and Jones, Halhed, Henry

Thomas Colebrook, and Charles Wilkins were all officials of the East India Company under his administration.[19] The German and eventually pan-European discourse of world literature is thus fundamentally indebted to and predicated on this British colonial project. These early forays into the world of Sanskrit textuality betray anxieties about what was at least initially a near-blind reliance on the native practitioners and specialists of what appeared to the emerging Orientalists to be an ocean of indigenous learning. The "secretiveness" of the Brahmins is a constant anxiety in the literature of the period, including in Jones's private correspondence, and the story of his gradual entry into the Sanskrit universe is often told as one of his winning over their trust and even love.[20] The relationship between the European scholar-administrator and "his" pundits, as they came to be called, constitutes the core institution of this early Indology, an institution that survived to some extent the great shift of the 1820s toward a textual-archive-based Indology, and already by the first decade of the century, Indian philology had begun to acquire a more firmly textual basis in Europe itself: in the 1780s, Jones and Wilkins could have acquired Sanskrit only in India; in the first two decades of the nineteenth century, Schlegel and Franz Bopp did so in Paris, and Wilhelm von Humboldt (from Bopp) did so in London. Through the 1770s, the linguistic focus of the new research in Calcutta had remained on Persian, the language through which the British had largely come to know the history of India.[21] It is only gradually in these decades that these early scholars became acquainted with Sanskrit textual traditions, whose very existence had largely been a matter of rumor and sometimes of wild speculation until then.[22] Some of the translations from this period whose ultimate source is a Sanskrit text or set of texts, such as Halhed's well-known compilation, widely read in Europe at the time, were translated from Persian versions of the Sanskrit originals, themselves often at more than one remove.

What this early generation of Orientalists encountered on the subcontinent was not one single culture of writing but rather a loose articulation of different, often overlapping but also mutually exclusive, systems based variously in Persian, Sanskrit, and a large number of the vernacular registers, often more than one in a single language, properly speaking.[23] Their writings reveal both a sense of elation and apprehension at this encounter with an unknown of almost sublime proportions. I think we may speak here of a sort of *philological sublime*, a structure of encounter with a linguistic and cultural complexity of infinitesimal and dynamic differentiations and of seemingly infinite proportions. Sympathetic chroniclers of these intellectual developments, even into the twentieth century, cannot resist the language of incalculability. "He stood," writes Garland Cannon of Jones at the threshold of his study of Sanskrit, "the pioneer and orienter [*sic*], before a huge, unexplored knowledge." Jones's famous third-anniversary address to the Asiatic Society in Calcutta in 1786, in which he broached for the first time the claim for a genetic "affinity" between Sanskrit and Greek and Latin—the germ of the idea of the Indo-European family of languages—was itself intended as the first of five annual discourses that would elaborate a vast comparative anthropology of, as Cannon puts it, "titanic scope" to encompass the ancient continent:[24]

> The *five* principal nations, who have in different ages divided among themselves, as a kind of inheritance, the vast continent of *Asia*, with the many islands depending on it, are the *Indians*, the *Chinese*, the *Tartars*, the *Arabs*, and the *Persians: who* they severally were, *whence*, and *when* they came, *where* they are now settled, and *what advantage* a more perfect knowledge of them may bring to our *European* world, will be shown, I trust, in *five* distinct essays; the last of which will demonstrate the connection or diversity among them, and solve the great problem, whether they had *any* common origin, and whether that origin was *the same*, which we generally ascribe to them.[25]

The famous prospectus of research that Jones had already penned during his passage to India is similarly expansive, covering such fields as flora and fauna, astronomy, geography, numismatics, and archeology.[26] And in these early records of his Eastern discoveries, at least, it is not simply "India" that is referenced but India, Asia, and the East more broadly, in a series of synecdochal enlargements. It is only in later decades that the idea of Indo-European affinity came to function explicitly as part of the cultural apparatus of colonial governance, mutating in the course of the nineteenth century into the full-blown theory of the Aryan conquest, in which race, language, and culture became indistinguishably fused.[27]

In the now-classic study *Rhetoric of English India*, Sara Suleri has spoken of Burke's famous involvement with the impeachment of Hastings as the occasion for an elaboration of what she calls the "Indian sublime." Implicit in the workings of the sublime in colonial culture, Suleri writes, is an "overdetermined fearfulness that the colonial imagination must experience in relation to its Indian novelty." To reduce experience to a list or itinerary thus becomes the "driving force" of Anglo-Indian narrative, such forms of the "catalogue" becoming the modality of "colonial self-protection" in the face of the sublime. Suleri calls attention to Burke's insistence on the failure of colonial description, to "the colonizer's pained confrontation with an object to which his cultural and interpretive tools must be inadequate."[28] The various philological "projects" (to borrow a term from Said) of the long nineteenth century, from these early excavations of Jones and his contemporaries, through the linguistic inventions of the College of Fort William, to which I return in the next section, and culminating in the monumental cultural cartography of G. A. Grierson's *Linguistic Survey of India* (1898–1928), are linked by their participation in the philological version of this overdetermined sublime and mark a variety of attempts to grapple with the unrepresentability of the sociocultural reality of the subcontinent in the terms of contemporary Western intellectual systems at various points in the history of its subsumption into the imperial domain. The birth of modern (European) *comparative* philology itself is linked to this philological sublime and may be traced to, first, Jones's thesis about the connectedness of Sanskrit to Greek and Latin (in the "Third Anniversary Discourse" of 1786) and, second, to the observations about the genetic relationship between Sanskrit and Persian (in the "Sixth Anniversary Address" of 1789).

The new Indology to arise out of and alongside Jones's involvement with India—the founding of the Asiatic Society of Bengal, the systematic study of Sanskrit by a number of officials in Calcutta, the "discovery" of Sanskritic aesthetics, the translation of works of imaginative literature or of a religious nature and their dissemination to European reading publics, the fixing of a newly canonized Sanskritic culture as the "classical" culture of the (singular) civilization of the subcontinent, the development of schemes for the transliteration of Indian texts (from various languages) in European writing systems, and last but not least, the establishment of legal codes for specifically defined religious communities in contemporary society through the translation of "classical" juridical works—proceeded to a great extent through an application to the "Indian novelty" of the theory of cultural difference and national "poetic genius" that Jones had developed in the early 1770s with regard to ancient (that is, pre- and early Islamic) "Arabia" and medieval (that is, early Islamic) "Persia." One consequence of this transposition (and generalization) from, strictly speaking, pre-Sanskritic Orientalism to the Sanskritic domain is that the Indo-Persian tradition, which in Jones's early essay had simply stood in for (contemporary) Indian culture as such, now appeared in a problematic light as the embodiment of a *nonnational* cultural imagination continuous with the cultures of the Near East and without deep roots in the subcontinent.[29] More than any other contemporary European thinker and scholar, therefore, Jones helped to install the *chronotope of the indigenous,* as I have called it in Chapter 1, a figure as much as a conception of a certain form of deep habitation in time, helping to establish it as the fulcrum of the new knowledge practices concerning the culture and civilization of Britain's newly acquired possessions in Asia.

Schlegel's *Über die Sprache und Weisheit der Indier* marks the culmination of this initial elaboration of the new Indology, the codification of the Indic complex as it operated throughout the nineteenth century. On the one hand, it identified Sanskrit as "the Indian language," identifying it, as Foucault noted, as the extreme case of an "inflectional language" (Chinese being the exemplar of the opposite juxtapositional or additive mode).[30] On the other, Schlegel linked Sanskrit to Old Persian and the languages of European antiquity as their common ancestor, "the earliest derived language, to the general source" (presumably something like "proto Indo-European"):[31] in other words, this work produced in a single stroke a mode of producing the *canon* of "Indian literature," that is, a conception of *the unique tradition* of the vast and complex society of the subcontinent, and grounded it in the notion of the Indo-European family of languages. While specific hypotheses, like the notion of Sanskrit as genetic ancestor to Greek, came to be refuted by later researchers, that correction took place within the larger structure of knowledge systematized in Schlegel's work from the material provided by Calcutta Orientalism, namely, general grammar and, more broadly, comparative philology.

Schlegel also marks the shift from India to Europe itself as the site for the study of Sanskrit and Indo-European philology—the world centers of Sanskrit studies would henceforth be in European cities and universities. He was taught Sanskrit by a veteran of Calcutta Orientalism, but in Paris, so his experience encapsulates this historical transition perhaps more neatly than that of any other individual. As is well known, this experience involves the person of Alexander Hamilton, member of the Asiatic Society in Calcutta, and the event of his arrival and stay in Paris in the first decade of the nineteenth century. Able to enter France in 1802 after the signing of the Peace of Amiens to study what was then the largest collection of Sanskrit manuscripts in Europe, which he subsequently helped to catalogue for the first time, Hamilton was detained when hostilities broke out once again and, through the intercession of leading scholars and public figures in France who were aware of his reputation for prodigious Sanskritic learning, as well as an appeal to Talleyrand by his namesake American cousin, was released and allowed to provide instruction to individuals in the language. It was with him that Schlegel studied Sanskrit and under his daily influence—Hamilton lived in his home for a while—that he wrote his instantly famous work.[32] Hamilton was allowed to leave France after the intercession of Sylvestre de Sacy and took up position as a professor at the East India Company's training college at Haileybury, the classically "Anglicist" institution designed to moderate the malign "Orientalist" influence of the College of Fort William in Calcutta (about which more in the next section) on the young recruits of the company.

What began to emerge in the work of the Calcutta Orientalists and its dissemination throughout the Euro-American world was thus the cultural system of English as a worldwide assemblage. *Asiatick*

Researches was among the first vehicles of this dissemination and therefore of this cultural system. It is in this manner, by providing the materials and the practices of a new cosmopolitan (as well as indigenist or particularist) conception of the world as linguistic and cultural assemblage, that English began to supplant the neoclassical cultural order on the continent in which above all others French and France had provided the norms for literary production. Crucially, it helped transform the role of Paris itself as literary center, which rapidly emerged, as both Schwab and Said noted a long time ago, as the most important locale for the systemization, institutionalization, and diffusion of the new Oriental learning, including, above all, Sanskritic Indology.

It is thus in English as cultural system, broadly conceived—namely, in the new Indology and its wider reception in the Euro-American world—that the subcontinent was first conceived of in the modern era as a single cultural entity, a unique civilization with its roots in the Sanskritic and more particularly Vedic texts of the Aryans. It is in the new Indology that the contemporary Western frames of thought that I have referred to as nation-thinking were first brought to bear on culture and society in the subcontinent. I cannot put it more starkly than this: the idea that India is a unique *national* civilization in possession of a "classical" culture was first postulated on the terrain of literature, that is, in the very invention of the idea of Indian literature in the course of the philological revolution. The dissemination throughout the European intellectual world of the new researches that began to emerge from Calcutta in the 1780s therefore constitutes the *first significant dissemination anywhere of the Indian national idea.* This invocation of an "Indian" tradition of sublime appearance and proportions consisting of both sacred and secular elements—this invention of the sacred-secular *Indic complex* as such—functioned historically as a massive collective act of interpellation, calling up into existence a specifically Indian intelligentsia for the first time and assuring its inculcation in the procedures and methods of nation-thinking. As I have already noted, the *Anglicist* project for the modern and Western education of segments of the elite classes in the subcontinent served as the means for the transmission of *Orientalist* knowledge to them. The history of this transmission—the process by which this particular historical consciousness, this emergent understanding of language, culture, society, and history, took hold within certain elite sectors of society in India itself later in the century—is an extremely complex story, being reconstructed in bits and pieces by literally dozens of scholars across several disciplines but still best understood in the formation of a new literary culture among the Bengali Hindu *bhadralōk*, the first properly colonial and thus first modern intellectual culture in India and perhaps Asia, which came eventually to refer to itself as the Bengal Renaissance.

The role of Orientalist knowledge in the fabrication of this colonial elite and the first, properly speaking, Indian intelligentsia in the subcontinent is copiously documented but understood largely in terms of the historiographical category of "influence." The narrative that lurks close to the surface in most of these accounts, as I have already noted, represents this cultural transaction as a selfless gift from colonizer to colonized of the latter's past conceived as History. Two generations of scholars of modern Hinduism—such as Partha Chatterjee, Tapan Raychaudhuri, Brian K. Pennington, Srinivas Aravamudan, Amit Ray, and Anustup Basu—attempting precisely to break free of this profoundly colonial narrative, have shown in recent years that the most famous products of the translation labors of the Calcutta Orientalists, such as Charles Wilkins's *Bhagvat-Geeta, or Dialogues of Kreeshna and Arjoon* (1785) and Jones's translations of *Śākuntala* and the *Mānavadharmaśāstra*, were acts of invention with far-reaching consequences of a different sort for the colonized society.[33] They acquired a prominence and uniqueness within the Orientalist conception and practices of the Indian "tradition" that had little or nothing in common with their authority and place in precolonial cultures in the subcontinent, in Bengal or elsewhere. This is true equally of forms of writing deemed sacred as of those deemed secular. And the process reveals the mutual interdependence between emergent secular-national and Hindu-religious identities. The conception of the *Gita* as a distinct and core scriptural text of the Hindus, for instance—a conception that allowed Gandhi even to juxtapose it to the scriptures of the monotheistic religions in his publicly ostentatious practice of religious ecumenicism—cannot be understood outside this, precisely speaking, *Orientalist* process of its extraction from its textual and social contexts and reconstellation at the core of a newly fashioned Indian national tradition.

More broadly speaking, Orientalism placed selected Brahminical texts, practices, and social and cultural imaginaries from ancient times at the core of the civilization of the subcontinent as a whole, establishing hierarchies not merely between diverse textual traditions within contemporary Indian society but between these various elite forms of textual authority and a vast range of lived socioreligious forms—in what was well into the twentieth century a largely non-literate population—hierarchies that continue to help reproduce elements of the colonial social order in postcolonial times. Orientalism thus helped to reproduce in secular-literary terms the authority of those social classes whose place in the hierarchy of precolonial society had been ensured by their religious-ritual connection to Sanskritic learning. It is thus not mere coincidence that the founders of modern *savarna* (literally, "same color") or upper-caste Hinduism—figures such as Bankimchandra Chattopadhyay, Swami Vivekananda, and Keshub Chander Sen—were enthusiastic readers and devotees of the European Orientalists.[34] The awe and even reverence in which these early "moderns" in the subcontinent held such eighteenth- and nineteenth-century European codifiers of this "Indian" tradition as Jones, Wilkins, Hamilton, Colebrooke, and Max Müller is an index of the Orientalists' *invention* of Indian literature and its insertion into an expanded and transformed world literary space. We might even say that the acquisition of this structure of feeling—a sense of awe and reverence for the labors of the Orientalists—is what it meant to be (colonial) modern for the first time in different regions and languages of the subcontinent at different times in the course of the nineteenth century.

Thus, when the colonial-nationalist intelligentsia began gradually to emerge in different parts of the country from the middle decades of the nineteenth century, it found fully formed a body of writing understood as "Indian literature" and a body of knowledge and cultural system for configuring language, literature, and culture in national terms. Put differently, this emergent intelligentsia was in a strong sense *schooled in Orientalism*, which constituted for it the very horizon of modern and Western humanistic knowledge. The nineteenth century in India can thus be conceived of in cultural and intellectual terms as the period of the *long emergence of the chronotope of the indigenous* and its installation at the core of a new middle-class intellectual culture of increasingly pan-subcontinental scope. Both the secular and the religious types of nationalism in modern times share this ground of the indigenous as facilitator of *the authenticity of tradition (paramparā)*, the shared ground that explains the ease of movement over the modern era from the one to the other political and cultural formation—from the religious to the secular in the early decades of the twentieth century and in the opposite direction in our own times.[35] The notion of world literature itself came to have a significant place in this culture of nationalism, stressed to varying degrees by different writers and thinkers, as that universal space to which India may be said to have made, in the form of its ancient Sanskritic culture, a distinct *national* contribution, as I have already noted with respect to Tagore.

But my larger interest here, to which I return in more detail shortly, is that this mode of insertion of the colony into the space of world literature, this distinctly *nationalist* resolution of the question of literature and culture, set the stage for the elaboration of contradictions (and eventually social conflicts) between national and nonnational social imaginaries in the subcontinent, in particular between the indigenized Indic complex and the Indo-Persian ecumene, of which the Urdu version of the northern vernacular (as opposed to its Hindi version) may be said to carry the most visible linguistic trace in modern times. Let us briefly consider the case of *Payām-e maśriq* (Message of the East, 1924), the great "response" in Persian to Goethe's *Divan* produced by Muhammad Iqbal, Tagore's approximate contemporary, in which "the East" as a whole is produced above all as a transnational Islamicate sphere. If Goethe's *Divan* of 1819 may be said, in its detailed and close engagement with the (fourteenth-century) *dīvān* of Hafez, to be the culminating gesture of the emerging European practice of world literature, taking the "national" literary complex of "Persia" to be a synecdoche for the "East" more broadly, Iqbal's cycle of poems returns the gesture "a century later," as he puts it in the preface, by placing an *Indo*-Persian (and, by implication, Indo-*Muslim*) literary and theosophical complex, in whose elaboration he himself had played a role for some two decades already, at the center of this "message" in response.[36] Iqbal's preface to the work offers a summary history of the so-called Oriental school in German poetry from Goethe to Friedrich Rückert and beyond and locates the necessity of his own work in the wake of "Europe's war," just as, he notes, Goethe had sought refuge in the East from the devastation of a whole continent in the great wars of his own times. But his own *dīvān* of poems, Iqbal asserts, has the "aim [*mudda'ā*]" of warning his readers in this time of crisis in both East and West against the "Eastern tendencies ['*ajamīyyat*, literally "Persianism"]" that "avoid the problems of life" and cannot "reconcile sentiment [*jazbāt-e qalb*] with the rational mind [*afkār-e dimāgh*]." As in a great deal of his verse, the challenge for Iqbal here is how to engage with the philosophical and poetic heritage of Sufism without succumbing to the Orientalist-Anglicist stranglehold of the "mystical East." In *this* practice of world literature on Indian soil, the tradition *(rivāyat)* of the Indo-Muslim poet, born in a family of Kashmiri Brahmin converts, leads through a circuitous route via Goethe back to the Persian Hafez—a fundamentally non-nationalist, because nonindigenist, resolution—and the so-called indigenous cultural materials of the Indian-*national* literary complex certainly make an appearance from time to time in Iqbal's verse, but as a framed (rather than framing) element.

In the remaining sections of this chapter, I shall return at length to the question of the divided vernacular of North India, namely, Hindi-Urdu, whose history in the nineteenth century is a record of a series of effects of the emerging logic of indigenization. But let us turn first to an Anglophone context for the early elaboration of the topos of the nation and consider briefly the case of Henry Derozio, the poet and famously charismatic teacher of literature at Hindu College in Calcutta. A young "half-caste" of mixed English, Portuguese, and Indian parentage, Derozio got caught up in the late 1820s in one of the first controversies in colonial India concerning the effects of Western-style education and will likely forever remain associated with the perhaps apocryphal image of his students, the sons of upper-caste Hindu families, allegedly consuming liquor and meat openly and ostentatiously in the marketplace. It is conventional to regard Derozio as a leading member of the generation known as Young Bengal and as the first Indian to write poetry in English. Hindu College itself was an early attempt to negotiate between Hindu orthodoxy and the new education. But this new culture of reading and writing became immediately associated with the scandal of iconoclasm and the breaking of caste rules. The new practice of *reading literature* is in tension here with fealty to a textually authorized religious orthodoxy. A mere four decades later, as Chatterjee has shown in his reading of the Bengali writer Bankimchandra Chattopadhyay, this seemingly insurmountable tension became, for certain classes of people in certain places in colonial India, a distant memory: for Chatterjee, Bankim is both the leading figure of the new Bengali literature that emerged in the second half of the nineteenth century and one of the founders of a modern Hindu neo-orthodoxy.[37]

"Anglicist" classicism comes into productive tension in Derozio's verse with "Orientalist" indigenism, poetic conventions that, for instance, Jones's Indian verse, especially the hymns to the figures of the Hindu pantheon—which appeared in several editions of his collected poems in the quarter century from 1799 on—had helped to popularize. On the one hand, the European classical imagery itself acquires a certain ambiguity. Are the "barbarous hordes" in the poem "Thermopylae" the Persians knocking on Europe's door or Europeans who have come to subjugate Persia's ancient neighbor? Are "Sparta's sons" defending Europe against the Asiatic horde or a model for Asia's sons themselves that shows them how "liberty in death is won"? Is the "patriot sword" in "Freedom to the Slave" a *gift of* the English language or *lifted against* it?[38] On the other hand, Derozio replicates Orientalist conventions by repeatedly invoking an Indian golden age. This is, for instance, the case with "To India—My Native Land":

> "My country! In thy day of glory past
> A beauteous halo circled round thy brow,
> And worshipped as a deity thou wast.
> Where is that glory, where that reverence now?
> ... Well, let me dive into the depths of time,

And bring from out the Ages that have rolled
A few small fragments of those wrecks sublime,
Which human eye may never more behold."[39]

Indian *national* sentiment—"My country!"—arises out of a *Western*
and in fact *English* literary model here, which in itself is the product
of an encounter between literature in the new sense and the Orientalists' philological labors. And a constitutive ambiguity is already
at work in this very early, properly speaking, nationalist text,
revealing the ambiguous and ambivalent reliance of nationalist
culture on the structures of colonial knowledge: how could "India"
appear to one of its "native" sons as an ocean full of "wrecks sublime"?
The national consciousness *finds* itself, so to speak, precisely by
adopting the colonizers' orientation toward "Indian literature" and
can therefore only be understood, to be more precise, as an *Orientalized* consciousness.

The historical trajectory I am interested in here, leading from the
birth of the new Orientalism in the late eighteenth century to the
fitful and regionally uneven emergence of a colonial-nationalist intelligentsia in the course of the nineteenth, is far from being a linear
or unidirectional one and cannot be said to conform to any notion
of historical necessity. And it unfolded across a social field marked
by contradictions at various levels. Perhaps most importantly, and as
Thomas Macaulay already understood, this process of acculturation
to indigenizing notions and practices was directed ultimately at a
small class constituted mostly from the precolonial social elites rather
than the subaltern mass of the people, turning the latter into the
popular *object* of the former's project of self-elaboration, which would
thus take national form. And this intelligentsia came eventually to
turn this national complex, including the Orientalist myth of a lost
Indian Golden Age that we have just encountered in Derozio's verse,
against colonial rule. The imperial overlords, furthermore, remained
as a whole highly ambivalent about these cultural developments, split
in the late nineteenth century, for instance, between the posture of
selfless tutelage of the natives and that of savage disdain for these
"chattering" classes, both of which we encounter, for instance, in Ru-
dyard Kipling's fiction as well as verse. But the fact that nationalist

intellectuals appropriated the work of the Orientalists selectively and in effect ironically, or with a view to their own perceived interests, does not in any way lessen the significance of a distinctly Orientalist pedagogy in their very emergence as a pan-subcontinental, "Indian" class.[40] When in the middle to late nineteenth century members of the emergent nationalist intelligentsia produced apologia in response to "Anglicist"—secular utilitarian or evangelical Christian—attacks on "their" religious and cultural traditions, they typically did so, as Pennington has argued, in broadly "Orientalist" terms, drawing on precisely the figures whose influence on colonial policy the Anglicists wished to displace.[41]

This logic of indigenization, first put to work with respect to society in the subcontinent, as I am arguing here, in the assembling of the Sanskrit-centered Indic complex, had far-reaching effects across the cultural and social field that came into being under the impact of colonial rule and across a range of contemporary vernacular formations. But Orientalism's linguistic and literary invention of India has in fact to be understood as a complex two-part, nonsynchronous process: the assembling of the Indic complex (Jones and his contemporaries and the wider discourse in the nineteenth century initiated by their work) and then, following the first significant transition in the history of this early Indology, the invention of the modern vernaculars through an enormous and multipronged project. This second phase of Orientalism's Indian "project" (in Said's sense) involved in these early years such colonial institutions as the College of Fort William in Calcutta (about which more in the next section), the Baptist mission at Serampore in Bengal, and the College of Fort St. George in Madras—the mission, for instance, undertaking a massive printing project in a large number of the vernaculars, inventing movable type for the first time for several of the languages and dialects of India. One tectonic impact of this dual process of indigenization in colonial culture—the Sanskritization of tradition, on the one hand, and the invention of the modern vernaculars, on the other—was the rapid decline and disappearance of Indo-Persian civilization, whose forms of cosmopolitanism, once the culture of vast segments of the literate classes in the subcontinent across the lines of religious affiliation, could now only appear under the sign of the nonindigenous, the elite and thus alien.

By far the most dramatic instance of this process of indigenization on the terrain of language, not surprisingly, is the effort to produce a linguistic and literary *center* for the emerging nation-space—the invention of modern *śuddha* (purified) Hindi as the language of the nation precisely under the sign of the indigenous. As Vasudha Dalmia has shown in her now-classic study of the colonial invention of standardized Hindi, *The Nationalization of Hindu Tradition*, since British officials in the nineteenth century were convinced that "Hindus" and "Muslims" in India were distinct and radically different populations, those tasked with educational matters in North India were in constant search for the "original" language of the Hindus, as opposed to the many existing forms of the actual lingua franca, which were understood to be variously degraded forms, mutilated by centuries of "Muslim" influence.[42] And if modern Urdu may be described for our purposes as the version of the northern vernacular that most visibly carries traces of the now mostly disappeared Indo-Persian culture, then the concept of indigenization helps clarify for us the distinct situation of Urdu since the middle of the nineteenth century as a set of linguistic, literary, and social practices at odds with the emerging practices of the nation.

It is therefore meaningful, as confirmed by a number of scholars of the emergent Hindi nationalist polemics, which were elaborated in a wide range of forms of writing, from poems and plays to pamphlet literature, that one of its distinct features was the *feminization* of Urdu, often anthropomorphized as an aristocratic and indolent "*bībī*" or "Begum Urdu" or even a louche and garishly made up courtesan, figures of the precolonial upper-class social milieu in the towns of North India that are inassimilable to notions of "national" productiveness and rectitude.[43] The larger issue here, however, is not simply that the fabrication of an Indian tradition was anchored by a (modern) Hindu religio-political identity but rather that these shifts in the contours of knowledge, language, and culture produced (and reproduced) *two* increasingly distinct social groups and social imaginaries among the new urban middle classes across the subcontinent, *each* marked by a newly standardized religious identity but only one of which came to see itself as being in possession, in a strong sense, of that *Orientalized* Sanskritic, and more broadly "Indic," heritage, and the other, because it could not replicate that *strong* claim to possession, came to see itself, and of course was seen by others, as not quite Indian in the emergent sense. The indigenization of language, literature, and culture is a core and canonical practice of Orientalist knowledge in the subcontinent with far-reaching effects across the social and cultural field.

The sociology of "communalization" in colonial India has most often focused on what it considers to be the partial and incomplete modernization of the *aśrāf* Muslim elites of northern India and their subsequent competition of unequals within the state with the ascendant Hindu middle classes. This way of understanding the Muslim question is in fact canonical to nationalism itself. I have argued at some length elsewhere that this argument is circular in nature, assuming the prior existence of those entities—"Hindu" and "Muslim" as religio-political identities—whose emergence it is meant to explain. Moreover, this account of a social fissure in the elite domains of colonial society cannot explain the "effectiveness" of communalized politics with respect to the masses at large or why this regional problematic could have been translated into a national one.[44] Such analyses lack an adequate understanding of the historical trajectory of the ideological elements of this process of social transformation, and it is their genealogy that I am trying to present in this chapter. As Ranajit Guha has argued, the politicization of the Hindu-Muslim question in the late nineteenth and early twentieth centuries marks one of the two "axes" along which the nationalist bourgeoisie failed in enacting a hegemonic project with respect to society, with the other, of course, being class.[45] My goal here is to develop a way of understanding the cultural logic that unfolds along this "communal" axis. The emergence of polarized religio-political identities in India in modern times, and of the two distinct and rival forms of the North Indian vernacular associated with them, that is, modern Hindi and Urdu, itself so decisive for the course of the larger processes that precipitated the final Partition of India in the middle of the twentieth century along religious lines, is in a strong sense a colonial development. This is a historical judgment, furthermore, that must not be confused with the more popular, and distinctly nationalist, habit of assigning the "blame" for the political split to British policies of Divide and Rule. But the precise unfolding of these processes of partition across the cultural, social, and political fields cannot be understood without reference to the conditions of colonial rule in the subcontinent. The entire dialectic of the indigenous and the alien, Hindu and Muslim, that is so defining of the cultural history of the second half of the nineteenth century is put into motion for the first time in the slow and massive realignment of the gears of knowledge and culture at its beginning.

Calcutta Orientalism, Phase II: What Is the "Language of Hindoostan"?

At least two levels of interaction are significant here, if we may return for a moment to the terms of analysis introduced by Casanova: first, this linguistic and cultural conflict may be viewed as evidence of a struggle to achieve preeminence in an emerging *national* literary space in the subcontinent in the course of the nineteenth century, a literary space whose (evolving) political milieu is provided by the development of the structures of the colonial state; and second, the emergence of this national space itself is inseparable from the process of its insertion into the *world* literary space in the period of the latter's massive expansion across the globe. Of course, to a large extent this process in India parallels developments in language and literature in Europe itself since the middle of the eighteenth century, from the ubiquitous collections of folk tales across the continent to the recovery of "bardic" traditions—the so-called Herder effect, in short.[46] And the celebrated "Ossian" forgery, which, given its initial popularity, acquired scandal-like proportions once exposed, in fact reveals the inventive nature of *all* philological fabrications of national traditions. But the paradox of the Indian situation is this: the process of vernacularization that we know to be inseparable from bourgeois modernization—and outside Europe, we may think of such language revolutions as the May Fourth Movement in China, *genbun itchi* in Japan, the *nahḍa* in Egypt and Greater Syria—produced in

India not one but two claimants to the status of lingua franca. To put it more precisely, it produced two versions of the same language complex, the northern Indian vernacular, in conflict and rivalry with each other over claims to social reach and social distinction in the emerging national literary space. These two supposed languages are in fact two lexically overlapping versions of the same *kharī bōlī* (upright speech) morphological subset of the vernacular of western Uttar Pradesh and eastern Punjab (including present-day Haryana), which the armies and Sufis of the Mughal sphere had helped to establish as the northern Indian lingua franca. Part of the difficulty of making this argument about Hindi-Urdu as spectrum, which is instinctually evident at various levels to native speakers, is that there is no name for this more encompassing and contradictory linguistic formation—whether Hindi, Urdu, or Hindustani—that is not subject to the terms of the conflict itself: Indian and Pakistani speakers, for instance, routinely use "Hindi" and "Urdu," respectively, to refer to exactly the same common speech forms. To acquire one or the other of these supposedly distinct languages as a native speaker is therefore not simply to learn a language as such. It is to learn ways of participating in *a language field constituted as a polemic.* It is now the settled social reality of the North Indian vernacular to be experienced internally by native speakers simultaneously as one single and two different languages.

Urdu cannot be conceived of as just another Indian language among others, as it were, since part of its historical reality over the past two hundred years has been precisely that it creates difficulties of a particular sort for the very terms in which the Indianness of language and literature have come to be conceived, difficulties that have repeatedly produced an embittered response in those who are committed to the production of a philology or literary history of a nationalist orientation.[47] In this connection, we may consider briefly the history of Urdu's relationship as a cluster of language practices and a textual corpus in the northern vernacular to the *mārga/dēśī* polarity (literally, "the way" / "of the place, local") operative in nationalist philology and literary history. A feature of Sanskritic culture since its rise to hegemonic status as the cosmopolitan cultural order in the subcontinent early in the first millennium CE, it acquired a

radically new valence and functionality in colonial-nationalist culture. Sheldon Pollock has translated this polarity into English as
"cosmopolitan/vernacular" and analyzed its ability to give an account
of the relation between Sanskrit and the rise of the vernaculars toward the end of the first millennium of the Christian era.[48] Since the
early nineteenth century, however, this conceptual binary has been
subject to the logic of indigenization that I have been attempting to
describe here and played a central role in Orientalist-nationalist philology. In the foundational work of such figures as Suniti Kumar
Chatterjee, for instance, it functions entirely within the terms of the
Hindi-Urdu polemic, with *both* the "cosmopolitan" and "vernacular"
functions and orientations (read: "Sanskrit" and the "new Indo-
Aryan languages" like Hindi, respectively) now carrying the force
of the indigenous as against the hybrid and alien forms of Urdu and
the Indo-Persian cultural sphere more broadly. Any attempt to conceptualize linguistic-literary relations between different cultural formations in contemporary South Asia in terms of the conceptual
structure of *mārga/dēśī*, as in G. N. Devy's *After Amnesia: Tradition
and Change in Indian Literary Criticism*, which is a pioneering attempt
to envision a practice of literary criticism that is capable of thinking
against and beyond what Devy calls the "epistemological stumbling
block" of colonial culture, finds its own stumbling block in the forms
of anomaly that from the perspective of nationalism seem to coalesce
in Urdu.[49]

The single most important institutional setting for an understanding of the inventiveness of Calcutta Orientalism in its second,
"vernacular" phase is the College of Fort William, which embodied
this first transition in its history from the decade of Jones and deserves a closer look from our discipline than it has gotten. (From
Said's account of the developments in Calcutta, it is missing entirely.)
The college was formed in 1800 as the first formal institutional
attempt to train the future officers of the East India Company. If
Governor-General Hastings is the patron of the first, that is, Sanskritic, phase of Orientalism, Wellesley is that of the second, vernacular one. In the course of a few years at the beginning of the century,
a small group of European lexicographers and translators, including
John Gilchrist, Edward Warring, and the Baptist missionary William

Carey, along with their teams of native assistants, including Mir Amman, Mir Sher Ali Afsos, Lalluji Lal, and Ramram Basu, produced the models for standardized prose in several of the vernacular languages of India. The very organizational structure of the college, which grouped its personnel into European "professors" and "teachers," on the one hand, and native "munshis" (scribes), on the other, was thus an acknowledgment of its articulation of vastly different intellectual cultures, subjectivities, and social temporalities— European intellectuals with the most "advanced" contemporary forms of Western humanistic education from such institutions as Oxford, supervising the work of munshis of various sorts, who were trained in the traditional manner of the late Mughal Empire, in the first formal institution of "modern" education in India.[50]

The effects of the college's work for language and literature in North India in particular were far reaching. Under the explicit instructions of Gilchrist, appointed professor of Hindostani in 1800, these individuals produced, for use as textbooks in the linguistic education of the young British recruits of the East India Company, a handful of prose works in two distinct forms of the North Indian vernacular, to be called "Hindi" and "Hindostani," which Gilchrist viewed as separate Hindu and Muslim languages, respectively, the one with Sanskrit as lexical source and the other with Persian and Arabic.[51] In aligning religion, language, and literature in this manner, Gilchrist was simply extending the terms of a wider Anglo-Indian discourse since the middle of the eighteenth century. In these early decades, the British often used "Moor" to refer to Muslims in India and "Moor's" for their purported language. Jones himself, in his 1786 address to the Asiatic Society, distinguished between the "Hindostani" language and the "Bhasha," and the Serampore missionaries, among them Carey, who joined the college as teacher of Sanskrit and Bengali, had already begun to highlight in their publications two distinct variants of the northern vernacular. But the Fort William project takes this process to a new level, and the narratives produced there are the first systematic instance anywhere of the standardization of the vernacular in two distinct forms marked by religious difference. And the fact that these works were published with individual munshis identified as *authors* of the works is already an indication of the at-least-minimal inroads toward the installation of a specifically "literary" space in India—a far cry from the anonymous pundits of Jones and his contemporaries when they started out a mere twenty years earlier. The Fort William project thus represents one attempt to impose order of a particular sort, in line with the methods of nation-thinking, on the "infinitely varied common tongue" of North India, as Alok Rai has put it quite memorably.[52] A critical reception history of the "Hindi" and "Hindostani" narratives produced at the college, which comprehends the modes by which these profoundly colonial texts entered and shaped the emerging vernacular literary cultures in northern India—their entry into school and college curricula, their canonization in the works of the new literary history—remains still to be written, as does a careful comparative philology that seeks to place these early colonial linguistic-literary projects (the Serampore and Fort William texts above all) alongside the range of contemporary literary practices at various degrees of remove from colonial institutions.[53]

As Shamsur Rahman Faruqi has shown, the term Hindustani had no such fixed currency within the indigenous culture itself, with the poets and *tazkira* (biographical anthology) writers of the period using a range of designations, including *rēkhta* (scattered or mixed), *zabān-e urdū-e muʿallā* (speech of the exalted camp/court), Hindavi or Hindui, and even simply Hindi to designate the language of their compositions, which was seen to be in varying ways distant from or proximate to a number of dialects and registers—Braj-bhasha or Braj-bakha, Avadhi, and Bhojpuri, among numerous others, often referred to, indiscriminately, as the *bākhā*.[54] Let us consider briefly the case of Inshallah Khan Insha's *Kahānī Rānī Kētakī aur Kuñvar Uday Bhān kī* (The Tale of Queen Ketaki and Prince Uday Bhan, 1803?), for instance, a text whose likely period of composition makes it a contemporary of the Fort William College narratives but whose social milieu lay at a relative distance from the social orbit and temporalities of the emerging colonial state. It played a not-negligible role in the production of the self-conception of Hindi nationalism in the twentieth century as having arisen out of a long indigenous tradition.[55] This Hindi canonization of Insha's tale is at the very least paradoxical, since otherwise he is widely regarded as one of the major codifiers of the Urdu tradition, due largely to his *Daryā-e laṭāfat* (The Ocean of Refinement, 1808), a *Persian*-language prose work establishing rules of *bon usage* in the northern Indian vernacular. This latter text is perhaps our most fecund source for understanding the range and emerging hierarchy of linguistic practice in North India in the early nineteenth century and has been subject to repeated excoriation in later Hindi literary history as evidence of the tangential nature of Urdu to the mainstream linguistic development of North India.[56]

But in the story, Insha appears to have proceeded with the opposite intention—to purge writing in the vernacular, as a sort of feat of linguistic prowess, of all "foreign" vocabulary originating in Arabic, Persian, and Turkic. It is of course this linguistic conceit that makes it available for later appropriation by Hindi nationalism: "It occurred to me one day to tell a story in which besides Hindavi no mixture of another way of speaking [*bōl*] should be encountered. . . . Neither any foreign speech [*bāhar kī bōlī*] nor the rustic [*gañvārī*] should be present in it." But what is meant by the "rustic" here is itself quite revealing, as we are told that a respectable older acquaintance of the author's had expressed his skepticism about the plausibility of such a linguistic adventure, in which "neither Hindavi-ness would be removed [*Hindavī-pan bhī na niklē*]"—that is, by "foreign" lexical elements— "nor the *bākhā* would come bursting in [*bākhā-pan na ṭhōñs jā'ē*]"[57] In this text, written at a certain remove from the workings of the properly colonial logic of indigenization at work in state-Orientalist practices—within elite social groups in Lucknow, but outside formal British rule, at the turn of the century—a very different sort of cultural logic seems to be at work. The danger inherent in the quest for "Hindavi-ness," that is, for a lexically de-Persianized and de-Arabicized practice of the *kharī bōlī* form of the vernacular, "as spoken formerly [*pahlē*] by the best of the best [*achchhōñ sē achchhē*] amongst themselves," is thus eruption of the "*bākhā*," coded as "rustic" speech. (And Insha's boastful response is of course that he is equal to the challenge of overcoming this peril.)

In other words, the register we now identify as Urdu is imagined in Insha's text as the guarantor of the social prestige and purity of *kharī bōlī* as such and is on a continuum with the register that is characterized here by its "Hindavi-ness," both forms needing to be vigilant about the popular and "rustic" forms identified collectively here as the "*bākhā.*" Insha's story thus seeks to render a whole range of existing forms, including above all Braj, as nonstandard, this being precisely Insha's task in *Daryā-e laṭāfat* as well. In other words, both the Urdu and "Hindavi" forms of *kharī bōlī* are *equally* capable of enforcing this hierarchy within the complex and heterogeneous linguistic space of the North Indian vernacular. The properly colonial logic of indigenization ("Hindavi," or "Hindi" in our contemporary terms) and alienization ("Hindustani" or "Urdu")—at work, for instance, in the contemporary Fort William College project—is nowhere to be seen in Insha's story, which is shaped instead by the effort to assure the prestige of elite language practices (both "Hindi" and "Urdu," in our contemporary terms) against subaltern, "rustic," or popular ones. And the fact that Braj, a court language of great social prestige across North India into even the nineteenth century, with a vast corpus of not only poetry but also prose, can nevertheless be rendered as "rustic" or subaltern speech reveals the social ascendancy of *kharī bōlī* forms by the turn of the century.[58] The nationalist historiographical convention that views each of these works of Insha's as contradicting the project of the other—one supposedly indigenizing the language, the other alienating it from indigenous forms—thus represents a profound misinterpretation, one made possible, and even inevitable, by nationalist-Orientalist conceptions of language and culture.

Taking a longer historical view, we might therefore say that the Fort William project shatters the linguistic continuum between varieties of *kharī bōlī* practice by positing, with the certainty and effectiveness inherent in the state-Orientalist truth-claim, the existence of distinct and vastly different, indigenous and alien, practices of speech and writing marked by religious difference. The later retroactive "Hindi" assimilation of Insha's story under the sign of the indigenous and popular and as a sign itself of a continuous historical development that also seamlessly includes the so-called Hindi narratives of Fort William thus misconstrues the fractures of this historical moment entirely, papering over the still-vast gulf separating the indigenizing logic of the colonial state from the precolonial logics of linguistic and cultural differentiation and stratification operating in vast segments of society in the subcontinent.

Modern Hindi thus emerged in conflict and competition, on the one hand, with Urdu, which, under the sign of the nonindigenous, it wished to *eject* from the space of the nation, but also, on the other, with a range of *other* forms of the northern vernacular about which it remained instead fundamentally ambivalent, wishing to *incorporate* them into its own prehistory—even though they are not *kharī bōlī* forms, properly speaking—but as premodern and thus *superseded* forms of the indigenous vernacular, inadequate to the linguistic and aesthetic demands of the modern world. This is the case above all with Braj, which was, along with the poetic corpus now identified as Urdu, one of the two dominant literary traditions in the eighteenth and early nineteenth centuries in the northern language zone but which now could only appear in Hindi nationalist culture under the sign of a premodern and popular "sweetness" of expression *(miṭṭha)* whose temporality is incommensurable with the, properly speaking, historical time of the nation.[59] This inability of early Hindi nationalists to see anything but *kharī bōlī* as the appropriate idiom—or, more precisely, as the only appropriate and authentic morphological base—for the speech of the nation in its modernity is thus in large measure the result, ironically, to say the least, of the already established and officially canonized modernity of *kharī bōlī* in its *Urdu* version, which was from 1837 a language of the colonial state in its function as the language of the law courts in North India. Put differently, because modern Hindi occupies the same morphological ground as Urdu, it replicates the morphological hierarchy of *bon usage* codified in the earlier emergence of Urdu in the late-Mughal eighteenth century and in its standardization in the nineteenth as a language of the colonial state, *reproducing (but also revaluing) Urdu's classification of Braj as primitive and rustic speech.* To put it somewhat differently, we might therefore say that at its moment of emergence in the middle of the nineteenth century, modern "Hindi" simply *is* "Urdu" in the process of being indigenized.

This process of linguistic differentiation and realignment was thus a gradual and laborious one and was by no means linear. This fact may be judged in an anecdotal way from a small but now-famous event from 1847 reported by several scholars of the language conflict. A group of Hindu students at Benares College—which a mere four decades later emerged as one of the centers of the Hindi movement—responded to the linguistic admonishments of their exasperated British educator by noting that since there were numerous forms of the spoken language, they did not understand what he meant by pure Hindi, and that in order to know which words to expunge in an effort to purify their language as he was requiring them to do— this *Orientalist* demand par excellence, as we have seen—they would have to learn Arabic and Persian. Even if this story were apocryphal, it would be enormously useful for understanding the logic of linguistic indigenization: for the native speaker, the route to the discovery of that which is meant to be properly one's own is a circuitous one, leading through precisely that which is to be rendered foreign and alien.[60] The overall process of the emergence of Urdu and Hindi as rival linguistic and literary registers identified with distinct and mutually conflicted religious identities represents a massive rearrangement of a layered, performatively contingent, and dynamic linguistic reality into a structure of binary oppositions. It is only quite late in the nineteenth century, as the notion of a lexically Sanskritized version of the northern vernacular built on the same *kharī bōlī* morphological ground as Urdu gradually gained ground among a segment of the intelligentsia as the only legitimate lingua franca, that the terms "Hindi" and "Urdu" came to acquire their present differentiations and meanings. To sum up this entire historical development, then, we might say that when a colonial intelligentsia emerged in North India in the second half of the nineteenth century that was schooled in the basic procedures of nationalism-Orientalism, which require, as we have seen, the dividing up of the space of culture between indigenous-Indic elements and alien ones— the so-called Hindi nationalist intelligentsia—it desired a language of the nation distinct from both any of the actually existing speech forms of the people and the range of extant literary practices of the precolonial elites. In conjuring up this language, however—a meticulously concrete effort in a range of philological and literary practices—it relied entirely on the existing linguistic hierarchy established in the rise and dominance of Urdu in late-Mughal and early-colonial times between *kharī bōlī* and all the other forms of the northern vernacular.

Finally, any attempt to give an account of the contemporary social situation of Urdu and Hindi as literary languages must confront the paradoxical fact that no literary history, properly speaking, can fail to locate their modern origins in the Fort William College narratives, written expressly not for an Indian reading public but rather for the linguistic and cultural training of young British officers of the East India Company. There was a lag of several decades after the initial publication of the narratives before they became available to "Urdu" and "Hindi" reading publics. Even some three decades later, the ornate language of Rajab Ali Beg Suroor's *Fasāna-e 'ajā'ib* (1831?), written in a prose-poetic style, was intended precisely as a repudiation of the purportedly conversational and pedestrian Fort William idiom. The very foundational acts of historicization that sought to produce for the first time the terms of distinct and independent histories for these two traditions—I am thinking here of such late nineteenth- and early twentieth-century figures as Ramchandra Shukla (Hindi) and Muhammad Husain Azad (Urdu), to whom I turn shortly—thus represent at the same time their anchoring in this colonial and Orientalist logic.[61] In a very real sense, then, prose traditions in the languages we have come to read and write as "our own"—I am speaking here as a person formed in the Hindi-Urdu polemic as a supposedly "native" speaker of "Urdu"—were invented for the purpose of colonial governance, and the task of criticism today is at the very least the untangling and rearranging of the various elements presently congealed into seemingly distinct and autonomous objects of divergent literary histories. The critical task of overcoming the colonial logics persistently at work in the formation of literary and linguistic identities today is thus indistinguishable from the task of pushing against the multiple identitarian assumptions, *colonial and Orientalist in nature*, of Hindi and Urdu's mutual and religiously marked distinctness and autonomy. A postcolonial *philology* of this literary and linguistic complex can never adequately claim to be produced from a position uncontaminated by the language *polemic* that now constitutes it and can only proceed by working through its terms.

This secular-critical task, furthermore, corresponds not to the erection of some image of a heterogeneous past but to the elaboration of the contradictory contemporary situation of language and literature itself. For the laborious historical process of creating two distinct language identities—a historical labor undertaken, as I have tried to show, first by Orientalists and then by Indian nationalists (and Muslim separatists)—remains still ongoing and incomplete. Despite the countless efforts at differentiation and countless applications of identitarian pressure across the linguistic and literary field in this enormous cultural zone in the subcontinent for well over a century, Urdu and Hindi remain intimately proximate and available to each other in a whole range of media and forms—in spoken language forms, in the so-called Hindi films of Bollywood cinema, but even in literary writing itself. The literary examples are legion, come from some of the most significant writers of the late twentieth and early twenty-first centuries, and I shall turn to a few of them shortly. A desire for Urdu (coded as refined and cosmopolitan) is inherent to modern Hindi, and a desire for Hindi (coded as popular and vernacular) inherent to modern Urdu itself. This coding of course marks the diffusion of a haze of misconceptions—after all, in Pakistan the institutionalization of Urdu as the national language has been achieved by sundering nearly all its former associations with the mannered *aśrāf* elite of northern India, Urdu is unselfconsciously the language of emancipatory caste politics among Muslim Dalits in India, and modern standard Hindi can hardly be equated with any genuinely popular form of the spoken language. But the misconceptions do not in any way diminish the fact that the encounter does daily and routinely take place. In this sense, Hindi and Urdu remain articulated as the elements of a single formation in contradiction, and the more the contradiction is heightened—by a myriad of nationalizing (and Orientalizing) processes operative at numerous social locations—the more the singularity (in contradiction) is affirmed and renewed, even though at yet one further level of remove from the phenomenal levels of social and cultural experience.

More broadly, then, it bears repeating the obvious, namely, that the chronotope of indigenousness, a temporal structure of deep habitation in time, marks an orientation in and toward *modern* culture, not a means of return to the origin from the displacements produced by the colonial process. As a modernizing modality, therefore, its installation in a sociocultural milieu in fact (and in effect) *intensifies* the sense of distance from the origin, even as it heightens the desire for its restoration. This is evident from even a cursory look at the history of indigenizing discourses and projects in India since the nineteenth century, which suggests that the more their concepts and categories become unquestioned in more and more sectors of society and implicit in social and cultural practices, the more anxious and even shrill the need for their reassertion, tending clearly toward a totalitarian view of society. And all attempts at the normalization of Urdu as the language of Pakistan as a *nation*-state stumble on the demand, built into the nation-state form, of the indigenousness of language, culture, and society. Thus, any invocation of the transparency of world literature need only be confronted with the very different reality within the subcontinent itself, where even literary works in the same language—Urdu in this instance—cross borders in line with the frames of nationalized literary histories, forms of nationalization of language, literature, and culture installed in this region precisely in and through the world-historical process that is the emergence of world literature. But what exactly are the modalities of indigenousness as chronotope, what in each case is its relationship to different cultural modes and genres of writing, and what, finally, are the prospects for nonindigenizing (that is, non-Orientalizing) forms of historical thinking about culture in postcolonial society? It is to some of these questions concerning indigenousness and form that I shall now turn.

Literary History and the Beginnings of Colonial Time

It is one of the most widely shared assumptions in literary studies that the transition to a properly speaking bourgeois literature in any language, and thus entry into the space of world literature, is announced by the rise of the novel form. Moretti's entire system, for instance, is based on this more or less explicit assumption. Aside from the usual western European cases cited most often—Spanish, English, French, German—this historical claim is also thought to hold true outside the West, in those languages and cultures that experienced the transition under colonial or semicolonial conditions, including, say, Japanese, Chinese, Arabic, and the Indian vernaculars. As I have argued at some length elsewhere, however, in Urdu and Hindi the picture is complicated by the fact that the otherwise "minor" form of the short story has long held some of the preeminence associated elsewhere with the "major" form of the novel. This lopsided distribution of genres is a result and a sign of the modes of emergence of modern Hindi and Urdu literatures as distinct (and conflicted) bodies of writing—the entire historical process of insertion into literariness that I have been charting in this chapter.[62] More broadly speaking, the historical thesis about the novel needs to be revised at the very least so that it does not resemble a sort of natural history of genre, in the manner, say, of Moretti's evolutionary schema, but rather takes a critical-historical approach to literary historicity itself. If, on the one hand, world literature has been an explicitly literary-historical question, on the other, literary history has been one of the modalities of the institution of world literature. Histories of "national" literatures were of course among the most prolific genres of writing of the extended Romantic culture in Europe in the late eighteenth and early nineteenth centuries. But precisely this genre is central to *world* literary relations as well. To be more precise, the entry of a body of writing into world literary space as a distinct literary tradition has characteristically taken place since the nineteenth century through its acquisition of a narrative of ("national") historical development. It is when a writing tradition has produced a literary history that its literary modernity, properly speaking, may be said to have begun.

Ranajit Guha speaks in his essay "A Colonial City and Its Time(s)" of nineteenth-century Calcutta not only as a territorially divided space but as a city split in time—between the rhythms of native society, exemplified to an extreme degree in the time of ritual and festival, and the time of *Ophish-para* (Officetown, the administrative center of the colonial metropolis), Guha tells us, named thus in the vernacular of the city as a marker of the latter's deeply divided nature. The social life of the city was thus elaborated along "a tangle of two braided temporalities," Guha notes, which were unequal and asymmetrically situated with respect to the urban world, but neither of which ever operated without its articulation with the other, each cutting across and interrupting the other's unfolding. *Ophisher bela*, or "office time," operated for the natives first of all in their relationship to the forms of labor solicited from them by the colonial rulers, as "*khansamans, bawarchis, ayahs, darzis, dhobis*, peons, *saises, malis*, orderlies, *babus*, and so on everyday in and around the bungalows, *kachehris*, cantonments, clubs and other institutions that affirmed the presence and power of their rulers in a colonial city." And even in the "residential parts" of the city, whose daily rhythms of "indigenous time" were reinscribed by the colonial rulers as "delays, inexactitudes, unpunctualities, and other vagaries which were a constant source of irritation to them," the ticking of colonial time was never far from the consciousness of the natives, reiterated most starkly perhaps in the hourly firing of the cannon in Fort William.[63]

In this essay, Guha raises the question of the temporal displacement of native society in the process of its absorption into the rhythms of colonial-capitalist social relations. But the essay proceeds—mistakenly, in my view—by invoking the seemingly solid ground of the *indigenous* as counter to the colonial formation and, as he puts it, the "primordial and inalienable privilege of a native speaker" against the powers of the colonial language, which "served the regime both as an instrument of dominance and an agency of persuasion."[64] In the remainder of this chapter, I take this opening up of the question of colonial temporality as my starting point in order to move into an overlapping but somewhat different terrain, namely, the question of literary history or, more precisely, the question of the ascription of historical temporality to a body of writing as literature.

In separate introductions to a joint translation of *Āb-e ḥayāt* (The Waters of Life, 1880) by Muhammad Husain Azad, which is often spoken of as the first literary history of the Urdu poetic tradition in the language itself, Frances Pritchett and Shamsur Rahman Faruqi bemoan what they see as the continuing influence of Azad's work over the imagination of Urdu literature, continuing, as they see it, even into our own times. This is, strictly speaking, a historically accurate statement, for Azad's work is discourse initiating for elaborations of the modern in Urdu poetics, every new poetic project attempting anew to struggle with and navigate the space opened in and by this work. The question of the "first" Urdu literary history is simultaneously a question about the disappearance of another form of writing, in Persian or in Urdu, concerned with the poets of what is variously called *rēkhta*, Hindi, or ultimately, Urdu, namely, the *tazkira*, an anthology and lives-of-the-poets genre, an element of the culture of (Urdu) poetic composition and circulation that bridged the transition from a manuscript culture to that of print over the course of the late eighteenth and early nineteenth centuries. The one and the other are in fact different ways of posing the same question. The basic facts of the fate of *tazkira-nigārī* (*tazkira*-writing) are well known: this form of writing came to a fairly rapid end sometime in the nineteenth century more than a hundred years after its first appearance in Urdu—an end understood as timely or untimely depending on who happens to be reporting the demise. This judgment itself—that is, the manner in which criticism orients itself toward the disappearance of this genre—is the site in Urdu of a politics concerning poetry and prose, aesthetics and society, tradition and modernity. I am attempting here to reopen once again this double question of the historicization of Urdu poetry, the question of the acquisition, by a non-Western and precolonial body of writing, of the attributes of *its own* unique and singular history.

The *tazkira* had come to the Urdu poetic tradition from Persian, although there is strong historical reason to believe that some of the earliest extant exempla of the Persian-language/Persian-poets *tazkira* were also composed on Indian soil and in the thirteenth century.[65] The first emergence of the *tazkira* as a biographical anthology of *Urdu*-language poets, written in Persian prose, is usually dated to the middle of the eighteenth century and conventionally located in the *Nikāt al-shuʿarā* of the poet Mir Muhammad Taqi "Mir." Faruqi has argued that the form of the *tazkira* is dramatically different from literary history, for not only does it not follow chronology in its assembling of biographical materials, but it has no recourse to the passage of time whatsoever as a structuring element and views the poetic text as existing simultaneously in the past and present. Faruqi attributes this to the status of poetry in the traditional Islamicate sphere—in Arabic, Persian, and Urdu, more precisely. The revelation of the Qur'an in language, he argues in an exposition of Arabic poetics, meant that all poetry pointed to the possibility of the perfection of language in the Qur'an, thus freeing it in a sense from its historical circumstances. But this argument has been made by others concerning the precolonial literary traditions of South Asia as a whole, for instance by Kamil Zvelbil with respect to Tamil.[66] And it accords with the precepts of the Ashis Nandy school on the differences between Indian and European civilizations. Moreover, such arguments are on a continuum with "perennialist" arguments about the one true tradition everywhere, a shared essence to which only the modern West does not conform and whose destruction it represents. In Urdu criticism itself, this viewpoint came to be associated most closely with the late work of Muhammad Hasan Askari, and Faruqi is generally considered to be a figure in the Askari tradition.[67] Such (perennialist) arguments are symptoms of the crisis of modern culture and made entirely on the latter's own terms rather than means of escape from it, as they typically claim to be.

Faruqi's exposition is notable for a number of reasons. First, in seeking to address the question of the origins of the Urdu poetic tradition by placing it in this strong manner in the Perso-Arabic sphere, he seems to replicate those very historical processes—the colonial transformation of Urdu literary culture that I have been discussing here—against which he appears to be defending the *tazkira* as an authentic form in the Urdu tradition. Second, to treat the *tazkira* and literary history in this manner as two free-standing genres of writing misses their mutual inextricability in the nineteenth century, the larger point I am making here. And third, and perhaps most decisively, to offer this particular genealogy of Urdu literary culture as emerging out of an exclusively "Islamic" source, while a recognizable gesture in Urdu criticism, with a distinct politics all its own, is hardly a convincing one.

The first literary history of "Urdu" poetry as a distinct tradition was written by Joseph Héliodore Sagesse Vertu Garcin de Tassy, who was well known in his own time in France but is relatively unknown today even in France, outside the narrow circles of Oriental studies and Indology. But he is not only not forgotten in the world of Urdu literary criticism and literary history; his influence continues to be visited and revisited from time to time, often in the midst of anguished attempts to excavate the tradition of Urdu literature and to forge a coherent link to its past—not, in other words, as detached exercises in historical reconstruction but rather as matters of survival for the critical project itself. Garcin de Tassy studied Arabic and Persian at the École spéciale des langues orientales vivantes with Silvestre de Sacy, the great modernizer of Oriental studies on the continent in the first half of the nineteenth century, whom Said has identified as the person who, by training an entire generation of scholars in Paris who would fan out to the major universities of the continent, established Oriental studies as a pan-European professional network. He was hired by his mentor in 1828 to a newly created chair for the study of "Hindoustani" language and literature at the École, a language in which he was entirely self-taught. His career thus unfolded in close proximity to the centers of the global Orientalist apparatus, and in fact from the early 1830s until his death in 1878, he functioned himself as the center of a vast network for the collection and distribution of information and knowledge on the living literature of the northern Indian vernacular, incorporating scholars throughout Europe, British colonial officials in the subcontinent and in Britain, and numerous native individuals, all of whom regularly channeled textual materials to him in Paris.[68]

Garcin de Tassy's *Histoire de la littérature hindouie and hindoustanie*, which was published in two volumes in 1838 and 1847, to be reissued in an expanded edition in three volumes in 1871, is, properly speaking, the first literary history of Urdu literature and marks an odd conjuncture. This text, written by a Frenchman and in French, is nevertheless multiply imbricated within the structures of the British colonial enterprise in the subcontinent. First of all, it was sponsored by British colonial authorities, and a large number of copies were bought in advance of publishing for the benefit of colonial officers at various levels of the colonial bureaucracy—a debt acknowledged by the author in dedicating the book to the Queen. And the text itself, written by an individual who had never set foot on Indian soil, is addressed to the needs of precisely those Europeans who would come into close contact with the language communities whose textual output it sets out to historicize. In this complex relationship to the British colonial enterprise, however, it is far from being unique among the works of French Indologists in the aftermath of the secure establishment of British authority in large parts of the subcontinent beginning in the late eighteenth century and especially after the end of the Napoleonic wars. Equally well known is the case of *Description of the Character, Manners, and Customs of the People of India; and of their Institutions, Religious and Civil*, written by a French missionary, the Abbé Jean-Antoine Dubois, and purchased and then published in English translation by the East India Company in 1816, the priest eventually retiring on a pension from the company.[69]

Garcin de Tassy's *Histoire* quickly produced significant effects in vernacular literary culture. A partial "translation" into Urdu was produced in 1848 at Delhi College, arguably the leading center of (Orientalized) modern learning and translation from English in North India in the decades before 1857.[70] As Sayida Surriya Hussain has shown, this was in fact a free standing work which took the *Histoire* as its source material.[71] This Orientalist historiographic enterprise, and its assimilation into the new Urdu public sphere, partial and fitful though it was, mark the beginnings of the shifts in knowledge practices that eventually put a final end to the *tazkira* by appropriating its materials. In that instant, as it were, of the emergence of the history of Urdu literature, the genre of *tazkira* was reconstellated and could henceforth only be judged to be a sort of debased literary history, devoid of the basic principles of rigorous historical research and writing. In the form of Garcin de Tassy's *Histoire*, literary history not so much repudiated the *tazkira* as assimilated it, raiding and appropriating its materials and establishing a new hierarchy, with the *tazkira* now appearing simply as an insufficient and inferior attempt at history writing. (The scholarly historical literature that has emerged in Urdu with recurring frequency ever since on the subject of the failings of the *tazkira* as historical writing constitutes an enormous archive on its own.) Furthermore, the epistemological basis of what had been a form of anthological compilation pertaining to a narrowly conceived and linguistically and socially delimited tradition of writing within a larger linguistic space—which I have been calling the northern Indian vernacular—was now converted into an instance of the "history" of a language as such and "its" literature. As Pritchett has argued in her discussion of Mir's *Nikāt al-shu'arā*, that text seeks to establish a relatively narrow constellation of poets of *rēkhta*, which it defines as poetry along Persian lines that is written in the "refined" vernacular of eighteenth-century Delhi, or Shahjahanabad, demoting and marginalizing, while unable to ignore entirely, the enormous body of *rēkhta* verse produced in earlier centuries far away from Delhi, namely, in Bijapur, Golconda, and Gujarat.[72] For the *tazkira* as a form offered not an account of the past (of poetry), let alone an account of the progressive development of a tradition, but rather a treasury of verse to be emulated and a common stock of anecdotal knowledge that was part of the history of reception of the verse. It was therefore inherently selective in nature in ways that do not conform to those of literary historiography.

It is against this background of the institution of literary history that Azad's precise role and accomplishment must be understood. Azad was a second-generation product of Delhi College. His father founded the first Urdu-language newspaper in Delhi, and from an early age, Azad himself was involved in the family's journalistic activities. On the sudden outbreak of the rebellion in 1857, the father half reluctantly threw in his lot with the rebels' cause; so when the British forces retook the city, he was summarily arrested and executed, and the family, including the twenty-seven-year-old Muhammad Husain, was thrown out of their house and the city. These events and the subsequent years of wandering and destitution are described by Azad toward the end of his literary history as part of a life narrative of his deceased teacher, the poet Shaikh Ibrahim "Zauq," a fragment of whose unpublished manuscripts Azad saved from the devastation in Delhi.[73] When Azad eventually resurfaced in Lahore in the early 1860s, it was as a protégé of local British officials, and he rose rapidly in the educational and cultural institutions set up by the state in Punjab—Government College, Oriental College, and above all, the Anjuman-e Panjāb (Punjab Association)—in the early decades of the region's incorporation into the colonial domain. The tenor of his writings of this early period are sycophantic in the extreme, endorsing the most racist ideas about the parental tutelage of the rulers over their Indian subjects. And for the remainder of his life, he seems to have struggled between a wholesale endorsement of "English" models for Urdu (and, more broadly, Muslim and Indian) literature and culture and fealty to older practices, institutions, and forms.

Pritchett has documented the ways in which numerous literary histories written in the twentieth century continued to produce judgments concerning the Urdu poetic tradition that can be traced to Azad. She notes the highly ambivalent statements made by such (Anglophone) historians of Urdu as Ram Babu Saksena and Muhammad Sadiq, among others, who cannot quite renounce what they simultaneously denounce as a morally compromised and rhetorically overwrought tradition. She speaks of the "ubiquity and inescapability" of Azad's colonial appeal for a "naturalistic" poetry along "English" lines and of the "passionate, hypnotic spell" he has cast over Urdu criticism for a century.[74] And Faruqi goes so far as to state that the "literary career of Muhammad Husain Azad can be described as a triumph of British techniques of management and control in India."[75] I will have occasion shortly to engage more closely with Faruqi's discussion of *Āb-e ḥayāt*, with which I agree in some important respects but not in others. At the very least, however, we should note here the fact that a long tradition of very "passionate" recapitulation of Azad's views seems to have solicited in these two introductions an equally passionate denunciation—they seem as caught up in the terms and politics of Azad's text as are the subsequent historians they excoriate. When I return to Azad shortly, I shall in part be concerned with understanding the structure of this debate, what it means for a postcolonial critique of Urdu's location in its social worlds, and the possibilities of escaping its seemingly centripetal force.

Azad's literary history of 1880 and the *Muqaddima-e śiʻr o śāʻirī* (Introduction to Poetry and Poetics, 1893) by his comrade in arms Altaf Husain Hali have a distinct place in the history of the world literary system, for they mark a colonial project of "reform" with respect to the very practices of "Oriental" writing whose "discovery" and assimilation into the European literary sphere had been so crucial an element in the very condition of possibility of world literature a century earlier. As I have already argued, given the profound involvement of nineteenth-century western European literature with the newly discovered literatures of the East, given the very invention of world literature precisely through the assimilation of these materials—from Jones's translation of *Śākuntala* to Goethe's gestures toward that text and full-scale engagement with the ghazals of Hafez—it is, to say the very least, an ironic development that when a literary-historical and critical practice emerged in Urdu along "Western" lines under the impact of colonial rule, it produced an *Anglicist* or more broadly "Occidentalist" critique of the lyric traditions of Persianate culture, the very "Oriental" corpus of the lyric that a century earlier had been utilized or evoked by a wide range of individual scholars, writers, and literary movements in Europe in a series of attempts to transform poetic practice in the modern West.

Despite the location of the ghazal in Urdu at the very center of the crisis of literary modernity in colonial society, it has proven to be a strangely persistent form, surviving wave after wave of excoriation and rejection by writers and critics of all hues for well over a century, from those "Hindi nationalists" in the nineteenth and twentieth centuries for whom it was "people's exhibit A" in their case against Urdu for having brought an alien (that is, Near Eastern) sensibility into an Indian language to those Urdu poets and critics themselves, like Azad and Hali, who, for various reasons, considered it a historically superseded form, incapable of giving expression to a distinctly modern subjectivity. At one level, the genre is definable simply as a form in the narrow sense, and the poet Agha Shahid Ali, whose Anglophone ghazal practice we shall turn to in Chapter 3, has delineated the structure with remarkable clarity: "It is composed of autonomous or semi-autonomous couplets that are united by a strict scheme of rhyme, refrain, and line length. The opening couplet sets up the scheme by having it in both lines, and then the scheme occurs only in the second line of every succeeding couplet—i.e., the first line (same length) of every succeeding couplet sets up a suspense, and the second line (same length but with the rhyme and refrain—the rhyme immediately preceding the refrain) delivers on that suspense by amplifying, dramatizing, imploding, exploding."[76] But the reformist critique of Urdu and Indo-Persian poetic culture is ironic in another sense as well: the anguished recognition that the corpus of Urdu verse has entered the space of world literature disheveled and disfigured—not on its own terms but on those of the world-literary system—and as such can henceforth be judged only as a relic of the past. In a revealing passage in the introductory section of *Āb-e ḥayāt*, Azad notes precisely these discrepancies: "My friends! I see that the exhibition hall of sciences and arts is open, and all the peoples have been displaying the handiwork of their literature. Don't you see on what level our language stands? Yes—you can clearly see—she lies there on the doormat!"[77] In other words, the act of historicization undertaken by Azad, this very process of the assimilation of the Urdu corpus into a knowledge system in which the literary production of "all the peoples" is placed next to each other and judged from the perspective of the system, is the very *agent* of its displacement and disfigurement. It is this recognition of the inescapability of the vernacular culture's alienation in the new world context that marks Azad's text with its characteristic tone of reproach—*self*-reproach, above all. The Fort William College enterprise—its narratives and such supplementary forms of its textual production as glossaries, dictionaries, and grammars—which, as I have argued, is the first instance anywhere of a standardization of the northern vernacular in two forms, each firmly marked by its basis in a conception of communities marked by denominational difference, was thus merely the first step in this process of conflicted vernacularization, which is completed in the historicization of this diverse textual corpus. More accurately, we should say that the first literary histories of the northern vernacular constitute an attempt *to provide a historical basis* to the supposedly distinct languages first standardized at Fort William. How, then, are we to understand this process of acquisition of literary history? What happens in that moment in which a textual corpus is reinscribed within a narrative of historical development?

The question of the literary history of the vernaculars arose in the colonial *disjuncture*, but its modalities typically consisted of positing a *continuity* of past and present—emphasizing transition instead of disjunction, papering over the heterogeneity of the moment, both enabling and disabling—that allows the very asking of the question. In other words, to ask the question—what is the history of Urdu literature?—is to mask the historical violence of the question itself; but it is a violence that cannot be papered over entirely, and its effects surface in all kinds of forms in the language itself over the next century and in fact into our times. In this process of the acquisition of literary history, the textual corpus acquires, first of all, the attributes of literariness. That is to say, as I have noted, it enters the world literary system as one among many other literatures, being subject henceforth to the requirements and measures of literariness, replacing the models and modes of evaluation internal to the textual corpus itself. Furthermore, in the moment of its historicization, it undergoes a shift of orientation within the larger social formation, being reinscribed within a discursive system for the attribution of a literature to a language, understood as the unique possession and mode of expression of a people.

With Azad's *Āb-e ḥayāt*, widely heralded as the first history of Urdu literature written by a native speaker and practitioner of the written language, the gesture embodied in the Orientalist establishment of the history of "Urdu literature" is imported back into Urdu itself as its foundational declaration of independence from its complex linguistic and literary environment. Whereas the *tazkira* had been a genre of writing devoted to commemorating and repeating the transmission of a particular poetic practice within a larger linguistic field, the vast and multiform North Indian vernacular, Azad's text transforms its investments entirely, producing instead a *proprietary* account of the poetic tradition of a distinct language. This is the significance of the seemingly bizarre historical claim about the origin of Urdu as a language out of Braj-bhasha that Pritchett has correctly identified as a fulcrum point in his text, around which its various lines of force are arranged. The "tree of Urdu grew in the ground of Sanskrit and Bhasha," Azad writes, and was born when Persian vocabulary and grammatical forms entered Braj-bhasha.[78] As Pritchett points out, in simply morphological terms, this statement makes no sense at all, since Braj is distinct—morphologically, geographically, historically—from the *kharī bōlī* of Delhi and eastern Uttar Pradesh that is the shared morphological ground of both modern Urdu and modern Hindi. But Azad's aim here seems to be quite other than philological precision. He is attempting to situate the origins of Urdu centuries ago in the Persianization of the North Indian vernacular, signified here imprecisely as (Braj) Bhasha, a historical process that intensified to the degree that "Bhasha and Urdu became as different as night and day," the one (that is, the former) a "sweet language," without metaphor and "exaggeration," and the other (that is, the latter) a treasure house of metaphorical elaboration.[79] What is sought in Azad's claim, in other words, is to resituate Urdu within a narrative of historical development in which its vernacular linguistic environment is remapped as a lost origin from which it has long broken free, Urdu now appearing as the (only) *modern* form of the northern vernacular. But since this cannot be the ever-present origin of indigenizing nationalist discourse, the corpus now known to us as Urdu can at best ever have an unstable and unsettled relationship to the nation. Or to put it more precisely, in the project of national literary historicization, Urdu inevitably acquires the attributes of *a literature in search of a nation.*

What is remarkable for both its historical irony and the lack of attention it has gotten by scholars of language and literature is the fact that when modern *kharī bōlī* Hindi began to declare its independence from Urdu, it replicated precisely this historical narrative of the development of the northern vernacular. The emergence of Urdu as a modern (that is, colonial) language thus required that its living connections to its larger linguistic environment be sundered and rearranged within an account of a (tenuous) relationship to a distant past. In this reconstellation of language, writing, tradition, and people, the *tazkira* became merely a source of *information*—imperfect and imprecise, needing decoding and evaluation—on the prehistory of a modern language and its literature. It is thus that with Azad, the *tazkira* finally comes to an end and an Urdu literary history, properly speaking, may be said to have begun. Therefore, by the time a full-fledged historiography of a tradition of writing called Hindi literature emerged in Ramchandra Shukla's *Hindī sāhitya kā itihās* (The History of Hindi Literature, 1929), which has been revisited in some recent scholarship as an originary act of independence, the terms for the establishment of separate literary histories out of the single but diverse and diffuse corpus of writing in the vernacular of the North—this colonial resolution of the question of language and literature—had long been settled, precisely by the official historiography of what is now to be called Urdu literature, by its internalization of the Indological premise and gesture. The very foundational acts of historicization that produced for the first time the terms of distinct and independent literary histories for these two traditions thus represent at the same time their anchoring in a colonial and Orientalist logic. The characteristic stance of this emergent national (and colonial) literary history thus reveals the *retroactive* nature of all literary historicization. Our task, on the other hand, or rather our question, is how to give a historical account of the acquisition of literary history, and in fact two supposedly distinct literary histories, by a vast, diffuse, and internally differentiated body of writing. What I have attempted in this section on literary history is a historical (and critical) account of the Orientalist ascription of historicality to the linguistic-textual corpus of the North Indian vernacular, an ascription structured around the chronotope of the indigenous.

It is therefore not a mysterious or inexplicable fact that Azad's text occupies the horizon-defining role that Pritchett and Faruqi have ascribed to it, against which each generation of criticism and literary history seems to struggle anew. But this is a problem not only in criticism and scholarship, but rather for literary writing practice itself. In each generation of writers, it seems, the problem of the colonial resolution of the question of language, literature, and history, whose icon and name within the realm of criticism is "Azad," is renewed and tackled in yet more novel and creative ways. Let us note here in passing a few prominent examples from the post-Partition period. Qurratulain Haider's epic novel *Āg kā Daryā* (River of Fire, 1959) represents an attempt to create a historical imagination in novelistic discourse that can take as its purview the entire society of the Indo-Gangetic plain in its historical evolutions over two thousand years, from the empire of the Mauryans to the decade following Partition. Given how stunning the chronological framing of its narrative is, that has received much of the attention of critics over the decades. But one of its more unique (though quieter) experiments is the development of a "high" Urdu vocabulary and mode of discourse for the expression of Hindu and Buddhist religiosity. In the poetry of Faiz Ahmed Faiz, as I have argued at length elsewhere, the conventional Persianized vocabulary of the Urdu tradition is abandoned from time to time, to be replaced with a linguistic register which can only be thought of as "Hindavi," and in fact these linguistic choices are often marked by direct reference to the thirteenth-century mystic and Hindavi poet Amir Khusrau himself.[80] And in an important late poem—"Ab tum hī kahō kyā karnā hai" (Now you say what is to be done, 1981)—in which he examines the entire arc of the twentieth century and the collapse of the utopian hopes for decolonization and the revolutionary transformation of society, the "Hindi" register is not medieval but contemporary, *kharī bōlī* in morphological terms but largely without the conventionalized Persian-Urdu vocabulary. It would simply be read as a Hindi poem were it not grounded to the Urdu tradition by the workings of the author-function, the identity of its author as a poet of Urdu. In the work of Jamiluddin Aali, this attempt to struggle against the colonial identity of language and literature takes the form of the adoption in Urdu of a historical poetic form, the *dōhā* or distich, whose identity in colonial-modern terms is entirely "Indic" or "Hindi." And Fahmida Riaz, among the greatest living writers in Urdu, has performed this attempt in both verse and prose fiction: her collection *Dhūp* (Heat of the Sun), written while in exile in India escaping persecution by the General Zia dictatorship in Pakistan, marks an act of deliberate experimentation (explained at length in the preface of the book), with the linguistic boundaries of modern poetry; while her trilogy of novellas attempts, within the temporal confines of the late twentieth century, something like Qurratulain's civilizational mapping, but what we get now from a late postcolonial location are fragments, *epic* fragments, perhaps, but not the synthesis of the earlier novel whose main mechanism is the device of reincarnation. It is hard to imagine more canonical figures, works, and practices in modern Urdu literature than the ones I have briefly outlined here, and yet, their very aesthetic energies and modalities raise the most fundamental questions about the identity (in the philosophical sense of this term) of Urdu as language, literature, and civilization. Overall we may therefore say that the question of aesthetic value itself in Urdu literary culture remains inseparable from such destabilizing and unsettling acts. And so to the extent that such works might find a place in world literature, it would be as attempts at dismantling its very effects on a linguistic and literary field in a colonial (and postcolonial) setting and therefore perhaps its entire historical development as such.

In light of this analysis of modern Indological practices and their imbrication in the social and cultural life of the subcontinent, then, we might say that Orientalism, broadly speaking, may be understood as a set of processes for the reorganization of language, literature, and culture on a planetary scale that effected the assimilation of heterogeneous and dispersed bodies of writing onto the plane of equivalence and evaluability that is (world) literature, fundamentally transforming in the process their internal distribution and coherence, their modes of authorization, and their relationship to the larger social order and social imaginaries in their places of origin. World literature in its historically received forms is therefore fundamentally a concept of exchange, that is to say, irreducibly a concept of bourgeois society—a concept that recodes an opaque and unequal process of appropriation as a transparent one of supposedly free and equal interchange and communication. And the Latinate term "literature" and the set of its cognates in the Western languages, together with a number of calques or loan translations in the languages of the Global South, now provide the dominant, universalizing, *but by no means absolute* vocabulary for the comprehension of verbal-textual expression worldwide.[81] As my analysis of the Orientalizing process in India, and in the specific case of Hindi-Urdu, has attempted to show, this is an ongoing and open-ended process, a determinate logic of the late-capitalist world, so that the critique of Orientalism (and world literature) too is best understood as open-ended and ongoing, rather than engaged in and accomplished once and for all.

3

Global English and Its Others

WHILE THE HINDI-URDU situation I have examined in Chapter 2 represents at many levels a fairly particular, if not exactly unique, historical trajectory, the broader historical situation of the Indian vernaculars, and their relation to English as literary language and cultural system, reflects a larger and now planet-wide reality. The nationalization of languages over the past two centuries all over the world has been accompanied by the globalization of English. This is only seemingly a paradox, for, as the genealogy I have traced here should have made clear, "English" is the preeminent cultural system for the assimilation of the world's languages precisely along these lines. Having transformed formerly extensive and dispersed cultures of writing, such as Persian and Sanskrit in the region we have been most concerned with here, into narrowly conceived ethnonational spheres, English seeks everywhere to become the preeminent medium of cosmopolitan exchange. And this global situation is replicated in different forms within individual countries, such as India, in the complex hierarchical relations that have come to be established in the postcolonial decades between globalized English and the so-called regional or vernacular languages, as Rashmi Sadana has described in her superb anthropological study of the politics of literary "language and location" in the country.[1]

Among the many signs of this dramatic historic shift—and I have charted some others in detail in the foregoing pages—is in patterns of circulation and of access to literary works beyond their immediate societies of origin, one of the sine qua non conditions, according to preeminent contemporary formulations, for ascent into world literature. To take one more or less concrete example, for instance, a hundred years ago at least some intelligentsias in the vast stretch of societies from the eastern Balkans, through Anatolia and Persia proper, including swathes of Central Asia and Afghanistan, and stretching across the northern belt of the subcontinent, may have encountered each other's textual creations in the original and directly—that is, in Persian, Arabic, or Ottoman Turkish. Today, readers in India, Pakistan, Iran, or Turkey will typically encounter each other's literatures only in translation in English (or in further translation from English), thus only if the works have received that metropolitan authentication. (It is fairly evident that the overwhelming majority of translations of world literature into the Indian languages, for instance, are actually translations from English versions.) Muhammad Iqbal, who is generally regarded as the founding poet and philosopher of the Pakistan idea, wrote much of his poetic output in Persian in the first third of the twentieth century, a far cry from the situation today, when most writers in Pakistan, to say nothing of the larger reading public, may well have encountered *Reading Lolita in Teheran* in the original or in Urdu translation but (with minimal exceptions) are almost entirely unaware of contemporary Iranian literature in Persian. (This is even true, to some extent, of Urdu-language writers, let alone Anglophone ones.) And Naguib Mahfouz's Nobel Prize (1988) and the spate of translations that followed certainly did help introduce modern Arabic literature to many Western readers for the first time, but this is also true of readers in many societies formerly part of the Perso-Arabic sphere as well. Lest this line of argument be mistaken, however, for nostalgia for a lost world—the Perso-Arabic ecumene—a specific case of the nostalgia that unmistakably characterizes certain lines of postcolonial thinking, the stakes here ought to be spelled out clearly: the absence of nostalgia for the past does not require that we submit to the realities of the present.

But these shifts in readership and circulation are largely surface phenomena that indicate the deeper tectonic shifts in language, literature, and culture that I have been concerned with here and that are the long legacy of the colonial empires and their logics of Anglicization (or Westernization) and Orientalization. It is a remarkable historical fact, for instance, that at either geographical end of the Persianate sphere—that is, in India and in Turkey—modern literariness was instituted precisely through controversies concerning the link to Persian (and thus also Arabic). Both modern standard Hindi at the turn of the last century and the Turkish of the Kemalist language reforms a few decades later were instituted in large measure through a de-Persianization and de-Arabization of the lexical base, literary influence and models, genres, writing practices of various kinds, and orthography of an existing language formation in order to enact a project of ethnonational or civilizational nationalism in linguistically diverse and multicultural societies. In both historical cases, the most radical linguistic innovations were conceived of as a return to the original language of the people.[2] To Erich Auerbach on his arrival in Istanbul in the mid-1930s, the language reform appeared "at once fantastical ur-Turkish ('free' from Arabic and Persian influences) and modern-technical."[3] But the second "and" in this phrase misses the mark slightly but significantly. For it is precisely because the Kemalist linguistic project was conceived as an attempt to indigenize and vernacularize the Turkish language that it may be said to represent a project of modernization and Europeanization as well. It is therefore hardly surprising that the first systematic case for such a project of indigenization of (Ottoman) Turkish was made by a British Orientalist, the Scottsman Elias Gibb, who, in his history of Ottoman poetry, unfinished at his death in 1901, on the one hand recommended this poetic corpus to Western readers for its aesthetic finesse and accomplishments, while calling at the same time, on the other hand, for the radical "reform" and, as he saw it, *vernacularization* of this written form of the Turkish language.[4] And of course we have already seen in the previous chapter the interest of the colonial state in the invention and institution of an authentically indigenous vernacular of North India, the rise of an indigenizing (that is, nationalist) intelligentsia being linked in complex ways to the state's linguistic, literary, and pedagogical projects from the early decades of the nineteenth century.[5]

A World of English

As I have argued at some length in earlier chapters, the entire question of the expansion of English (and a handful of other Western languages) or, more accurately, the question of their assimilation of non-Western cultures of writing—the process I have identified here as the unfolding of the double logic of Orientalism-Anglicism—is largely ignored in contemporary accounts (such as Casanova's or Moretti's) of the emergence and expansion of world literary space and in such frameworks for the consideration of literary and linguistic diversity as Anglophone literature, World Englishes, or Global English. A serious consideration of this historical process is obstructed by the ubiquitous persistence of nation-thinking, which naturalizes the historically contingent contemporary situation into a landscape of peoples in possession of their "own" languages and literary traditions. The supranational role and presence of English escapes scrutiny precisely in the ascription of authenticity to "local" practices of writing through figures of multiplication, either "other" languages than English or the multiplication of the terrain of English itself— "Anglophone literatures" or "World Englishes." Such acts of multiplication cannot quite dispel the suspicion that the language continues to be conceived of as a single organism, with its origins on a little island in the North Sea, whose subsequent history in the world can be charted as a continuous evolution or unfolding.[6] Before turning to the question of Anglophone writing per se, however, I want to start by posing the broader question of what English is in the situation of literature and culture worldwide and how we can understand its relation to its various others.

There is a powerful moment in Tayeb Salih's novel *Season of Migration to the North* (*Mawsim al-hijra 'ila al-šamāl*, 1966) that condenses into a single image this entire problematic of English as cultural system and the situation of global postcolonial culture.[7] The novel is, famously, an inversion of the narrative movements (in time as in space) of *Heart of Darkness*. The Kurtz figure, as it were, appears in the person of Mustafa Said, the novel reversing the direction of the journey into the heart of darkness, this time from colonial Sudan to pre–World War I London.[8] In England, Mustapha reverses the originary and ongoing violence of colonial occupation through sexual conquest, claiming to liberate Africa with his penis—mentioned only in ellipsis in the novel—seducing and ultimately driving to suicide a long series of English women, precisely by manipulating, intensifying, and finally shattering their Orientalist (and primitivist) fantasies about him as an Arab and African, confirming their desire to see him and his world as the very antithesis of their own, as the purest expression of the barbarous, animality, and nature itself. Convicted finally for the murder of his English wife—who had turned the sexual tables on him and had managed, as he puts it, to convert him from hunter to quarry—Mustapha serves his prison term and returns to the Sudan, settling down in a remote village along the banks of the Nile, where the narrator, a younger native of the village who himself has just returned from England with a Ph.D. in English poetry, encounters him for the first time. The story of his early life is revealed fitfully in exchanges between him and the narrator and at later moments in the latter's encounters with the former's Sudanese friends and acquaintances from his England days.

But this attempt of Mustapha Said's to reinvent himself as an authentic son of the soil and to erase the legacy of his devastating colonial encounter utterly fails in the end. After he has gradually revealed to the narrator this past, entirely unknown to the peasant folk among whom he has chosen to live, including the local young woman he has married, let alone the sons he has had with her, Mustapha disappears, presumed to have drowned in the seasonal floodwaters of the Nile. But Salih leads us to wonder if he had perhaps died, or even simply disappeared, while answering the siren call of the West, of illicit desire, of conquest and sexuality. His widow, in the meantime, who is a local village girl, is forced after his assumed death to remarry against her will with an old man in the village, but she kills both him and herself when he tries forcibly to consummate their marriage on their wedding night. In the wake of this devastating event, the narrator, having discovered that he himself had fallen in love with the now dead woman, returns to the village and enters a room in Mustapha's house that has always been kept locked and sealed from the outside world. It is the jarring juxtaposition of what he discovers in this room in this farmer's house in this village on the banks of the River Nile in the heart of Africa that is of interest to us here. The room is a perfect replica of an English study and sitting room, down to the last architectural detail: "A fireplace—imagine it! A real English fireplace with all the bits and pieces, above it a brass cowl and in front of it a quadrangular area tiled in green marble, with the mantlepiece of blue marble."[9] It is an authentic replica down to the last object it contains, from the paintings and tapestries on the walls to the furniture, carpets, and mementos carefully placed on floor, tables , and mantlepiece. But what shakes the narrator to the core is the library it contains, the books that are everywhere in the room:

> Good God, the four walls from floor to ceiling were filled, shelf upon shelf, with books and more books and yet more books. . . . I could see in the light of the lamp that they were arranged in categories. Books on economics, history and literature. Zoology. Geology. Mathematics. Astronomy. The Encyclopedia Britannica. Gibbon. Macaulay. Toynbee. The complete works of Bernard Shaw. Keynes. Tawney. Smith. Robinson, *The Economics of Imperfect Competition*. Hobson, *Imperialism*. Robinson, *An Essay on Marxian Economics*. Sociology. Anthropology. Psychology. Thomas Hardy. Thomas Mann. E. G. Moore. Thomas Moore. Virginia Woolf. Wittgenstein. Einstein. Brierly. Namier. Books I had heard of and others of which I had not. Volumes of poetry by poets of whom I did not know the existence. *The Journals of Gordon. Gulliver's Travels*. Kipling. Housman. *The History of the French Revolution*, Thomas Carlyle. *Lectures on the French Revolution*, Lord Acton. Books bound in leather. Books in paper covers. Old tattered books. Books that looked as if they'd just come straight from the printers. Huge volumes the size of tombstones. Small books with gilt edges the size of packs of playing cards. Signatures. Dedications. Books in boxes. Books on the chairs. Books on the floor. What play-acting is this? What does he mean? Owen. Ford Maddox Ford. Stefan Zweig. E. G. Browne. Laski. Hazlitt. *Alice in Wonderland*. Richards. *The Qur'an* in English. *The Bible* in English. Gilbert Murray. Plato. *The Economics of Colonialism*, Mustafa Said. *Colonialism and Monopoly*, Mustafa Said. *The Cross and Gunpowder*, Mustafa Said. *Prospero and Caliban. Totem and Taboo*. Doughty. Not a single Arabic book. A graveyard. A mausoleum. An insane idea. A prison. A huge joke. A treasure chamber.[10]

What Salih attempts to condense in this extended image is *the immense library that is the humanistic culture of the modern West* and the fate within it specifically of those forms of historical difference that come marked with the non-Western or non-European origins of the languages in which they are produced. The passage stages the global dominance of this culture, which seems here to include not only the corpus of bourgeois literature and culture but also the internal radical critique of Western society—"Robinson, *An Essay on Marxian Economics*"—*as well as* the specifically Third Worldist, radical, and internationalist critique of Western colonialism—"*The Cross and Gunpowder*, Mustafa Said." Above all, what this remarkable passage points to is *a generalized condition of culture in the contemporary world.* We see now the enormity of the problem: the non-Western text is available to us only within this immense library—"in English," in Salih's resonant words, that is, *in translation*, assigned its place as "Oriental" text-object within the architecture of the Western "universal" library. The passage thus brings to light the situation of the modern Arabic writer and of postcolonial writing and culture more broadly: it raises the possibility that the book in which we encounter it will itself inevitably find its ("translated" and assigned) place in this library, so that the act of writing would have to be a struggle to produce a text that is not merely a dead letter, an epitaph, as it were, words carved on a tombstone. In the final pages of the novel, the narrator, having escaped from the "graveyard," "mausoleum," "insane idea," "prison," "joke," and "treasure chamber" of Mustafa Said's universal library, enters the Nile in a state of semiawareness, nearly drowns midstream, and in the last lines, comes back to consciousness of himself and his surroundings and decides to fight physically to stay alive. The passage thus offers an allegorical rendering of the wider struggle to achieve *historically* validated social and cultural forms as opposed to fantasies of authenticity.

The Moroccan writer and historian Abdallah Laroui, in his classic work of Arab cultural criticism, *L'idéologie arabe contemporaine* (Contemporary Arab Ideology, 1967), published within a year of Salih's novel, attempted to describe this crisis of the intelligentsia in the Arab world on the threshold of decolonization in philosophical terms. His discussion will be of some use to us here in our attempt to understand the meaning of Mustafa Said's library. Although Laroui resists the claim that his conclusions might have a "general value" for the "entire Third World"—a value he believes has been incorrectly ascribed to "the book by Frantz Fanon," presumably *The Wretched of the Earth*, published posthumously four years earlier—the analysis nevertheless has such a value for societies whose modern culture is characterized by the crisis of a textually authorized tradition, the societies, as he puts it, "possessing a classical culture expressed in a national language," including, beyond the Arab countries, "Iran, modern Greece, or the Sicily given expression by its writers from Pirandello to Lampedusa, countries where the past crushes with its splendor a painful present that is lived in forfeit [*un présent douloureux vécu comme une déchéance*]."[11] The dominance of this fundamentally Orientalist ideological structure—a Golden Age in a more or less distant past that provides a permanent counterpoint to a fallen and inauthentic present—implies that no attempt to comprehend the Self in such historical situations can bypass the Other, that is, "the West."

Laroui identifies three main lines of ideological force in Arab society: religious purisms, statecraft and politics, and developmentalist technophilia. Despite the seemingly different relation in each case to the Other that is the West, all three are in fact situated within the generalized sociocultural situation of postcolonial societies that he describes through the "concept of future anterior—of a future already outlined elsewhere and which we are not at liberty to reject." No self-described attempt to "return" to tradition, religious or secular, can sustain its claim to be autonomous of "the West" as Other, Laroui writes, not even claims to authenticity based on gestures of return to the purportedly uncontaminated doxa of religious tradition: "In contemporary Arab ideology, no form of consciousness is authentic: no more so in the religious intellectual [*clerc*] than in the technophile; he reflects a different image of contact with the West, but the center of his thought is no more his own than that of the technophile belongs properly to him."[12] No attempt at self-definition and self-exploration can therefore bypass a historical critique of the West and its emergence into this particular position of dominance. And, in this sense, the critique of the West and the logics of its imperial expansion from a postcolonial location is in fact a *self-critique*, since this location is at least partially a product of that historical process.

This is the task that is undertaken in *Orientalism*, which attempts, as we have already seen, to "inventory the traces upon [him], the Oriental subject, of the culture whose domination has been so powerful a factor in the life of all Orientals." From our present perspective, then, Edward Said's *Orientalism* may be read as an attempt to understand the architecture of Mustafa Said's library, the library that one owns by virtue of being a product of the postcolonial world and by which one is owned in turn. In the original text of Salih's novel—that is, from the perspective of modern literary Arabic—it is of course this catalogue of *English* (and more broadly European) names that appear as estranged and foreign, requiring translation, with the Qur'an, made to stand in here for the entire Arabic-Islamic tradition, undergoing a double estrangement, a double translation. And the *hijra 'ilā al-šamāl* (migration to the north) invoked in Salih's novel parallels what is glossed in Said's work by "the voyage in," the emergence of a worldly oppositional consciousness that is neither fully inside metropolitan culture nor entirely outside it, a critical consciousness that will undertake a radical critique of the Other-as-Self as a condition for exploring "contemporary alternatives to Orientalism, to ask how one can study other cultures and peoples from a libertarian, or a nonrepressive and nonmanipulative, perspective."[13] For Laroui, this is the task of a "double critical consciousness," directed both at the various ideological positions in the Arab world and at the cultural complex that is the modern West.[14]

With respect to the mutual relationship of English and the Indian vernaculars, a now-notorious statement published some years ago by Salman Rushdie might inadvertently offer us some further clarity regarding the contemporary situation of the languages and literatures of the postcolonial world. In the introduction to an anthology of post-Independence Indian fiction, Rushdie offered his readers his considered opinion that the only contemporary Indian literature of significant worth was being written in English: "prose writing . . . by Indian writers *working in English*, is proving to be a stronger and more important body of work than most of what has been produced in the 16 'official languages' of India, the so-called 'vernacular languages,' . . . and, indeed, this new, still burgeoning, 'Indo-Anglian' literature represents perhaps the most valuable contribution India has yet made to the world of books."[15] At least a dozen of these vernaculars happen of course to have literary cultures with traditions of writing that are up to a millennium old, of which Rushdie could not have been entirely unaware. Rushdie's remarks came clothed in a mood of sincerity frustrated: the editor of a projected anthology, having searched exhaustively, was forced to admit in the end that there was nothing in these literary languages that was worth including in the volume. The one exception to this general rule, Rushdie informed his readers, was the Urdu short story "Ṭōbā Ṭēk Siṅgh" (Toba Tek Singh, 1955?) by Saadat Hasan Manto, a translation of which was consequently included in the collection—not exactly an original selection or the result of particularly strenuous deliberation, given the story's mass popularity in the subcontinent, including in multiple English translations, and the fact that it had been produced as a short film for Channel Four in Britain a decade earlier for the fortieth anniversary of the Partition of India.

It is tempting to dismiss Rushdie's remark as a sign simply of arrogance or silliness, but I believe it bears much closer examination. It is not, strictly speaking, an Orientalist statement but is rather an Anglicist one, to return to the terms of the imperial debate in the early nineteenth century about colonial governance and native education. If there are echoes of Thomas Macaulay here, this is far from being accidental. Macaulay's judgment of 1835 about the relative merits of Occidental over Oriental literatures had expressed the distinctly *colonial* logic inherent in Europe's encounter with its Asiatic possessions: "I have no knowledge of either Sanscrit or Arabic—but I have done what I could to form a correct estimate of their value. I have read translations of the most celebrated Sanscrit and Arabic works. I have conversed both here and at home with men distinguished by their proficiency in the Eastern tongues. I am quite willing to take the Oriental learning at the word of the Orientalists themselves. I have never found one among them who could deny that a single shelf of a good European library was worth the whole native literature of India and Arabia."[16] Although Macaulay's text is critical of the Orientalists' case for continuing the natives' education in Asiatic languages and traditions of writing—the narrow issue in contention in the administrative debate—it nevertheless *relies on and reproduces the terms of the Orientalist reinvention of the world literary system* and the placing of the "literatures of the East" within it. Macaulay's formulation expresses very precisely the relative hierarchy and discrepancy of power in the colonial era between, on the one hand, the European languages and above all English and, on the other, major languages of Asia and the Middle East, so that "the whole native literature of India and Arabia" could be *judged in terms of*, and therefore *assimilated into*, "a single shelf of a good European library." It is an image of the *subsumption* of the writing traditions of the world into the European cultural system.

In Rushdie's comments about the quality of literature in the Indian vernaculars, which reveal the reality of a larger linguistic and cultural situation in our times, Macaulay's judgment is updated for the twenty-first century—in an exact sense, giving expression to the now *postcolonial and global* logic through which the Indo-English novel has come to be represented to the outside world in recent years, and to some extent (and increasingly so) to Indian society itself, as the authentic and, more importantly, *authenticating* literature of India. Rushdie, whose *Midnight's Children* (1980) first introduced world audiences to the global ambitions of the Anglophone Indian bourgeoisie at the threshold of the neoliberal restructuring of the Indian economy, seeks to establish the proper relationship in the world literary system between English and the Indian vernaculars: it is on the ground of English as cultural system—and, more precisely, as medium of literary expression—that, for Rushdie, the literariness of the "vernacular" languages must now be adjudicated. Far from being an idiosyncratic and isolated statement, this declaration in fact reflects fairly accurately dominant tendencies in the processes and institutions of world literature. Every spectacular event in the life of global Anglophone literature—such as the much-celebrated recent emergence of the Pakistani novel in English, to which I return shortly—reinforces or even intensifies these tendencies.

No consideration of the Anglophone novel with links to South Asia can bypass entirely the question of the role of English education as "an instrument of colonial rule . . . related to colonial dominance not only as a means of persuasion, but as an arm of its coercive apparatus as well," as Ranajit Guha has put it.[17] As Gauri Viswanathan has demonstrated in her classic study, the teaching of English literature as a subject itself was pioneered in India, in part as a substitute for Christian proselytization, which was looked on with anxiety by administrators for the violent reaction it might produce among native populations of different religious denominations.[18] And as I have already argued, English education, as embodied in individual practitioners and institutions, although typically associated by historians with the Anglicist side of the colonial debate, in fact contained Orientalist projects within it as well. Macaulay's concession to the Orientalists' knowledge therefore catches that complicity between the two poles of the debate at the level of discourse quite precisely. The association of English education with loss of tradition (and even with debauchery and perversity), in the early decades of its institution in India, and especially in Calcutta, extends to the Orientalist dimension of education as well, for the latter invariably meant a reorientation—scholarly or intellectual as well as ritual and customary—toward one's own newly discovered "tradition." It is of course commonplace in the language of politics in contemporary India for partisans of Hindi (as the national language) and the vernaculars (as regional and state languages) to deride the Anglophone elite as "Macaulay's children" and its cultural products as the nation's continuing colonial burden. (A recent Google search of the phrase produced results well in excess of 100,000.) But, as I have argued earlier at some length, the "vernacular" side of this debate is itself implicated in a colonial genealogy and cannot sustain its claim to an "authentic" position uncontaminated by the colonial process. A critical engagement with the Anglophone novel must therefore take place on grounds other than those of authenticity. What is the political scene of the Anglophone novel's emergence, not only at its beginnings in the early twentieth century but every time it is renewed and refurbished into our own times? Rushdie's remark seeks to recode this inherently *political* scene of the mutual relations of English and the vernacular languages in the subcontinent in terms of (uniform and supposedly universal) aesthetic *value*, and it is this question of the Anglophone novel (from South Asia) as the site of a fraught politics of language to which we shall now turn.

"Out of the Garrets of Bloomsbury": The Anglophone Novel from Anand to Aslam

The Indo-English novel has become in recent decades a global form and tradition with a vast accumulation of cultural capital. For readers of world literature outside the subcontinent, in particular (though not exclusively) in the countries of the North Atlantic, it is Anglophone fiction above all, read in the original or in translation in various European languages, that carries the aura of Indian literature. This is in part a result of the preeminence of the novel form as such in world literature as against poetry or drama. And in turn, this global market for the work of writers in the subcontinent writing in English has significantly affected their writing practices. British and American editors now routinely descend on the major cities of South Asia in a frenzied search for the next big first novel, the next *God of Small Things*, a process that is now a routine part of the lives of aspiring young Anglophone writers, affecting in all kinds of concrete ways the writing that gets produced. Sectors of the English-language publishing industry in India itself now work seamlessly with major publishers overseas. But there are continuities with earlier forms of the novel as well. From the first real beginnings of the Indo-English novel in the 1930s, it has represented a series of attempts to explore the possibilities of the novel as such as an "epic" narrative form, capable of giving an account of social totality. If, in the early phases, it offered itself as the epic of a society on the seemingly inexorable path to decolonization and political sovereignty, in its later phases, it has represented a multivalent questioning of the modes of establishment of the nation as community. Throughout its history, therefore, it has struggled with the *social distance* that separates the authorial context from the realities of social and cultural worlds marked as vernacular.

The social situation of English in the societies of the subcontinent, the social geography of access to the language in a range of cultural spheres, is of course irreducibly linked to class, caste, religious-communal, regional, gender, and urban-rural politics. If, on the one hand, elites and segments of the middle classes rely more and more on English as a marker of their identity and place in society in the postcolonial decades, on the other, the desire for English has become an unmistakable mark of the desire for social mobility at other levels of the class spectrum, leading, for instance, to the growth of a vast private-sector school industry, purveyors of English-language education of very dubious quality. The widening of the sphere of English seems to simply reinforce the privilege of those with regularized and steady access to it at all levels of education.[19] The writing of Anglophone literature in these societies, the only aspect of this social complexity that gets to be seen outside the subcontinent, therefore sits atop this enormous social volcano, to which it has an uneasy relationship. Successful Anglophone writers are thus almost inevitably of urban and middle- or upper-middle-class origin, often even linked to individual elite institutions of secondary and higher education, such as Aitchison College (Lahore), Karachi Grammar School (Karachi), the Cathedral School and St. Xavier's College (Mumbai), the Doon School (Dehradun), and St. Stephen's College (Delhi).[20]

Remarks such as Rushdie's represent, first of all, an erasure of this specific class politics of the acquisition of language itself in contemporary South Asia and, second, a naturalization (in "value" terms) of the asymmetrical situations, the vastly different material and symbolic resources, of English and the "vernaculars" as literary languages—including Hindi and Urdu, the putative national languages, respectively, of India and Pakistan—an asymmetry not just in global terms but within South Asia itself.[21] By "vernacular," I of course do not mean simply indigenous or native, for vernacularization, as we have seen, is a complex and fraught historical process that is differently oriented within, but no less immune from, the broader colonial (and postcolonial) process and the assimilative powers of the English cultural system than is Anglophone writing. English shapes the identity of the Anglophone intelligentsia as, properly speaking, the *national* (rather than a provincial or regional) intelligentsia precisely through the circulation of its cultural products in *world* literary space (Rushdie's "world of books"). Furthermore, the remarks are an attempt at disavowing the heterogeneity of the Anglophone novel's *own* linguistic environment in places such as the subcontinent (and, we might add, Africa)—English (or for that matter French, Portuguese, or Afrikaans, among others) in Asia and Africa is never written or spoken out of hearing range of a number of its linguistic others—a heterogeneity that often gets packaged within the form itself as one of its supposedly exotic pleasures, most famously in Rushdie's own works, whose characteristically "Indianized" English stages the presence of modes of speech that the author and the novels themselves repeatedly characterize as the distinct street Hindustani (that is, a sort of "neutral" form of Hindi-Urdu) of the city of Bombay (now Mumbai). Amitav Ghosh's *Calcutta Chromosome* (1995) is perhaps unique in its own generation of Indo-English fiction in that it explores thematically precisely this manifestation of the vernaculars in Anglophone practices, which it characterizes as a *ghostly* presence.[22]

This mode of appearance of the vernaculars within the discourse of the Anglophone novel can be adequately understood only against the long historical arc that I have been tracing in this book. From eighteenth-century Oriental tales, both "original" compositions and those tied in a more or less loose manner to a work or a textual tradition in an Oriental language, through the vernacular "versions" produced (in "Hindi" or "Hindustani") in the early nineteenth century at Fort William College from one or another of the "classical" languages of the subcontinent (Arabic, Persian, Sanskrit, or Braj), to the first self-described attempts to write novels in the vernaculars in the second half of the nineteenth century, the history of narrative forms linked to the societies and cultures of the subcontinent is a series of inversions and tensions—not simply between English and the vernacular languages as media of literary expression, or between "Occidental" form and "Oriental" life-worlds or materials (pace Moretti), but also between versions of the individual and of totality and, finally, between the inherent "novelty" of the novel in relation to more broadly "epic" formal possibilities. The Anglophone novel, properly speaking, is a late appearance in this historical process but carries within itself the tensions it has inherited (and recalibrated and rearranged) from those earlier forms.

The first novelist we shall turn to is Mulk Raj Anand, a figure of considerable interest with respect to the questions that are of concern to us here. A pioneering writer of Anglophone fiction, he was also a cofounder of the Indian Progressive Writers' Association (1935), the umbrella organization of anticolonial writers; played a small role in the United Front antifascist writers' movements of the mid-1930s in Europe; and was at the forefront of Indian writers' and artists' involvement in progressive literary internationalism of the "Bandung" variety from the mid-1950s.[23] *Untouchable* is conventionally treated as the first significant Anglophone novel by an Indian author, the taking-off point in the 1930s for a coherent novel tradition in English. But, as Meenakshi Mukherjee has shown, the form has a prehistory extending at least to the middle of the nineteenth century, with novelistic fictions being published not only from the main metropolitan centers but by small publishers in provincial towns as well and often serialized in periodicals.[24] The Anglophone fiction that emerged in the 1930s—and Anand and Raja Rao are among the key figures—constitutes a sort of declaration of independence from those colonial writing practices. The overarching horizon of these works is of course the problematic of nationalism, and the novels explore the difficulties of the nationalist resolution of the crises of culture and society. At their core is thus the question of the very possibility of representation: they lead us to ask how it is possible for nationalism, the political movement of the Anglicized bourgeoisie, to "represent" the Indian masses in the political sense, an act that is indissociable from its right and ability to produce representations of "the people" in an aesthetic sense.

In this regard, Mahatma Gandhi's reported comment to Anand on experiencing his manuscript of *Untouchable* that his subaltern protagonist—an "untouchable" latrine cleaner and sweeper in a provincial garrison town in North India—sounded too much like a "Bloomsbury intellectual" is more than just an amusing throwaway remark and is of more than casual interest to us here, for it identifies a central tension of the Indian (and world) Anglophone novel as a form.[25] It is Rushdie's distinct place in the history of the Anglophone novel that he attempts to explode this problematic entirely by an ostentatious performance of a "vernacular" Indian speech. But something carries over; the tension and problem are merely displaced to another level, as we shall see in a moment. The temporal structure of the narrative in Anand's novel is itself an attempt to suture together the vastly distant social worlds of the nationalist writer and intellectual—a consciousness that seems to oscillate, or is at best unable to decide, between Gandhian-populist and Nehruvian-technocratic views of society and politics—and the subaltern protagonist living at the abject margins of society: it is an assertively realist narrative that is nevertheless based on the canonical modernist temporal expanse of a single day. In *Mrs. Dalloway*, Virginia Woolf placed London at the center of a world empire—the novel opens with a "shindig" in a pub involving a "colonial" who had made an audible insult to the House of Windsor, and during Clarissa's party later in the day a guest shares her concern, repeated almost like a refrain, about the "state of India," a reference to the rise of Gandhian nationalist agitation.[26] Anand takes us to the colonial periphery itself, the novel thus marking *a double displacement of Bloomsbury* as aesthetic complex and social milieu, the dominant metropolitan literary and intellectual culture for this emergent Indian nationalist intelligentsia: from the West End of London to a dingy little colonial garrison town in North India and from the peregrinations of a middle-aged socialite through streets lined with bespoke establishments to the fraught and perilous walk through the center of town by a young latrine cleaner, cowering in the presence of his caste oppressors but dreaming of better days. These two protagonists, Bakha and Clarissa, represent perhaps the two extreme ends of the social hierarchy of the globally extensive social order of the British Empire. In an address delivered to the second conference of the Indian Progressive Writers' Association in Calcutta in December 1938, a remarkable document of modern Indian literary history, Anand coined an extraordinary image for the emergent aesthetics of his generation and their attempt to give it political-organizational form: "It is almost uncanny to look back upon those dark foggy November days of the year 1935 in London when after the disillusionment and disintegration of years of suffering in India and conscious of the destruction of most of our values through the capitalist crisis of 1931, a few of us emerged from the slough of despond of the cafes and garrets of Bloomsbury and formed the nucleus of the Indian Progressive Writers' Association."[27] The Indo-English literary imagination appears in this image as the *unconscious* of contemporary British culture, with Indian social realism emerging out of a sort of talking cure of (European) modernism. There is no strong or naïve claim to autonomy here; on the contrary, it marks a recognition of the mutual imbrication of "Indian" and "English."

As for the framed appearance of "vernacular" modes of life and speech in the discourse of the world Anglophone novel in our own times—the *inverse* social scenario from latrine cleaners sounding like Bloomsbury intellectuals—it is an essential structural feature of the form, whose exact treatment can be subject to a fairly wide range of experimentation but whose overall structure does not undergo very dramatic variation. At a certain level of abstraction, we could say that this is merely a subset of the broader feature of novelistic discourse that Mikhail Bakhtin identified as the inherent discursive plurality of the novel form as such, its simultaneously "centripetal" and "centrifugal" arrangement of vastly different discourses in a hierarchical but dynamic structure—tendencies, on the one hand, toward a common and "unitary language" and, on the other, toward "social and historical heteroglossia."[28] But it is among the tasks of a social stylistics of the (South Asian) Anglophone novel as a form to identify, first of all, the *modes* of such discursive suturing specific to it and, furthermore, the social significance and *valences* to which they correspond as well. The representation of vernacular speech and life forms within the discourse of the Anglophone novel, which is perhaps most ordinarily achieved through a speaking person marked as subaltern, is a means of *bridging a certain type of social distance* characteristic of postcolonial society, either within the nation-state or across a wider geopolitical landscape.

We can make a few pertinent observations here about this feature of novelistic discourse in the Indo-English novel of India's own boom years. This globalized form of the South Asian Anglophone novel dates more or less to the publication of Rushdie's *Midnight's Children* (1980), though it has important precedents in G. V. Desani's *All about H. Hatter* (1948) and the works of R. K. Narayan. Perhaps no other Anglophone novel has come to be associated to this extent with the idea that it bends the English language toward another language, terms like "chutney," "masala," or "hot" English being routinely used to describe this feature by numerous readers and by the author himself.[29] There are many characters, major and minor, in the novel, whose life-worlds, speech forms, and "ideologically freighted discourse" are marked as subaltern, but perhaps none is as paradigmatic as Padma, the lover, caretaker, and even, in a certain way, amanuensis of the narrator, Saleem Sinai, as he races against time to write down the story of his life and that of the Midnight's Children Conference, the psychic assembly of the most magically gifted individuals of India's first post-Independence generation.[30] Being a part of the narrative milieu, Padma is therefore one of the most constant presences throughout the novel, second only to Saleem himself, trying constantly to feed him and keep him alive while witnessing his physical disintegration. Here is a somewhat typical passage involving Padma from near the beginning of the novel, her very first appearance in the story:

> Padma—our plump Padma—is sulking magnificently. (She can't read and, like all fish-lovers, dislikes other people knowing anything she doesn't. Padma: strong, jolly, a consolation for my last days. But definitely a bitch-in-the-manger.) She attempts to cajole me from my desk: "Eat, na, food is spoiling." I remain stubbornly hunched over paper. "But what is so precious," Padma demands, her right hand slicing the air up-down-up in exasperation, "to need all this writing-shiting?" I reply: now that I've let out the details of my birth, now that the perforated sheet stands between doctor and patient, there's no going back. Padma snorts. Wrist smacks against forehead. "Okay, starve, starve, who cares two pice?" another louder, conclusive snort, . . . but I take no exception to her attitude. She stirs a bubbling vat all day for a living; something hot and vinegary has steamed her up tonight, thick of waist, somewhat hairy of forearm, she flounces, gesticulates, exits. Poor Padma. Things are always getting her goat. Perhaps even her name: understandably enough, since her mother told her, when she was only small, that she had been named after the lotus goddess, whose most common appellation amongst village folk is "The One Who Possesses Dung."

For all the talk of blowing up literary English, it is pretty clear in this passage, first of all—and examples from this novel could be multiplied almost endlessly—that there is a clear distinction of diction, rhythm, and grammatical structure between the ideological (and therefore) social field that Bakhtin calls authorial discourse, which is not to be confused simply with "narrative voice," and the discourse we glimpse in Padma's speech, the latter being represented by means of the former. The preceding passage is in fact followed immediately by this one:

> In the renewed silence, I return to sheets of paper which smell just a little of turmeric, ready and willing to put out of its misery a narrative which I left yesterday hanging in mid-air—just as Sheherazade, depending for her very survival on leaving Prince Shahryar eaten up by curiosity, used to do night after night! I'll begin at once: by revealing that my grandfather's premonitions in the corridor were not without foundation. In the succeeding months and years, he fell under what I can only describe as the sorcerer's spell of that enormous—and as yet unstained—perforated cloth.[31]

On the one hand, there is the earthy one, "thick of waist," "Who Possesses Dung"; on the other, there are references to the *Thousand and One Nights*. First of all, since this is first-person narrative, we might say that in this extended passage one character in the novel—the narrator, Saleem—is not revealing (and cannot reveal) large segments of his social and cultural worldview, the ideological contents of his own specific discourse, to the (social) "other" that is Padma, contents that can be shared, of course, with the reader. (The implied reader is thus much more likely to be Saleem's social type rather than Padma's.) And the *Nights* itself appears here as a sign of a certain *Western*, because Orientalist, learning. Furthermore, in one remarkable little imperative phrase—"Eat, na, food is spoiling"—Padma's very first spoken words in the novel, we see Rushdie's entire strategy for the introduction of a recognizably Indian English idiom into his language. In fact, there are two distinct techniques at work here. The phrase "food is spoiling" is an instance of the syntax of one language being mimicked in another—a common feature of Indian English speech forms. The Hindi-Urdu phrase being "translated" here could, for instance, be, "khānā kharāb ho rahā hai." Even more interesting, however, is the imperative phrase—"Eat, na"—where a *morphological* element of a conjugated verb from some unidentified North Indian language (though probably again Hindi-Urdu), the emphatic *nā*, is attached to an English verb in its imperative form. And there is a *comma* separating the English verb from its emphatic "foreign" (that is, Hindi-Urdu) suffix—the hilarious nature of the claim that this suffix might settle into English morphology being highlighted by the comma that separates it from the verb.

These are of course common features of what even sociolinguists have come to call "Hinglish," the lexical, syntactical, and morphological mixing in speech forms in India between English elements and those of the northern vernacular. But more specifically, they are habits of urban *middle-class* Indian (and, more specifically, Bombay) English speech. What we get in this passage from *Midnight's Children*, therefore—and this is a typical feature of Rushdie's novelistic language across his works—is the attribution of an urban middle-class idiom to an illiterate subaltern (and here, a woman and of peasant background) who should typically not be able to speak any kind of English at all. This is not a question so much of "the linguistic authenticity of fictional characters," a question that resurfaces repeatedly in polemical form in the literary language debates in India, as of mapping the social valences of their speech forms and patterns.[32] In the case of Rushdie's writings, we might then say that a middle-class urban Indian idiom is represented in the discourse of the Anglophone novel as a genuinely subaltern speech form or as its "translation" into the Anglophone discourse of the novel. When middle-class South Asian readers respond to this aspect of the novel, therefore, they are recognizing their *own* speech forms. In what is merely the most recent instance of this type of reception, Deepa Mehta, the director of the film based on the novel, told a journalist of her first encounter with the book in 1983, "It's the first time I had read a novel where I felt the English language had been chutney-fied or actually had been reworked with Hindi in such a way that it made it very personal to Indians."[33] And in the case of other Rushdie characters—Gibreel Farishta in *The Satanic Verses* (1988), for instance—this sociological link of a character's language to the Anglophone middle-class are more patently apparent. It is now a fairly routine judgment that before the moment of Rushdie's emergence practices of representing Asian and African life-worlds in English-language fiction had either exoticized those realities (including linguistic ones), that is, made the other thoroughly familiar through figures of the exotic—in *Cry, the Beloved Country* (1948) by Alan Paton, for instance, or even Pearl S. Buck's *The Good Earth* (1931)—or, in the case of a writer like Narayan, had projected the bullock-cart temporalities of the so-called eternal life of the Indian village or small town onto the life of the nation as such. The new fiction, it is then suggested, burst out of the constraints of those earlier novelistic practices and put the reader directly into contact with the "hot and messy and vulgar and crowded and noisy" reality of India, to quote Rushdie's recent comments about the writing of *Midnight's Children* once again.

While I do not disagree with some of the conventional perceptions about the historical novelty of Rushdie's fiction, I do think that one of its distinctive and much-heralded features, namely, the mode of appearance in it of "vernacular" speech forms and life-worlds, is not, as I have attempted to show in the foregoing analysis of one passage from *Midnight's Children*, exactly what it has often been taken to be. The "chutney-fied" English strewn throughout the novels is not to be confused for the authorial discourse itself, which may *cite* the former from time to time in unmarked ways but is never identical to it. Authorial discourse in these novels may not unfold in what Rushdie himself has called the "cool" language of E. M. Forster's novel of India, but its claim to "subaltern" status needs decoding: it is nothing more (but also nothing less) than a staking of a claim to autonomy within international Anglophone literary culture.[34] In this one limited sense, therefore, it seems to me that Rushdie's is not a more radical experiment than Desani's in *All about H. Hatter*, often mentioned by Rushdie himself as an important predecessor.

The genius of Rushdie's execution in *Midnight's Children* is a double and even contradictory one: it lies in calling attention to the social distance between elite and subaltern as social, cultural, psychological,

and linguistic realities and, on the one hand, *exploring* it thematically in terms of the lifelong struggle between Saleem and
Siva—the former having usurped the latter's privileged legacy when
the two were exchanged at birth—while offering us, on the other, a
myth of its overcoming at the level of novelistic discourse. And in this
one aspect, it is also not as distant as it might be expected to be from
such a canonical work of national realism in Hindi as *Ādhā Gāūñ*
(Half the Village) by Rahi Masoom Raza, whose famous presentation of the "Bhojpuri" speech forms of eastern Uttar Pradesh remain
limited to the speech of individual characters, with the authorial context provided entirely in "high" literary *kharī bōlī* Hindi. And the
technique of Ghosh in the first two (already published) novels of
the *Ibis Trilogy*, where sociolinguistic registers, from the Bhojpuri
dialect of eastern Hindi to Cantonese pidgin English, are reduced
almost to the level of idiolects associated with individual characters,
perhaps takes this procedure to its fullest realization. But this is
a paradoxical achievement, to say the least. In the first book of the
trilogy, *Sea of Poppies* (2008), for instance, we see the return of
the glossary, whose elimination from postcolonial Anglophone fiction was sometimes touted as a sign of its declaration of independence
from metropolitan literary English, with the added innovation now
that it is in fact incorporated into the novel itself, taking the form of
the "chrestomathy" of the *Ibis*, the ship on which the lives of all the
novel's characters, like their languages, intersect and commingle. To
this extent, it is possible to say that these new modes of representation
of vernacular speech forms in literary English therefore also mark
simply a new modulation in the larger and historically longer preoccupation with vernacularization—and "Anglicism," we might say,
reveals its complicity with "Orientalism" once again.

But the treatment of the social distance separating the social mi-
lieus of Anglophone novelistic discourse from vernacular spaces and
practices can of course take many forms in the contemporary novel
other than that of the (subaltern) speaking person and its discourse.
In the novel of immigration (from South Asia to Britain), for instance, the distance takes literally geographical form in the vector
of the immigrant's journey from his or her homeland in the global
periphery to the metropolis. To take one example, in *Brick Lane*

(2003), the social and cultural distance between the working-class London inhabited by Bengali immigrants and the rural Bangladeshi hinterland of their origin is given the shape of *temporal* difference, the almost mythological temporality of the opening chapter, which takes place entirely in the ancestral village in Bangladesh, being in sharp contrast with the "empty, homogeneous" realist narrative temporality of the rest of the novel. And the same individual characters "speak" differently in the novel's English in the two different places, as if to characterize the difference between their pre- and postmigration lives as ontologically distinct universes.

Finally, we need to address the singular fact that in a large number of important Anglophone novels linked to the subcontinent the question of a possible approach to the "vernacular" takes the form of a fascination and engagement to varying degrees with one single linguistic and cultural formation, Urdu literary culture and *poetry* in particular. Among the postcolonial writers, these include such important works as Rushdie's *Midnight's Children* and *The Enchantress of Florence* (2008), Anita Desai's *In Custody* (1984), Mohsin Hamid's *Moth Smoke* (2000), Nadeem Aslam's *Maps for Lost Lovers* (2004), Aravind Adiga's *The White Tiger* (2008), and Kamila Shamsie's *Burnt Shadows* (2009), to name only the most important examples and to say nothing of such earlier canonical works as *A Passage to India* (1924), *Untouchable*, or Ahmed Ali's *Twilight in Delhi* (1940), the latter in fact another Bloomsbury work, first published by Hogarth Press. It is hard to think of any other vernacular literary culture of the subcontinent receiving such persistent attention in the Anglophone novel tradition. What are we to make of this predilection, and what exactly is its significance for the larger set of issues that concern us in this book? To begin with, we may note that the modes of appearance of Urdu in the more recent group of novels are far from identical or uniform. In Desai's novel, for instance, Urdu appears cast as a degenerating (formerly elite) culture, given concrete form in the disintegrating life and domestic relations of the poet Nur, resident of Shahjahanabad, the old walled city of Delhi. Interestingly, in the novel's own terms, Hindi and Urdu are mutually antagonistic but nevertheless overlapping literary registers and cultures, on a continuum with each other rather than inhabiting noncoincident worlds: Deven Sharma, the protagonist of the novel, is a poor college teacher of Hindi in a provincial town but his true love is Urdu poetry, especially the verse of the once-great Nur. This association of Urdu with degeneration is a distinctly Indian possibility, nearly impossible to imagine within a Pakistani cultural framework (for instance in Aslam's novel), where, if anything, Urdu is of course experienced as the dominant literary culture in the country from the perspective of the various regional languages.[35] As I have noted in Chapter 2, this association of Urdu in India with a social order in decline—the cliché of its inculcation of *navābī* or semifuedal *mentalités*—reveals in fact a haze of misperceptions about the social realities of Urdu in the country, let alone in the subcontinent as a whole, from the location of the mainstreams of national culture. But it is also a notable fact that Desai uses Urdu, rather than Hindi or any other more (nationally speaking) "representative" literary culture in India, to reflect on the fate of the vernacular languages as such in the transition to the globalized economic, social, and cultural forms that are visible only in incipient or chrysalis form in the novel.

In Adiga's *The White Tiger*, the appearance of Urdu takes the form of citations of Urdu and Persian poets, including Asadullah Khan Ghalib but especially Muhammad Iqbal, as part of the elaborate joke that is the opening conceit of the novel—Balram Halwai's letter to the Chinese Prime Minister, an invitation, we might say, to collaborate in the creation of a sort of "capitalism with Asian values." The "values" here are provided by Iqbal's philosophy of historically meaningful action rather than, say, the romantic and lyric verse traditions associated in Desai's novel with Nur. And in Aslam's *Maps for Lost Lovers*, a certain sense of melancholia identified repeatedly as derived from Urdu literary culture comes to pervade the mood of the narrative as a whole. Here the preeminent figure is Faiz Ahmed Faiz—militant, worldly, and yet the creator of exquisite lyric verse. The field of affect generated by the scene of separation from the beloved, this characteristic and well-known preoccupation of the Urdu ghazal, provides in the novel the vocabulary for the experience of diasporic communities displaced from the newly decolonized societies of their origin—India and Pakistan, in the case of the major characters—to the former imperial center, the slow-burning fuse of their loneliness, despair, and disorientation. The sudden disappearance and slow discovery of the fate of the "lost lovers" of the title is in turn itself a figure for the temporalities of Urdu verse, closing the circle from verse to prose and back to verse again. To sum up, then, these English-language novels' attraction to the Urdu poem and its social lives reveals the life of Urdu quite beyond the terms imposed on it by the nation-state system in the subcontinent, namely, that it may be conceived of as either the exquisite but superseded and ghettoized expressivity of "the Muslims" as minority within the nation-state or the powerful medium of their normalization as a majority within a separate nationalism and nation-state. Urdu continues to cross the borders of this system, offering to Anglophone novelistic discourse a strange image, in a distorting mirror, of its own reach across the terrain of Britain's former imperial realm in the subcontinent. Within the practices of the most visible form of South Asian world literature, therefore, one form of the literature of the Hindi-Urdu vernacular of North India keeps making an appearance, a language and literature fundamentally of and in exile, failing to be adequate to the demand for indigenousness under any national project in the subcontinent, the demand that is inseparable from the history of world literature itself and which we have been charting in this book.

More broadly speaking, then, we might say that in world literature the (South Asian) Anglophone novel as a form marks a sort of *translation* of non-Anglophone and vernacular social and cultural spheres and life-worlds into the novelistic discourse of English and its cultural system more broadly. As such, it is subject to a *politics* of translation. On the one hand, the modes of appearance of vernacular realities in the novel's Anglophone discourse signify attempts variously to harness linguistic, cultural, and social inequality and heterogeneity through "ethnicized" assimilation that gets recoded and reproduced as linguistic diversity, in the interests of a global cultural system in which the regional Anglophone elite now wishes to participate on equal terms. It is an asymmetrical situation unimaginable in reverse, that is, a similarly instrumental assimilation of English into the discourses of vernacular fiction. On the other hand,

the force and social prestige of vernacular literary expression continually exerts a certain pressure on Anglophone expression, forcing
a reckoning with its social reach and claim to authenticity. The colonial cultural logic, that is, Orientalism-Anglicism, that we have
been examining in this book has been reinscribed in our own postcolonial times at one level in the argument (of unequals) about the
respective rights, representativeness, and value of English and the
vernaculars, an argument that now gets staged globally, not just
within the nation-states of the subcontinent. Indeed, Amit Chaudhuri responded to Rushdie's proclamations with an anthology of his
own, expanding its range to include precisely the vernacular literatures Rushdie had so summarily dismissed.[36] On the one hand,
Anglophone literary expression, the end product of an epochal historical process of *assimilation*, is packaged in the world literary
system—including in departments of literature in the West—as an
instance of pure diversity; on the other, South Asian languages,
especially in the nationalized forms of Urdu and Hindi, stake their
claim to *authentic* national expression against the alien presence of
English.

This script was performed once again in February 2015 in the con-
tretemps between Rushdie and the Marathi-language writer Bhalchandra Nemade, winner of the 2014 Jnanpith Award, India's highest
official literary prize, which is awarded annually. Nemade, himself
for many years a teacher of English literature at the university level,
had made extreme "nativist" comments at a public gathering, calling
for the elimination of English from the school curriculum as part of
the promotion of Marathi in its native state of Maharashtra. He described English as a "killer language" and denigrated the value of its
literature: "What is so great about English? There isn't a single epic
in the language. We have 10 epics in the Mahabharata [*sic*] itself.
Don't make English compulsory, make its elimination compulsory."
In the cultural politics of literary language in India, such remarks
cannot fail to be read in a right-wing "Hindu nationalist" register,
especially since the return of the Hindu nationalist Bharatya Janata
Party (BJP) to national power in 2014. One of the slogans of the
Hindu right, after all, has long been "Hindi, Hindu, Hindustan." But
Nemade went further, accusing the most famous "Indian" Anglo-

phone writers, namely, Rushdie and V. S. Naipaul, of "pandering to the West" and dismissing the quality of Rushdie's novels since *Midnight's Children*. The reaction of Naipaul, who has never even wanted to be called a Caribbean writer, to being called an Indian one is not known, but Rushdie's response came soon via Twitter: "Grumpy old bastard. Just take your prize and say thank you nicely. I doubt you've even read the work you attack."[37] Again, as if on cue, this little exchange reignited the "politics of language" debate in the country, with writers taking one or the other side and the state government threatening to take legal action against Rushdie for using abusive language against a revered writer. Meanwhile, the BJP government's attempt to impose Hindi on the central bureaucracy in place of English has been met with loud protests from non-Hindi-speaking states, especially those in the South. The multivalent roles of English in Indian society now include appearing to be a sort of neutral mediator between the "regional" languages and nationalized Hindi, suspending in the very performance of that function the political scene of its dissemination.

In fact, *neither* end of the polar structure of this debate between English and the vernaculars can do the work it is marshaled to do within the globalizing cultural logics of the late-capitalist postcolonial world. Neither framework allows an understanding of the Indian vernaculars themselves as "conscripts of modernity"—if I may borrow a phrase from the anthropologist David Scott from another context—conscripted into the cultural system of English and the world literary relations it makes possible.[38] While dislocated and displaced subjectivity is much touted by Rushdie and others as the great problematic of the Anglophone novel, it is in fact no less pertinent (and poignant), and perhaps more so, for our understanding of vernacular literary practices themselves.[39] For, as I have argued at various points in preceding chapters in some detail, the indigenization of language and culture in the subcontinent is irreducibly a colonial process, a radical innovation in the name of return to the origin. And as I shall argue in the remainder of the book, this historical reality calls for forms of critical thinking that are attentive to those forms of social experience that are fundamentally at odds with nationalist (that is, indigenizing) resolutions of the question of language

and culture. The problem with Rushdie's triumphalist claims about
the Anglophone novel, repeated in various forms in his novels themselves as editorial asides, is that they are part of the *myth* of the form
and as such preclude a real historical understanding of it, including
its actual successes and achievements but above all the multiple internal tensions that characterize it as a genre.

With some important exceptions, the significant writers of this
boom in Anglophone fiction from the subcontinent have been from
India rather than from the smaller countries of the region, with important exceptions from Sri Lanka and Bangladesh. But over the
past few years, this situation has changed dramatically, as media and
cultural institutions worldwide have been heralding the arrival of a
new breed of writer—from Pakistan—and the birth of a distinctly
Pakistani literature. The appearance over a few years of such novels
as Mohsin Hamid's page-turner *The Reluctant Fundamentalist* (2007,
now turned into a Hollywood film), Muhammad Hanif's brilliantly
funny satire *A Case of Exploding Mangoes* (2007), Shamsie's historical
novel *Burnt Shadows*, and Daniyal Mueenuddin's short-story collection, *In Other Rooms, Other Wonders* (2009), among a handful of other
works, produced the collective sense that there was a new cultural
force to be reckoned with in the subcontinent. The global reputation of Pakistan as the home of community-sanctioned gang rapes
of peasant women and public flogging of teenaged girls in the name
of Islamic values adds to the surprise of these literary developments
for metropolitan readers, a mode of response repeatedly expressed
by reviewers in the Anglo-American press. The specter of jihadi
Islam provides a certain frisson in the global reception of these works.

The process of international validation is already quite advanced—
endorsements of metropolitan authorities of various sorts have been
coming fast and hard. Individual books and the group of writers as
a whole have received, for instance, the imprimatur of William Dal-
rymple, the new dean of popular history writing in the subcontinent and an organizer of the Jaipur Literary Festival, and of Rushdie
himself, who has declared publicly that it is now in Pakistan that ex-
citing things are happening. And even the Indian publishing world
has been caught up in the excitement. The general feeling is that the
hegemony of the far-better-known Indian writers has been put into

question. Metropolitan readers could be forgiven for thinking that these writers represent the first green shoots of literary creativity in Pakistan. Very little, if anything, ever gets translated into English from Urdu and the other literary languages of the country—Pashto, Punjabi, Saraiki, Sindhi, and Balochi, to name only the most prevalent ones—either overseas or within the country. Lacking a central institution of the ambition of India's Sahitya Akademi or National Book Trust, which undertake a significant project of translation between and from the country's literary languages, the Pakistani literary landscape remains fragmented into linguistic spheres. But the fact that even the Indian media seem to believe the myth about the new writing reveals the extent to which English is now established as the region's literary vehicle for the journey to world literature. The shift in the literary landscape within the country itself is a dramatic one. When the poet and novelist Fehmida Riaz wrote her remarkable little study of Pakistani literature in the 1980s, she did not feel the need to even mention writing in English. Even a history of Pakistani literature in English written in the same decade by a sociolinguist had to make strenuous efforts to assemble its materials beyond Zulfikar Ghose and Bapsi Sidhwa, both long settled overseas.[40]

Given the complexity of the emergence of the new Pakistani writing in English into visibility out of the historical processes I have been tracing in this book—its imbrication in such institutional networks of world literature as publishing, editing, translation, distribution, marketing, reviewing, and the awarding of prizes but also, more broadly, its involvement in the colonial (and postcolonial) logic of Orientalism-Anglicism—how can we understand its significance on its own terms? Are these works a flash in the pan or the harbinger of a stable and more lasting contribution? The encompassing question that seems to hover over this entire body of writing concerns the distinctness and *scope* of "Pakistani" historical experience and whether it can be given coherent form in literary narrative, a question that, if answered in the affirmative, raises another question, namely, what literary *form* is its appropriate medium? In formal-generic terms, we might therefore say that the question of the Pakistani Anglophone novel is *whether* there is such a thing as a *Pakistani epic*, a question that emerges from and addresses the peculiar historical conditions of possibility of the country as the "nation-state" of "the Muslims of India."[41] The young novelists we are concerned with here have already, fairly early in their careers, experimented with different strategies for handling this question: Shamsie taking as background a vast historical landscape across continents and decades *(Burnt Shadows)*, she and Aslam revisiting canonical moments of the pre-Independence Indian-national historical narrative as the prehistory of distinctly Pakistani experience (*Burnt Shadows* and *Maps for Lost Lovers*), and Hanif exploding the epic ambition of (national) narrative as such into satire *(A Case of Exploding Mangoes)*.

In this regard, and seemingly without being aware of it, the new writing in English echoes aspects of an earlier preoccupation with precisely this question in Urdu literature. In such renowned (and different) works as Qurratulain Haider's novel *Āg kā daryā* (River of Fire, 1959), which I have briefly discussed in Chapter 2, Intezar Husain's story "Ēk bin-likhī razmīya" (An Unwritten Epic, 1950–1951), and Riaz's trilogy of novellas from the 1990s on, the question was not only raised but also answered (controversially) in the *negative*. For Haider's novel, if Pakistan was the nation-state of Indo-Muslim civilization, then the "Indic" element of its history was as pertinent to its cultural elaboration as the "Muslim" one was. (Not coincidentally, the novel's publication marked the writer's permanent departure for India over a decade after Partition.) The narrative unfolds against an expanse of time stretching from the fourth-century BCE reign of Chandragupta Maurya, who defeated the Macedonian satraps who ruled northwestern India in the wake of Alexander's death, to the upheaval of India's Partition in the twentieth century. The series of events narrated across this unwieldy time frame are held together, at one level, through the device of reincarnation, the *Orlando*-like means for the appearance of recurrence and repetition as historical themes that, despite the author's many protestations in this regard—she always claimed not to have read Woolf's novel when she wrote her own—also takes us to Bloomsbury as milieu of literary possibility. Within the fraught politics of religious identity in the subcontinent, the device of reincarnation itself, marked as "Hindu" religious belief, acquires socially significant meaning by undermining the possibility of notions of an autonomous "Muslim" historical development.

In Husain's story, the Partition, far from being an event that inaugurated an epic history, turns out to be one that put an end to precisely this hope and possibility. What starts out as a standard third-person narrative of a few weeks or months in a small North Indian village called Qadirpur around the time of the Partition, centered around the local fraternity of traditional wrestlers and their leader, Pichwa, ends abruptly two-thirds of the way through and becomes a series of dated first-person, diary-like entries. In these, the narrator, now in author persona, reflects on the impossibility of the story completing itself and his own inability in the end to produce an epic tale in the form of a novel—"my Mahabharata," he calls it—of Pichwa's befuddled reception of the idea of Pakistan and death at the hands of assassins on his return to India in the midst of communal violence. And Riaz's novella trilogy, each volume focused on one of the three successors to British India—namely, India, Pakistan, and Bangladesh—pushes against the impossibility of showing, let alone naming, the totality that contains them all. And even Rushdie, trying to write a "Pakistani" novel nearly three decades ago after his iconic "Indian" novel (that is, *Midnight's Children*), proclaimed in *Shame*, as I have already noted, "that Indian centuries lay just beneath the surface of Pakistani Standard Time."[42]

Could it be possible that now, more than six decades after the creation of the country, the judgment elaborated in Husain's story—"Pakistan" as an "unwritten epic"—is beginning to be reversed in writing in English? Is this new generation of writers collectively producing in English an epos of the nation? And, more broadly speaking, could even the violence, extremism, and overall fissiparous social tendencies that are currently tearing the country apart also be understood as the birth pangs of a new cultural independence from Pakistani society's "Indian" past? It may be too early to answer such questions with any degree of certainty. And it is also not yet evident whether the new writing is capable of the kind of ambitious act of historical imagination that can harness these disparate aspects of social experience into an original form. As the global reception of this generation of writers draws them further and more seamlessly into world literary spaces, in what ways can their writing continue to respond to the lived realities of Pakistani life? Above all, it remains very much to be seen whether they can engage in meaningful ways with vernacular social and cultural imaginaries, including those produced in the literatures of Urdu and the regional languages. This question about the Pakistani Anglophone novel is thus also of course in the end a question about the instincts and *capacities of the new Anglophone middle class*, forged in the foundry of globalization over the past several decades from which these writers have emerged, and whether it is capable of deep engagement with the cultural and social worlds that surround it. British and American publishers seem willing for the moment to publish and market aggressively virtually anything written by a talented young Pakistani writing in English. And the machinery of translation into the European languages is also in motion. There is no doubt that this is a highly talented group of writers, each in her or his distinct way, but the institutional conditions through which the work is acquiring a global audience will pose a tough set of challenges for them: how to survive the effects of early celebrity; how to resist writing according to the formulaic demands of the global market; and how to repudiate the opportunistic peddling of Islam and jihadi militancy to the global audience. They will have to perform a fine and precarious balancing act between writing about the fundamental issues facing Pakistani and South Asian society—among which religion, sexuality, politics, and violence surely constitute an important cluster—without playing to the metropolitan fascination with the specter of Islam and stereotyped Muslim sensibilities.

It seems pretty incontrovertible to say that the novel as a form has a preeminent, and perhaps even predominant, place in world literature, that is, both in the various forms of systemic literary relations across the world and in the academic discourse that addresses itself to this cultural reality. In the former case, it seems fairly evident that whether a society has something of worth to "offer" world literature—a constant trope in the discourse of world literature from Goethe to Rushdie—is now first and foremost decided on the basis of the novel, even though in many parts of the world poetic forms and practices of various sort still have a far more crucial place in local literary cultures. (I shall turn to the question of the "survival" into bourgeois modernity of one such form, namely, the ghazal in Urdu, in the remaining pages of this chapter.) And in the latter case, the novel is, for instance, at the core of Moretti's entire effort to conceptualize world literature, his "conjectures" taking the form of trying to answer the question of what exactly it is that happens when the novel "emerges" in a language or country for the first time.[43] But how exactly are we to understand this preeminence or to conceive of the novel as a global form, as perhaps the global form par excellence? In a study of the Latin American novel in a global frame, Mariano Siskind speaks of the novel as the "hegemonic [literary] form" of bourgeois modernity, the very (cultural) vehicle for "the world historical globalization of the European bourgeoisie." I have already noted that Siskind's use of the word "globalization" with reference to the (colonial) processes of the nineteenth century seems to collapse the historical differences between that phase, and those modalities, of the expansion of bourgeois culture and those specific to our own times. To speak, for instance, of "the global novel" in the nineteenth century is to obfuscate, by projecting back from the present, the social and cultural distance that separated colonial centers and peripheries and the aesthetic differences that corresponded to them, often inscribed in literary form itself.[44] And despite the evident preeminence of the novel on a world scale, it can hardly be said to have achieved "hegemony," strictly speaking, across all the modern literary languages of the world. In the subcontinent, for instance, the *novelty* of the novel as form is still available to the form itself as an object of reflection.

The Anglophone novel is, as I have tried to demonstrate here, defined by its paradoxical historical situation: it is a cultural and formal *innovation* that nevertheless emerges out of a long historical process of linguistic and cultural *assimilation*. Given its prominence, the form has been subjected to extensive critical and theoretical interpretation, including often in the novels themselves, especially in Rushdie's works, which never shy away from telling the reader how they ought to be read—as "postcolonial" (that is, postnationalist) Indian fiction, cosmopolitan world literature, or novel of immigration, to note only some of the registers to which his novels draw attention. If we turn from novel to poetry, however, we are forced to confront the fact that nothing like the highly elaborated conception of the novel, including its self-conception, is immediately available to us. In (Anglophone) poetry, we are forced to confront rather different elaborations of time and space and therefore rather different possibilities for conceiving of the space of world literature. If the form of the (South Asian) Anglophone novel contains (temporal and spatial) elements of the epic, how may we conceive of contemporary poetic expression and its relation to space and time? In order to pursue this line of thinking, I shall turn in the next section to the question of "lyric" poetic practices and their relationship to the history of Orientalism (and world literature) that I have been elaborating in this book. By engaging with a small number of poems by one poet, I shall suggest a possible line of thinking about the question of lyric as a modern norm at the intersections of languages and cultures in the colonial and postcolonial worlds.

The Ghazal among the Nations

In line with the distinct quality of "lyric" expression, it would be appropriate to begin here in a small way and at a certain remove from these larger questions, with just a few lines of verse:

> Someone, finally, is here! No, unhappy heart, no one—
> just a passerby on his way.
> The night has surrendered
> to clouds of scattered stars.
> The lamps in the halls waver.
> Having listened with longing for steps,
> the roads too are asleep.
> A strange dust has buried every footprint.
>
> Blow out the lamps, break the glasses, erase
> all memory of wine. Heart,
> Bolt forever your sleepless doors,
> tell every dream that knocks to go away.
> No one, now no one will ever return.[45]

A few simple observations seem appropriate here: the lines are divided into two stanzas of unequal length, in each of which the speaking subject addresses an other, but this other is identified as the former's own "heart," qualified as "unhappy" on its first appearance, in the first line. There is, in other words, an elocutionary feel to the language, a self addressing an other, even if that other is also revealed to be the self itself. We might say that in this very doubling, the self is made receptive to the possibility of an other, a truly other, with all three—namely, the self, the self as other, and the awaited or expected other—existing together within a world that contains them all. Second, in this *social* world, properly speaking—for two is just a dyad, but three is a society, as Georg Simmel once said[46]—the condition of the self is one of solitude, which itself seems to be not simply the absence of others but rather a *dialectic* of expectation (of the arrival of an other) and the failure of this expectation to be actualized. Third, we are introduced in the first stanza to elements of a material world, or a built environment, to be more exact: "roads," "halls," and the flickering light of "lamps," and it is through this world that a stranger may have passed, raising and then negating the expectation of some known other's arrival, an other who for some unknown reason does not arrive.

The second stanza displays a marked alteration of tone. Its forceful images perform a disassembling of the scene of expectation, the prospective social gathering into which the other was to be received, which would have been actualized precisely in the other's arrival: the lamps that would have lit up the dark, the glasses that would have carried the wine, the doors left wide open to receive the guest. The final judgment is, well, final: "No one, now no one will ever return." And at the end of this last line, in the very last word, something crucial is revealed: the expected (but thwarted) arrival was in fact to have been a *return*. Some of the images—flickering oil lamps, glasses or cups of wine—seem at least a little odd, alien, or out of place in this little lyric poem written in English. What could "strange dust" possibly mean? The poem, which is presented in its entirety here, on its own terms seems to court melancholia, but the very forcefulness of the final judgment, even the image of the bolting of doors, seems to speak of much more of an openness to life and effort than a melancholic orientation, properly speaking, would imply. Longing and its dialectical unfolding, disappointment and its dogged acceptance—these are some of the elements of the poem's structure of feeling. There is no strong claim on the world here, just an assertion of the right to hope, even in the face of strong disappointment.

We might begin to add a second layer to our reading by noting that these lines were written by Agha Shahid Ali, who died in Amherst, Massachusetts, in December 2001. He succumbed to brain cancer, which, by a bizarre coincidence, had killed his mother only a few years earlier, an event and a loss his readers are familiar with from his poems. He was just shy of fifty-two years old when he died. His early death seemed to have been followed by a quick consolidation of a broad and expanding reputation, which culminated in the publication of his collected verse in 2011. The news of his sudden passing was received with a proliferation of testimonials by people who had known him to one extent or another. In my own case, the encounters had been few and very brief: once at a poetry reading in the East Village and the second time on the Columbia University campus when I ran into him in the company of Edward Said, of whom he was a close friend. On that second occasion, we made jokes back and forth, in the manner of *dēsīs* (that is, South Asians) far from home taking each other's measure. And yet, despite this brief encounter, I have always felt his passing as a personal loss—as the disappearance of someone I could have, and should have, known. It feels like a failure that I did not.

This is at least anecdotal evidence of the force of his writing as of his life, which he commented on extensively in his verse. Shahid—as he is generally referred to and as he referred to himself when he wrote in the ghazal form, which requires one appearance of the author's conventionalized poetic name, or *takhallus*—was raised mostly in Srinagar, the capital of the Indian part of the troubled and contested region of Jammu and Kashmir, and he also spent some years in Delhi. In the American phase of his life, he sometimes referred to himself as a "Kashmiri-American," a gesture of solidarity with the ongoing Kashmiri struggle for *āzādi* that emerged in 1990—*āzādi* is an overcoded signifier in the Kashmiri context, a first level of whose meanings could be limned simply as freedom or independence—and a repudiation both of the Indian state's savage and ongoing repression of the Kashmiri Muslim population and of the equally callous and stupid manipulation of the Kashmiri struggle by the Pakistani state, which facilitated a violent global jihad in Kashmir that not only fractured Kashmiri society along Hindu-Muslim lines but has now rebounded on the Pakistani state and society themselves. This event coincided exactly with the end of the first Afghan war, the U.S.-Saudi anti-Soviet global jihad, making available a host of militants hailing from places as far afield as Saudi Arabia, Chechnya, and Uzbekistan for this new jihadi front. The call for *āzādi* is in one sense a sort of prayer to be rid of this eternal and obsessive conflict between two vicious political entities. Shahid's poetry registers his anger and despair, but also his insistent hope, in response to all these developments. Meanwhile, in Kashmir itself, Shahid has come to acquire something of the status of national poet. It is said that on news of his death, activists of the Jammu and Kashmir Liberation Front (JKLF) showed up at his residence in Massachusetts, asking to be allowed to accompany his body home. (He was buried in Amherst.)[47] If this story is indeed more than merely apocryphal, it resonates powerfully with his remarkable cycle of poems titled "From Amherst to Kashmir," which constitutes a record of the psychic journey of accompanying his mother's body back home from the United States just a few years earlier.

Although Shahid was by no means a political poet per se, his corpus of writing raises profound questions about the political landscape of contemporary South Asia and of the world at large. He paints a vast and complex emotional canvas. Loss, distance, recuperation, grief, love, and shimmering perceptions of inner and outer worlds—these are the elements of his poetic universe. The cultural references of his verse are widely ecumenical, ranging from Western literatures and histories to Arabic, Persian, and subcontinental ones, above all Urdu. Many of his poems record the process of his discovery of Urdu poetry, which came to acquire a powerful and luminous presence in them. Returning to the lines of Shahid's that I started with, we may now elaborate a few more layers of reading. This text in English is not, in fact, original. Called "Solitude," it is presented to us as an attempt to translate, or rather "adapt," the Urdu of a poem by Faiz, titled "Tanhā'ī," a word that carries the sense of solitude as a purely objective condition, certainly, but also of loneliness as a subjective condition, though somehow without the English word's sentimentality.[48] Shahid has spoken of his adaptational strategy as one of "unfaithful" fidelity, a precise description of the relationship between the two corresponding texts, the Urdu and the English. As a strategy, it is perhaps most clearly at work in the case of engagement with Faiz's ghazal poems, a lyric genre and a question in itself to which I shall return later.[49] It was on these terms of unfaithful fidelity, in his own terms, that Shahid sought the latter's permission for the exercise. He has given us a snippet of Faiz's response: "You are welcome to make your adaptations of my poems which I shall be happy to receive."[50] Bot Shahid and Faiz thus speak explicitly of adaptations rather than translations. While this particular poem of Faiz's is not a ghazal in genre terms, it abounds in that elusive quality of the form, *taġhazzul*—some of the recognizable things usually evoked by the term "lyric" but also the particular affective map of the ghazal universe that is situated in the form often in a highly conventionalized depiction of a social world. It is an early poem, from Faiz's first published collection of poetry (1941), therefore written probably when he was in his twenties. It is one of the poems from the second part of the collection, so arranged because they come after a turning point in his early development as poet, a turn marked by the famous poem "Mujh sē pahlī sī maḥabbat mērī maḥbūb na māñg" (Love, do not ask for that old love again), a programmatic poem in which Faiz transforms the self-enclosed world of the lyric by opening it up to the outer, social world, imbuing the lyric self with the life of the social.[51]

Some of Shahid's choices stand out and merit a bit of discussion. Take, for instance, "strange dust" in the eighth line. Faiz's phrase is "ajnabī ḵhāk," where "ḵhāk" could be rendered as dust or even earth in some contexts (as in the English "khaki"), and the noun "ajnabī" (stranger) is here used adjectivally, so perhaps the phrase could be rendered, a little awkwardly, as "stranger dust" or, more fluidly, "foreign" or "alien" dust. What could this possibly mean? A clue may be had in another of Faiz's poems from exactly this period—in fact, they sit two poems apart in the same collection of his verse—which speaks

of living under the tyranny of "ajnabī hāth" (alien hands), a phrase
that has usually been understood as a reference to foreign colonial
rule. If this is the case in "Tanhā'ī" as well, then a whole new possibility of reading the Faiz "original" might be opened up. In the image
of the bolting of doors, we might then say, Faiz is shutting the door to
the historical past and inviting his reader to live without the all-
consuming expectation that it might return. An "alien dust" has "obscured" all footprints, all those traces of the past. Faiz's poem could
thus be understood to be concerned with the whole cluster of issues
that coalesce in a colonial (and postcolonial) society around the idea
of a crisis of tradition, the problematic, we might say, of the broken
vessels and the desire for their restoration. Fanon famously detailed
the perils and potentialities of this situation and cautioned the artists and intellectuals of societies emerging from colonial rule that
"it is not enough to try to get back to the people in that past from
which they have already emerged; rather we must join them in that
fluctuating movement which they are giving shape to, and which, as
soon as it has started, will be the signal for everything to be called
into question."[52]

If this reading of the Urdu "original" is sound, then it has implications for our reading of the English "adaptation" as well. For the
image of "return" is Shahid's—Faiz simply speaks of an arrival, even
though he clearly distinguishes this present situation from the past,
whose traces have become increasingly obscured in the present but
not entirely erased. So in taking this license in the translation, Shahid
has in fact heightened a certain element in the original, the same effect also being produced by his insertion of a stanza break where
there is not one in the original, increasing the effect given in the lines
that follow that a firm *decision* has been taken. And I have come to this
understanding via a reading of the original and its comparison to
the adaptation. In other words, it is not just that the "adaptation"
has taught me something about the "original"; it is also that the latter
now tells me something about the former. Could we thus perhaps
think of this as one text in two languages, written by two individuals
and in two phases or stages, with the second coming decades after
the first, and the two modes of expression situated unequally and
asymmetrically with respect to each other, multiply and laboriously

articulated rather than constituting an organic whole? The conventions of institutionalized publishing flatten out many such ambiguities carefully arranged here when they assign the author function to Faiz and that of translator to Shahid. To know that you come from something, that in some strong sense you belong to it, and at the same time to know that you have no unmediated access to it free of the distorting and refracting filter of "alien dust"—it is this fundamentally exilic perspective on postcolonial life that our double text seems to have elaborated. In it, the essential homelessness of Urdu, which, as we have seen, cannot pass the test of indigeneity in either nation-state where it is spoken and written—too Arabo-Persian in its effects in India and too (North) Indian in Pakistan—meets the homelessness of the "Kashmiri-American" language of Shahid's poetry.

One of the more pronounced, complex, and distinct aspects of Shahid's verse is its use of Kashmir as signifier, perhaps most intensely in the collection *Country without a Post-Office* (1998). It is by far the most often recurring geographical reference in his work. It comes in many forms—from invocations of its fabled natural environment to ruminations on the Kashmiri origins of paisley design and various events and personages of the history of the region in precolonial, colonial, and postcolonial times. These motifs and preoccupations constitute an expansive set of coordinates that a strong "Indian literature" framing is unable to read in any satisfactory way. And since Shahid seems most often to be speaking of his homeland as an outsider and from a distance from it, that could too easily be assimilated into the frame of "diasporic" literature. But the work of "Kashmir" as poetic signifier is far more complex here and far more intriguing. It draws on a vast North Indian mythology of Kashmir as a fabled and legendary place in the mountains, a mythology that is precolonial, perhaps even ancient, but appears here mediated through its colonial (and Anglophone) reinscriptions.[53]

Many of the poems in *Country*, written at the height of the counterinsurgency, are detailed elaborations of grief tied to the violence: at the news of massacres and other outrages committed by security forces, the loss of loved ones, most often young men, and the army's confiscation of the poet's relatives' homes—all the dullingly repetitive scenes of the brutality of life in a society under siege. One extraordinary (and perhaps climactic) passage is almost unreadable out loud because it consists simply of multiple spellings of the same word. "Let me cry out in that void, say it as I can. I write on that void: Kashmir, Kaschmir, Cashmere, Qashmir, Cashmir, Cashmire, Kashmere, Cashmire, Cushmeer, Cashmiere, Cašmir. Or Cauchemar in a sea of stories? Or: Kacmir, Kaschemir, Kasmere, Kashmire, Kasmir. Kerseymere?"[54] "Kashmir" is a name to be cried out, said, or written into and against the void, but as a name, it has no stability. By drawing attention to the unsettled spelling of the place name in European languages—and by reducing the poemic content almost entirely to orthographic variation—the poem unsettles the significations of the name as such. Kashmir is an indeterminate name not because of a paucity of signification but precisely because of an excess of it. In fact, we might say, Shahid's Kashmir is literally an excess of the state-cultural system of South Asia. For in this place, *other* imaginings become possible, sweeping imaginings of past, present, and future. To repeatedly invoke Kashmir in this manner is to invoke a place between nation-states or a place in which two states overlap and their respective sanctioning narratives—the claim to the Indic origin and commonality of all Indian cultures, on the one hand, and a strong-nationalist claim to Muslim distinctiveness from the Hindu-Indic, on the other—have to somehow live together. It marks a sort of utopian space that violates the territorial logic of the modern state system, whose genealogy passes through the post-Westphalian order. Both states seem to agree that *this* Kashmir cannot be allowed to exist. "Kashmir" in Shahid's writing is thus the name for this entire complexity, the complexity of South Asian, of Indian, modernity: the indigenization (that is, rooting) and alienization (that is, uprooting) of cultural and social practices and imaginaries, the slow imposition of the modern state form on society. Its meticulous and loving invocation in Shahid's verse invites us to wake, however briefly, from the *dream*, as Stathis Gourgouris has called it in another context, of national belonging.[55] The cliché of everyday political life in South Asia is that Kashmir is the unfinished business of Partition. It is an ugly cliché, raising the possibility of another violent uprooting of peoples that, as Hannah Arendt once noted, is the "deadly sickness" of the nation-state form since the early twentieth century.[56] The proliferation of Kashmir as signifier in Shahid's verse, in fact, his strenuous untangling of its work as signifier, turns this cliché on its head: Kashmir as a future beyond Partition. Our desire for "Kashmir," so consistently engaged in Shahid's verse, is then perhaps also the desire, which only occasionally becomes available for conscious reflection, to escape from the hell—the fears, suspicions, obsessions, and compulsions—imposed on society by the (still incomplete) normalization of the nation-state form in the subcontinent.

For all the knowing looks that the political activism of Arundhati Roy can produce for her being a celebrity writer and intellectual with global reach, she has been exemplary in openly denouncing the state repression in Kashmir, which has included rape and killing of tens of thousands of persons by security forces over twenty-two years but does not appear to be on many people's radars worldwide, except of course the global-jihadi Islamists, who routinely list it alongside Palestine as one of their geopolitical grievances. She has also been exemplary about drawing international attention to the peasant rebellion among "tribal" (ādīvāsī or aboriginal) populations in east-central India and its brutal suppression by the state acting in the interest of multinational corporations. A small detail of her instantly infamous visit with a group of Maoist fighters on forest trails in Chhattisgarh state should be of particular interest to us in connection with the questions I am attempting to raise here. Roy tells us in her published account of her time with the rebels of listening together with them to a recording of the protest poem "Ham Dēkhēñgē" (We shall see) by Faiz, the voice of the singer Iqbal Bano and the defiant chant of her live audience in General Zia ul-Haq's Pakistan in the 1980s reverberating uncannily across the forest.[57] The scene is replete with a variety of political tensions: Roy is a globally celebrated *Anglophone* writer from Delhi, a general gadfly whose *international* celebrity is relevant to the encounter because it grants her a certain protection from state repression of the sort visited regularly on her companions, who are a group of young *tribal peasants* deep in a forest in central India at war with their local social oppressors as well as the postcolonial state over the theft of their resource-rich land, and they are listening to a "high" literary *Urdu* text (by Faiz) being sung by Iqbal Bano, one of his important interpreters in *Pakistan*. It is a scene of cultural transmission and solidarity—across the mesh of class, language, and nation-state borders, at the very least—that is neither

legible as "world literature" in any of its dominant metropolitan formulations nor assimilable to the frames of literature as *national*
institution that are promoted by the state and reinforced, as we have
seen, by discourses and practices whose frame supposedly is supranational. Neither set of reading practices is adequate to the multiple
resonances of this extremely simple yet extraordinary event.

But perhaps the most unique aspect of Shahid's poetic practice is
his turn to the possibilities of the ghazal form, an engagement that
grew stronger and more developed after the completion of the Faiz
translations. It includes *Ravishing Disunities*, a volume of 107 English-
language engagements with the form, mostly by American poets,
edited by him. This preoccupation with the ghazal runs like a leit-
motif throughout his own work. In a number of his own poems from
fairly early in his writing career, Shahid reflects on the nature of the
form, its wide presence (as song) in North Indian society, and his own
slow discovery of it. The collection of Faiz adaptations includes Shahid's versions of a number of Faiz's ghazals as well. For a bilingual
reader of this particular transaction, the paradox is that Shahid's
reworkings of Faiz's ghazals into English are very unsatisfying in
their attempt to render something of the Urdu. They are uniformly
in free verse, for one, about as far as you can get in formal terms from
the genre. Given Shahid's own stringent insistence on formal fidelity
to the requirements of the genre, should we say that his translations
of Faiz's ghazals are not themselves ghazals? Paradoxically, where he
gets closest to the world of the Urdu lyric is in his own *original*
"ghazals" written in English. *This* success seems to be born out of *that*
failure.

As with many individuals in South Asia, especially (though not
exclusively) those in the middle class given a largely colonial education in English, Shahid's introduction to Urdu poetry came through
ghazal as song. In an elegy for Faiz, he writes of his discovery:

> When I learned of her,
> I was no longer a boy, and Urdu
> a silhouette traced by the voices of singers,
> by Begum Akhtar, who wove your couplets
> into ragas: both language and music were sharpened.[58]

In another poem, written in memory of Begum Akhtar, arguably the greatest ghazal singer of the twentieth century—whom Shahid knew personally and seems to have loved—who had single-handedly reinvented ghazal singing for the modern age, that is, the age of recorded music, he writes,

> Do your fingers still scale the hungry
> Bhairavi, or simply the muddy shroud?
> Ghazal, that death-sustaining widow,
> sobs in dingy archives, hooked to you.
> She wears her grief, a moon-soaked white,
> corners the sky into disbelief.[59]

With great delicacy, Shahid manages to convey his affection for the arc of the singer's life, the transformation of Akhtaribai Faizabadi—the very form of the given name signaling her origins in the world of the courtesan-singer—into Begum Akhtar (Lady Akhtar), the doyenne of "semiclassical" singing in the second half of the twentieth century and a national monument. The singer's name occurs repeatedly in Shahid's verse, invoking the uniqueness of her sound and even her technical accomplishments, as in the foregoing extracts. Sexuality and desire as such as an affective terrain are marked out in indirect and elusive ways in Shahid's verse, and this ambiguity seems to reflect the ambiguousness of the Urdu ghazal's own exploration of desire and its sexual or gendered dimensions, moving easily between heterosexual and homosexual images of desire, between physical and platonic versions of love as emotion, and between devotion for the human beloved and that for the divine presence.[60] The emotional perspectives of the identified female figures in his verse—from historical personages like Begum Akhtar to his own mother and grandmother—acquire political overtones in becoming the ethical counterpoints to the hypermasculine demonstrativeness and violence of both the insurgents and the postcolonial state.

It is not an exaggeration to say that Shahid's practice of the ghazal form in English is unique in the now-long history of metropolitan engagement with the form in the European languages. These poems collectively stage a haunting and uncanny encounter between "English" and "Urdu"—as social imaginaries, ways of

thinking and feeling, and, of course, media of poetic expression—
without ever giving the impression of dabbling in the exotic. Let
us take a closer look now at one of these poems, called "Tonight"
after its *radīf* or refrain, in which the encounter assumes a stun-
ningly intimate form:

Where are you now? Who lies beneath your spell tonight?
Whom else from rapture's road will you expel tonight?   (1)

Those "Fabrics of Cashmere—" "to make me beautiful—"
"Trinket"—to gem—"Me to adorn—How tell"—tonight?   (2)

I beg for haven: Prisons, let open your gates—
A refugee from Belief seeks a cell tonight.   (3)

God's vintage loneliness has turned to vinegar—
All the archangels—their wings frozen—fell tonight.   (4)

Lord, cried out the idols, Don't let us be broken;
Only we can convert the infidel tonight.   (5)

Mughal ceilings, let your mirrored convexities
multiply me at once under your spell tonight.   (6)

He's freed some fire from ice in pity for Heaven.
He's left open—for God—the doors of Hell tonight.   (7)

In the heart's veined temple, all statues have been smashed.
No priest in saffron's left to toll its knell tonight.   (8)

God, limit these punishments, there's still Judgment Day—
I'm a mere sinner, I'm no infidel tonight.   (9)

Executioners near the woman at the window.
Damn you, Elijah, I'll bless Jezebel tonight.   (10)

The hunt is over, and I hear the Call to Prayer
fade into that of the wounded gazelle tonight.   (11)

My rivals for your love—you've invited them all?
This is mere insult, this is no farewell tonight.   (12)

And I, Shahid, only am escaped to tell thee—
God sobs in my arms. Call me Ishmael tonight.[61]   (13)

Clearly, a remarkable wit is at work in this poem, as in many of Shahid's works. It is a deeply ironic sensibility, acutely aware of the instabilities and inversions that mark poetic expression. And a pious mentality might even identify elements of the sacrilegious here, a sort of ecumenical and equal-opportunity searing of the foundational beliefs, practices, or stories of a number of world religious traditions. The first, third, fifth, seventh, eighth, and ninth couplets in particular sound like they could originally have been written in Urdu, so faithful is their replication of the rhythms and the structures of feeling that are characteristic of its poetry. It is not uncommon for Shahid's Anglophone readers to wonder if they are reading translations from some other language. For the bilingual reader, it is nothing short of an uncanny experience. And the poem ends by invoking perhaps the most famous opening line in American literature—but this is simultaneously an Islamic reference as well, evoking the Qur'anic story of Abraham's willingness to sacrifice Ishmael, inverting the relationship of Ishmael to God, who has after all commanded his sacrifice: it is God who submits to Ishmael, sobbing in his arms, rather than Abraham, through Ishmael, to God. The Islamic-religious meaning seems to be hiding within the American-literary one, as tenor to vehicle in this metaphorical construction.

We could approach this very complex poem from a range of perspectives. However, a core of themes and images seem to predominate: belief and unbelief, God's rivalry with "idols," believer and infidel, the passage from belief to apostasy. I am drawn in particular to a handful of couplets that seem to be elaborating this dialectic. If I follow this route, isolating a few lines from the rest of the poem, that would be an *Urdu* strategy for reading an *English* poem, the ghazal couplet being typically treated in Urdu as a more or less autonomous unit of poetic elaboration. Shahid's own rigorous adherence to the genre's formal strictures seems to have allowed me—or compelled me, perhaps—to follow this interlingual and intercultural direction. First of all, God is an intimate interlocutor here, for the "I" of lyric enunciation (in couplet 9, for instance) but also for "the idols" (in couplet 5). Furthermore, the religious and the secular appear to be inseparable in a strange way, elements of each type repeatedly morphing into those of the other. Couplets 1 and 12 seem to be thematically secular, for instance, with no overt divine or more broadly religious reference. But given the inherent and notorious polysemy of the ghazal's elaboration of love or devotion, which simultaneously points in earthly and heavenly registers and directions, we would be remiss not to pursue a theological possibility here as well. Could couplet 1 be addressed to God, for instance, designating him a thrower of spells on mortals and as an enemy of "rapture"? That would be a far-reaching critique of religiosity as such, as both a hypnotic state and an ascetic one. And could couplet 12 too be similarly addressed to God, or the reverse possibility, that is, in the voice of God himself, chastising the departing believer for rubbing it in, as it were, by inviting God's many rivals to the farewell gathering in which the believer is to take his leave of his erstwhile divinity? One effect of this series of inversions is the fact that the nonbeliever ("refugee from Belief," "infidel") appears to be a *mediating* figure, with a foot in both realms, the religious and the secular.

The monotheistic God is at the very least in a difficult situation here, beset from all sides by rivals, inconstant believers, outright infidels, saffron-clad (that is, Hindu or Buddhist) priests, and calls to prayer that fade into the cries of a "wounded gazelle." This is a lonely God, seeking comfort in the arms of the one who was to be sacrificed to him. And while both God and the believer/unbeliever see the idols as the former's rivals, it is precisely they to whom he must turn in hope of changing unbeliever into believer. In the terms of this remarkable poem, then, for the one true God to become involved in the life of humanity is to enter a polytheistic world. *The monotheistic creed is therefore an impossible proposition on its own terms*, constantly compelled by its own logic to acknowledge and address its other. The poem thus elaborates the dialectic of belief and unbelief as the ground of belief itself. And at another, more historically concrete level of signification, we may view this effort as a reworking of the mutual relations of polytheistic and monotheistic religious traditions in the subcontinent. The core images of the foundational story of Islam's emergence in seventh-century Arabia within and against a polytheistic environment—a *hostile* polytheistic environment—are repeated obsessively in orthodox Islamic culture in the subcontinent as representations of its relation to its own world, especially in modern times. In the Urdu ghazal from its inception, and especially in its more overtly Sufi forms, these orthodox images and gestures have been routinely undermined, with "idol" *(ṣanam)* in fact becoming one of the names of the beloved in both its forms, human as well as divine. Shahid's poem therefore represents a remarkable transposition into English verse of attitudes and orientations that have been characteristic of the Urdu ghazal as a form since its canonization in the vernacular of North India in the eighteenth century. In Shahid's English, this "medieval" structure of feeling in Urdu becomes available for an exploration of the *modern* dialectic of belief and unbelief, self and other, and belonging and community.

We might therefore say that in Shahid's work, "ghazal" is the name (and the form) of this transposition from Urdu to English. And this effort at translocation reveals something essential about the ghazal form itself. For the colonial reformers' accusation that the Urdu ghazal was a historically superseded (and thus decadent) form, inadequate to the demands of the emergent social and political experiences of the modern (that is, colonial) world amounts to no more than the perception—correct in my view—that it was inadequate to the *national* reorientation of culture and society under colonial rule. To note that the genre has somehow survived the violent colonial disjuncture is therefore simply to note its transformation from a premodern and precolonial (and, thus, in a strictly chronological sense, *prenational*) form to a postcolonial and fundamentally *nonnational* one whose adequate reading therefore requires a nonnational—that is, *exilic*—social imaginary. Such an imaginary would be neither "transnational" in global terms nor "civilizational" in South Asian terms: for the latter, with its assertion of a shared ancient cultural past or heritage, is produced entirely within the terms of nationalist discourse, as we have seen at some length in earlier chapters, and the former typically leaves intact the nation-space while promising an easy crossing of its borders. "Exile" is thus the frame *adequate* to these social, political, and cultural realities because it captures simultaneously the violent exclusions of the national frame, the material reality of its (physical as well as symbolic) borders, the dire need to overcome its destructive fixations, and its inescapability in the present moment. It is to the possibility of such an exilic philology that I shall turn in Chapter 4 by engaging with the work of Auerbach and Said.

As for Shahid himself, he may indeed be in the process of being lionized by a younger generation among the Anglophone middle class in Kashmir as their "national" poet, but with reference to Kashmir, this means something very different from what it might mean in many other parts of the world. If the nonnational form of the Kashmiri question as I have outlined it is ever resolved into the terms of a distinct and "autonomous" nationalism, that is, if it is ever assimilated into the terms of the nation-state system in the subcontinent, it would have to repudiate the orientations so carefully cultivated in Shahid's oeuvre. In a sense, then, Shahid's attraction to Faiz above all other poets in the subcontinent is far from accidental or idiosyncratic, for we might say that the younger poet picks up in English where the older had left off—but in another language.

One of the great accomplishments of Shahid's oeuvre is thus the way in which it performs a series of relays between "English" and "vernacular" spaces or practices, thereby helping us to bring to the fore the submerged network of relations between the cultural system of English and vernacular spaces in, for instance, the subcontinent. In his poetic practice, Anglophone poetry perceives its own environment as a multilingual one, a perception elaborated most explicitly perhaps in another of his ghazal poems, "Beyond English":

No language is old—or young—beyond English.
So what of a common tongue beyond English? (1)

I know some words for war, all of them sharp,
but the sharpest one is *jung*—beyond English! (2)

If you wish to know of a king who loved his slave,
you must learn legends, often-sung, beyond English. (3)

Baghdad is sacked and its citizens must watch
prisoners (now in miniatures) hung beyond English. (4)

Go all the way through *jungle* from *aleph* to *zenith*
to see English, like monkeys, swung beyond English. (5)

So never send to know for whom the bell tolled,
for across the earth it has rung beyond English.   (6)

If you want your drugs legal you must leave the States,
not just for hashish but one—*bhung*—beyond English.   (7)

Heartbroken, I tottered out "into windless snow,"
snowflakes on my lips, silence stung beyond English.   (8)

When the phrase, "The Mother of all Battles" caught on,
the surprise was indeed not sprung beyond English.   (9)

Could a soul crawl away at last unshriveled which
to its "own fusing senses" had clung beyond English?   (10)

If someone asks where Shahid has disappeared,
He's waging a war (no *jung*) beyond English.[62]   (11)

To begin with, we might note that the *radīf* or refrain has a somewhat different effect here than it does in "Tonight"—it feels like an
almost maniacal repetition of a phrase that seems to acquire in its
very repetition an imperative force. Each couplet points the reader
beyond the borders of "English," a space where all manner of perception, conception, and affect seem to become possible. Of the five
italicized words of foreign origin in this poem, only one occurs twice
(in couplets 2 and 11)—*jañg*, a word of Persian origin that is the most
common word for "war" in more or less all the languages of the
northern subcontinent and certainly in Hindi-Urdu. (We might also
note that the poem does not in any way highlight the "foreignness"
of words of Greek or Latinate origin.) At least two of the couplets (4
and 9) seem to place the composition of the poem in the aftermath
of the conquest of Baghdad in the Second Gulf War, although the
first of these also invokes the infamous "sack of Baghdad" by the army
of the Mongol chieftain Hulagu Khan, son of Genghis and brother
of Kublai, in 1258 CE, which laid waste to the capital (and consequently the remarkable civilization) of the Abbasids. The poem thus
evokes and links these two acts of occupation and destruction of the
city at the hands of barbarous armies, two acts of destruction seven
and a half centuries (and five couplets) apart. If we further note the
reference to Ernest Hemingway's novel of the Spanish Civil War in

couplet 6, it becomes pretty clear that war is one of the recurring motifs in the poem, invoked in five couplets (2, 4, 6, 9, and 11). The space of language and culture, and certainly the space of intercultural interaction, thus seems to appear as a space of war, that is, of the display, deployment, and exercise of force. The ubiquity of force in the life of human beings is one of the more persistent perceptions and motifs in Shahid's verse, even in moments of lyrical exultation in landscapes, friendships, or loves.

In another remarkable ghazal poem, titled, "In Arabic," Shahid seems to attribute to the language and its culture a sort of gravitational pull over a vast civilizational field across the centuries, bringing into its orbit figures as diverse as Moses Maimonides, Anton Shammas, Federico García Lorca, Jorge Luis Borges, and Yehuda Amichai:

A language of loss? I have some business in Arabic.
Love letters: a calligraphy pitiless in Arabic.   (1)

At an exhibit of miniatures, what Kashmiri hairs!
Each paisley inked into a golden tress in Arabic.   (2)

This much fuss about a language I don't know?
   So one day   (3)
perfume from a dress may let you digress in Arabic.

A "Guide for the Perplexed" was written—believe me—
by Cordoba's Jew—Maimonides—in Arabic.   (4)

Majnoon, by stopped caravans, rips his collars, cries
   "Laila!"   (5)
Pain translated is O! much more—not less—in Arabic.

Writes Shammas: Memory, no longer confused,
   now is a homeland—   (6)
his two languages a Hebrew caress in Arabic.

When Lorca died, they left the balconies open and saw:
On the sea his *qasidas* stitched seamless in Arabic.   (7)

In the Veiled One's harem, an adultress hanged by
   eunuchs—   (8)
So the rank mirrors revealed to Borges in Arabic.

Ah, bisexual Heaven: wide-eyed houris and immortal
   youths!   (9)
To your each desire they say *Yes! O Yes!* in Arabic.

For that excess of sibilance, the last Apocalypse,
so pressing those three forms of S in Arabic.   (10)

I too, O Amichai, saw everything, just like you did—
In Death. In Hebrew. And (please let me stress) in Arabic.   (11)

They ask me to tell them what *Shahid* means: Listen,
   listen: (12)
it means "The Belovéd" in Persian, "witness" in
   Arabic.[63]

Here, once again, the space of intercultural interaction is imagined
as a force field, or even minefield, with the desire for crossing over,
for rediscovering the self in the midst of the other, intact despite and
in the midst, as we saw in "Beyond English," of "war." "Hebrew" and
"Arabic" are locked in a death grip that is also a "caress" or embrace.
In three couplets (4, 6, and 11), Arabic is put in relation to Hebrew
as the scriptural, intellectual, and literary language of the Jews, and
these links are both historical (in al-Andalus) and contemporary (in
Israel-Palestine). In one couplet (12), Arabic is linked to Persian in a
way that concisely and perfectly reveals the internal structure of the
Perso-Arabic civilizational complex: lawgiving as Arabic ("witness"),
mystical love as Persian ("The Belovéd"). In three couplets (4, 7,
and 8), there is a counterposition to Spanish. In addition, we might
say, Arabic is in relation with English in every single couplet, as the
historical lives of the former are elaborated in verse in the latter. In
couplets 1, 5, 7, 8, 9, and 12, Arabic is, in one way or another, viewed
as a language of loss and love, but in couplet 12, as just noted, it is
viewed, in counterposition to Persian, as a language of law. The name
Shahid is an Arabic noun of great importance in Islam that means
"witness," etymologically and morphologically linked to *śahīd* (martyr)
and the *śahāda* (the basic profession of monotheistic faith and belief in Muhammad's Prophethood) itself, the entire cluster of words
linked to the trilateral root verb "to witness." But this set of broader

historical, literary, linguistic, and religious associations remain tied in the poem to a very personal and subjective register, tied in fact to the persona of the poet himself: the speaker's tastes in literature and art, for instance, the recurring turn to the language of love and desire, and also, perhaps, in the delicious alliteration of couplet 10 (the lines marked by a rhythmically released "excess of sibilance"), an exaggerated performing of the poet's own slightly discernible lisp—as if, in reading these lines out loud, the reader's speech begins to approach the speech patterns of the poet himself. Finally, the fact that the houris and youths promised in heaven to those who are pious in this world will speak a breathless Arabic is already quite funny (9). But there is another twist here: the opening phrase of this couplet—"Ah, bisexual Heaven"—suggests both that Heaven is "bisexual" and that "bisexuality" is heaven. The couplet elaborates a fantasy of fulfillment in which Heaven is the place or state in which the expression and fulfillment of desire are free of external (or internalized) social command, the object of desire a generalized one, on whom are now cathected all of life's ascetic and prescribed privations. It is not a fantasy of the complete disappearance of socially determined and socially legible (gendered) differentiation so much as one of desire itself freed from its rigid subjugation. The "bisexual" therefore is also a figure for a civilizational ambidextrousness or, alternatively, an agnosticism of cultural affiliation.

There are entire worlds to be discovered "beyond English," not in some geographically distinct and distant place but right next to you, wherever you may happen to be, and even in your own (English) speech itself. Thus, if the attempt to look, think, or feel "beyond English" involves a sort of warfare, that is, an effort that implies a certain arrangement of force, it is also, by the same token, already a matter of *love*, that is, a *suspension of force* in the very midst of a force field. This is possibly the great secret of Shahid's practice of the ghazal form, although, perhaps more accurately speaking, his is a *citation* of the ghazal form as such at the level of form. Love and its involvement in force constitutes the terrain on which this intercultural movement takes place, the movement in which Urdu appears in the midst of English. In the preceding chapters, I have attempted to construct a critical history of the concepts of the force field that is world literature in its reliance on the social situation of English in the world since the Industrial Revolution. The forms of writing and reading that we now call Urdu poetry, in their double "Persianate" and "Hindi" genealogy, have a complex relationship to this force field since its inception in the late eighteenth and early nineteenth centuries, aspects of which I have elaborated in this chapter and Chapter 2. By bringing the (Urdu) ghazal (back) into English, Shahid thus appears to close a great historical circle, whose instantiating moment saw the "discovery" of precisely this "Oriental" corpus and its placing at the center of various programs, from William Jones to Goethe and beyond, for the transformation of poetic practice in the western European languages. His ghazal poems seem to express a desire for a *world culture* but see it as a space of disturbance and conflict, their very movement turning margins into centers, turning received notions of influence and dissemination on their head, and leaving us with a world English that is just a bit less naturalized as the language of poetry. Finally, Shahid's verse makes clear that the question of the civilization of the subcontinent and its place in world literature can now only be posed in *exilic* terms, by taking an unsentimental look at the image of a lost home, in terms that will not help reproduce the structures of violence—physical, cultural, or symbolic—of the nation-state system of homelands in the subcontinent. And it is to the task of developing a concept of philology as homeless practice that I myself shall turn in the final chapter.

In light of the historical analysis of the cultural logic of Orientalism-Anglicism operating in the long, fitful, and ongoing process of bourgeois modernization in the subcontinent that I have attempted here, the task of criticism with respect to the field of culture and society in the region is therefore to adopt *partition as method*, to enter into this field and inhabit the processes of its bifurcation, partition not merely as event, result, or outcome but rather as the very modality of culture, a political logic that inheres in the core concepts and practices of the state. The modern state is majoritarian—a *nation*-state—establishing *some* set of social and cultural practices as normative and representative of the people as such. Majoritarianism is thus itself the minoritization of some other social group, set of practices and social imaginaries. And the crisis of minoritization leads to the partition of society (and sometimes, of state). Society as such is thus always in excess of the representative claims of the nation-state, and the political logic of partition is inherent in the latter as a form.

As Etienne Balibar has argued, primarily with a view to the emergence of a European political, legal and social space, the border as we know it today is a historical institution rather than simply a place or location, an institution that has already undergone several transformations since its first appearance in Europe alongside the modern state in early modern times. It can thus be made the object of a politics of transformation that would seek to democratize this "absolutely nondemocratic" institution that is the very *"condition of democratic institutions"* within the national political and legal space.[64] Sandro Mezzadra has attempted to take this line of argument further by arguing, against all the happy talk of the emergence of a "borderless world," that our present condition is in fact one of the *proliferation* of borders, which is no longer to be experienced at the periphery of the national territory but rather "running . . . through urban environments but also traversing wide continental and global vistas." These borders thus "cut and cross those that exist at the territory's edge but also establish regional and fragmented spaces of economics, politics and law that do not necessarily display the continuity or boundedness of territory."[65] Any attempt to understand the social life of the border in the subcontinent must take into account this global situation of the border as a now *universalized* institution. Even as the need for irregular labor in the Middle-East and Europe produces flows of humanity that must cross the Partition borders in the subcontinent, the state undertakes, with a sort of psychotic intensity and repetitiveness, a concretization of the institution of the border at the periphery of national territory, which is now visible to the naked eye at night in outer space.[66]

For culture and society in the subcontinent, therefore, partition is not merely a historical event (or events) in the past—which has been the approach of much recent revisionist historiography—but rather the very condition of possibility of nation-statehood and therefore the ever-renewed condition of national experience in the subcontinent. It continually instantiates and intensifies processes with far-reaching effects across the social field, both within and across the postcolonial states of the subcontinent. We need to ask in particular how Partition has affected and how it continues to affect our understanding of culture and society across the subcontinent. What forms of knowledge does it preclude and what forms does it make possible? The question of the homeland has appeared in South Asian postcolonial discussion mostly under the sign of the ever-present or overbearing homeland—as the repository of too much religion, too much culture, too much history and too much textuality. This is a far cry from the exilic perspectives on culture and society that Said relentlessly called for, which he once described, in a moment of luminous clarity, as the scrupulous renunciation of "the quasi-religious authority of being comfortably at home among one's people."[67] The homeland of criticism is for Said a *missing* homeland.[68] Said reassembles the paradoxes of exilic experience, of coming from a place that does not, strictly speaking, exist, into the orientation of a critical consciousness for our times. What would it mean for us to understand and experience "India" too as a missing homeland, as too little, not too much, homeland?

In a myriad of forms today, society and culture in the subcontinent continue to function at least in tension with the terms of partitioned society. Even the long arm of Islamic militancy, which stretches compulsively across the border that it claims to want to defend and eternalize, is itself enacting a form of cross-border sociality, a *negative* sociality, when it insists on inflicting pain on its undifferentiated enemy. And as Roy reports in the same essay that recounts the experience of listening, with Maoists in a forest in central India, to Iqbal Bano sing Faiz for her Pakistani audience, even the police in one district in Chhattisgarh state refer to a Maoist controlled area as Pakistan.[69] To argue for partition as method is, therefore, to argue for extracting submerged modes of thinking and feeling from the ongoing historical experience that is partition. Shahid's life's work has been to invite us into such ways of thinking and feeling, extracted with great labor and at much cost by making the achievements of one language available to the possibility of writing in another.

4

"Our Philological Home Is the Earth": World Literature from Auerbach to Said

ERICH AUERBACH IS AMONG the more enigmatic figures of European intellectual history in the twentieth century. His more-than-a-decade-long stay in Istanbul, precipitated by his firing from his academic position under the Nazi racial laws in the mid-1930s, has long been subject to a fierce debate about the meaning and significance of this "exilic" experience for his subsequent work, turning the particulars of Auerbach's life, as Seth Lerer has noted, "into a legend of the writer in exile, remembering the texts and context of a past."[1] Always a meticulous philologist typically immersed in the historical minutiae of the languages of the Latin and Romance worlds, he has left behind works that are nevertheless also resonant with some of the most pressing and encompassing social questions of his time. But these questions, from the historical decline and self-destruction of European civilization to the very possibility of the survival of humanity in the wake of the catastrophes of the century, appear and are handled in these works in elusive and *parabolic* ways that call for demanding and sympathetic modes of explication. He thus remains vulnerable to a desiccating form of reading that is not responsive to these larger concerns and remains fixated on this or that detail of his many accounts of European literary history, thereby missing their overall point more or less entirely. His great masterwork, *Mimesis:*

The Representation of Reality in Western Literature, in particular, remains vulnerable to such reading practices, given its infamous evasion of explicit conceptual framing or overall conclusions.

As the world seems once again, in the second decade of the twenty-first century, to be hurtling toward some as yet indiscernible but also possibly unpreventable catastrophe, the great themes of Auerbach's writings seem urgent and germane to our times as well: the internal conflicts of the monotheistic tradition and its agonistic relations with its pagan or polytheistic others; the fate of European civilization as it lives through and tries to survive the consequences of its own history; the ever-increasing replication of the same social and cultural forms across the world, accompanied by escalating social and political conflicts; the challenge for the Western humanities to produce adequate accounts of the historical crisis even as they are passing through it; the great overarching question of the "inner dream," as Auerbach called it, of world history of the last millennium; and, finally, our very ability to think "the world" and the human as such in the wake of catastrophe.[2] Auerbach's elliptical writings are alive with these issues but call for care and imagination in their untangling and the explication of their treatment. It is such wider historical concerns of Auerbach's works that, as Lerer has argued, "separate him poignantly from his contemporaries, Leo Spitzer and Ernst Robert Curtius . . . all three [being] often grouped together as the great exponents of a German philological tradition."[3] And Harry Levin was already quite astute in this regard in his comparison of Auerbach and Spitzer's personalities and careers.[4]

Given the great conceptual effort that Auerbach expended in rethinking the entire history of the concept and practice of world literature, it is a noticeable fact that the major contributions to the contemporary debate do not seem to rely in any significant way on this work and often even bypass it entirely. The latter is the case, for instance, with Franco Moretti's *Distant Reading*, Pascale Casanova's *The World Republic of Letters*, and even (to a lesser extent) with David Damrosch's *What Is World Literature?*[5] Emily Apter's chapter on Auerbach and Leo Spitzer in *The Translation Zone* is more concerned with the emergence of modern comparative literature (in Istanbul in the 1930s and 1940s) than with stakes in Auerbach's concept of world literature per se, while the section on Auerbach in her more recent *Against World Literature* is concerned with attributing to him a Jewish "*Welt*-theology" on the basis of a number of his essays dealing with Biblical materials. And James Porter, the editor of the important recent collection of new translations of Auerbach's selected essays, whom Apter draws on, seems most concerned to return him to a "German" or even "Jewish" discussion, seeking to rescue him, as he seems to see it, from breezy talk of worldliness or the secular— the terms in which, for instance, Said sought in a number of his writings to reframe Auerbach's career.[6] Finally, after years of being ignored or actively derided as a philologist and humanist from the perspective of the culture of theory in the academy, Auerbach seems to be undergoing ascension to its canon of thinkers, authorized partly by the imprimatur of Jacques Rancière's engagement with him and partly as a result of the rethinking of early Christianity as a site of contemporary theoretical elaboration, which has been undertaken in recent years in the work of such thinkers as Alain Badiou and Slavoj Žižek. But much of this reception focuses on *Mimesis*, above all, and secondarily on such works as the long essay on the history of the idea of *figura*, more or less avoiding his great "autumnal" synthesis, as Said once called it, namely, the essay "Philology and *Weltliteratur*" ("Philologie der Weltliteratur," 1952), of which Said was the cotranslator.[7] Thus, if, on the one hand, Auerbach has been strangely underrepresented in the discussion around world literature, on the other hand, his actual analysis of world literature is largely absent from the considerable Auerbach reception of recent years.

To some readers, Auerbach has appeared as a paragon of the traditional scholarly virtues, the literary historian of almost encyclopedic reach, a decidedly conservative and elitist figure, return to whom allows one to escape, however briefly, from what is regarded as the long nightmare of theory and of the political as such. For others, notably such critics as Said and Paul Bové, he is a figure who is exemplary of what it means to cultivate a critical consciousness and thus a significant resource for any project of cultural criticism in our times that views itself in oppositional terms, in a posture of negation toward the dominant forms of culture and society.[8] For these latter critics, the very erudition, often described as magisterial, that is foregrounded by the traditionalists should be revalued as a precondition for criticism in the oppositional sense. Furthermore, perhaps most unexpectedly from the perspective of Auerbach's traditionalist readers, he continues to exercise a certain gravitational pull on "postcolonial critics who followed in the wake of *Orientalism*," as Herbert Lindenberger has noted with respect to the present author and others.[9] It would not, in other words, be an exaggeration to say that in the contemporary discussion, Auerbach remains in a very real sense an indeterminate figure—conservative humanist and persistent critic of modern culture, nineteenth-century philologist and twentieth-century modernist, cosmopolitan and exile, central European mandarin and Jewish refugee.

The One World and the Ends of World Literature

"Philology and *Weltliteratur*" is arguably one of the great critical essays of the twentieth century, a masterpiece of the essay form, in Theodor Adorno's sense of the essay as a form of writing that is open to and immersed in the always-ongoing processes of social life, open-ended and without the false comfort of first principles.[10] It marks a complex attempt to comprehend the question of society and culture in its global or planet-wide ramifications from the historical perspective of the mid-twentieth century. It is here that Auerbach raises the question of the possibility of conceiving of the world as such in humanistic and philological terms on the threshold of the postcolonial era, and it is therefore this essay that I shall examine closely here. Having attempted in the course of the preceding chapters to expose and challenge many of the unspoken assumptions and even pieties of the contemporary debate on world literary relations by insisting on a historical reckoning, I return in this chapter to the concept of world literature itself by way of Auerbach's dramatic reformulation, and arguably the most significant rethinking, of the received Goethean notion. The stakes for Auerbach in what could otherwise have been treated as a narrow and specialized discussion in (European) literary history are nothing less than our ability to think the human itself in the aftermath of catastrophe, human life understood through its sedimentation in the "documents" of its many civilizations. When I turn to other aspects of Auerbach's project and career in this chapter, it will in part be in order to clarify their relationship to this "autumnal" synthesis.

Said's engagement with Auerbach, which sometimes even took the form of a claimed *return* to him, remained for a long time largely ignored and unexamined, Bové's *Intellectuals in Power* being one of the few significant exceptions. At precisely the moment when the literary discipline in Britain and North America seemed to be turning most decisively to an establishment of theory as its common language, a shift in which Said himself had played a not inconsiderable part, he placed Auerbach at the beginning of a book of essays, namely, *The World, the Text, and the Critic*, many of which challenge that disciplinary turn, invoking the German Jewish philologist in exile as the icon of what criticism once was and ought once again to be. Said is reported to have been challenged publicly on one occasion on precisely this count by Paul de Man, who suggested that Walter Benjamin would have better served Said's purposes—a misunderstanding, in my view, of what those purposes actually were.[11] For others of a more political bent than de Man, Said's was a perverse gesture. Many considered it explicitly as a politically retrograde move, and others responded to it with embarrassed silence. As I have noted in the prologue, I attempted in an essay published in the late 1990s to clear this logjam, arguing that Said's engagement with Auerbach was crucial for us to understand and that his invocation of "Auerbach in Istanbul" in particular was a symptomatic one, containing important clues about Said's core inclinations and concerns.[12] Auerbach became for Said exemplary of the relationship between criticism and exilic consciousness, not just in his literal displacement to Turkey on being fired from his position at Marburg, a displacement that meant he would survive the coming European genocide but in the forms of exile that are already inscribed in Jewish life in prewar European society.[13] I called this form of exile, which carries the potential of its own literalization in physical uprooting, *minority*.[14] This set of issues—that is, the possibilities that exilic consciousness offers criticism as a vocation and orientation in society—are at the core of Said's critical enterprise, and even his distinct mode of critique of imperialism and

Orientalism, as I have suggested in the prologue, could be traced back to it.

Auerbach's essay is profoundly a text of the early postwar years: its historical location is this moment marked by the rapid (and violent) disintegration of the colonial empires, the accompanying expansion of the global system of nation-states, and of course the wake of the war itself, in Europe and elsewhere, and in particular the aftermath of the Holocaust. It is thus infused with the melancholic perception that a certain European life and European order, and with it a certain idea of Europe, are coming to an end. It deals, we might say, with three sets of problems pertaining to the concept of *Weltliteratur*, dealt with in successive fashion: the first concerns the historical *conditions of emergence* of a new concept of world literature, linked to but distinct from the one attributable to the Goethean humanistic tradition; the second is what Auerbach views as the *practical* problems and difficulties raised for the conception and its practice under the new historical conditions; and the third concerns a possible approach to these methodological questions—a new approach to the *possibility of synthesis* in an age of microspecializations. (The Said translation inserts numbered sections to mark these transitions where there are none in the original.) The essay then concludes in a somewhat cryptic manner after raising the problem of what we may call critical consciousness or, to put it another way altogether, the knowledge-subject appropriate to this new philology of world literature. As I shall attempt to show, Auerbach seems here to touch on the relationship between the critical humanities, the possibility and practice of humanism, and different modes of being in, and attached to, the world.

To a certain extent, Auerbach's essay can be compared with a very different kind of text contemporary with it—different in language, discipline, and larger sensibility—namely, Claude Lévi-Strauss's *Tristes Tropiques* (1955), and it would be useful to linger with that work briefly before we return to Auerbach. Lévi-Strauss's text presents the postwar, postcolonial European subject as a cosmopolitan figure abroad in the world, exemplified in the figure of ethnographer, that is, a critic of Western ethnocentrism. In Auerbach's essay, on the other hand, the European subject appears in the role of philological humanist, a critic of the narrowness of attachments to the viewpoint of "national" language and literature. After a few opening sections in which Lévi-Strauss reflects on the context of his first introduction to Brazil, as a lecturer of sociology at the University of São Paulo, and on his many Atlantic crossings over the years, including the decisive one escaping from Vichy France, he comes to the core of the issues that animate the work—the "quest for power" and conquest that has animated Europe's history in the modern era and the consequent destruction of the world's diverse social forms:

> Now that the Polynesian islands have been smothered in concrete and turned into aircraft carriers solidly anchored in the southern seas, when the whole of Asia is beginning to look like a dingy suburb, when shanty towns are spreading across Africa, . . . what else can the so-called escapism of traveling do than confront us with the more unfortunate aspects of our history? . . . The first thing we see as we travel around the world is our own filth thrown into the face of mankind. . . . So I can understand the mad passion for travel books and their deceptiveness. They create the illusion of something which no longer exists but still should exist. . . . There is nothing to be done about it now; civilization has ceased to be that delicate flower which was preserved and painstakingly cultivated in one or two sheltered areas of a soil rich in wild species. . . . Mankind has opted for monoculture; it is in the process of creating a mass civilization, as beetroot is grown in the mass. Henceforth, man's daily bill of fare will consist only of this one item.[15]

The very possibility of (anthropological) knowledge of human societies, Lévi-Strauss argues, is implicated in this process, the peddling of the exotic in fact being one of the modalities of the destruction of genuine social and historical differences. The desire to preserve and experience the authenticity of the other itself facilitates the latter's assimilation and is caught from the beginning in an inescapable "circle": "When was the best time to see India? . . . For every five years I move back in time, I am able to save a custom, gain a ceremony or share in another belief. But I know the texts too well not to

realize that, by going back a century, I am at the same time for-
going data and lines of inquiry which would offer intellectual
enrichment. . . . The less human societies were able to communicate with each other and therefore to corrupt each other through
contact, the less their respective emissaries were able to perceive the
wealth and significance of their diversity."[16] For Lévi-Strauss—and
for Auerbach, as we shall see shortly—the investment seems to be
in the refashioning of the Western subject of knowledge in the era of
(postcolonial) globalism, and each of their respective works represents an attempt to understand (but also define) the new "predicament of culture" in the emerging world.[17] Suffice it to say here that
this new world is characterized for them in part by the loss of the
centrality of Europe and Europeans that had been the sine qua non
of the colonial world and of the European humanities in that era,
and in part by the necessity of confronting the consequences of the
new visibility of the formerly colonized peoples, the continent's
various historically constituted others, on the twentieth century's
historical stage. In other words, both works are located within, and
concerned with, the transformed field of culture on the threshold
of the postcolonial, "globalization" phase of the world capitalist
economy. They in fact belong to a larger set of contemporary works,
within which we could also place Hannah Arendt's *Origins of Totalitarianism* (1951), each of which is concerned in it own distinct way
with the fate of an aspect of modern European civilization in the
aftermath of the self-destruction of society on the continent.

Because Auerbach's remarkable essay belongs to and addresses the
early years of the emergence of our contemporary era, it still speaks
urgently to us. It begins by drawing attention to its own conjuncture, opening with a question whose very condition of possibility is
historical transformation: "It is time to ask what meaning the word
Weltliteratur can still have if we relate it, as Goethe did, both to the
past and to the future" (PWL, 2).[18] The very presupposition of the
concept was "mankind's division into many cultures." But today, "our
earth, the domain of *Weltliteratur*, is growing smaller and losing its
diversity" (PWL, 2). In the final chapter of *Mimesis*, Auerbach had
written that the "strata of societies and their different ways of life
have become inextricably mingled. There are no longer even exotic

peoples. A century ago . . . Corsicans or Spaniards were still exotic; today the term would be quite unsuitable for Pearl Buck's Chinese peasants."[19] Now, the verdict is an even more urgent one: "The presupposition of *Weltliteratur* is a *felix culpa:* mankind's division into many cultures. Today, however, human life is becoming standardized. The process of imposed uniformity, which originally derived from Europe, continues its work, and hence serves to undermine all individual traditions" (PWL, 2). Moreover, the explosion of nationalisms across the continent and the world in recent decades, in which each sociopolitical entity seems to be asserting its own individuality, is in fact nothing more than the means for the establishment of the most rigid forms of uniformity:

> To be sure, national wills are stronger and louder than ever, yet in every case they promote the same standards and forms of modern life. . . . The European cultures, which have long enjoyed their fruitful interrelation, and which have always been supported by a consciousness of their worth, these cultures still retain their individualities. Nevertheless, even among them the process of leveling proceeds with a greater rapidity than ever before. Standardization, in short, dominates everywhere. All human activity is being concentrated either into European-American or into Russian-Bolshevist patterns; no matter how great they seem to us, the differences between the two patterns are comparatively minimal when they are both contrasted with the basic patterns underlying the Islamic, Indian or Chinese traditions. (PWL, 2–3)

Auerbach thus takes as the starting point for the essay—I shall return presently to his notion of the point of departure—the paradox that the defining characteristic of the era of supposed national differentiation turns out to be a sort of leveling, the pressure for replication of the same political and cultural forms everywhere.

The essay as a whole is thus profoundly affected by, and concerned with examining, the major historical forces and events of its time. But it is also marked by the events of Auerbach's own life and its relation to those larger forces. Clearly, these opening reflections on modernization are deeply informed by his recent more than a decade of experience and work in Turkey, which provided almost laboratory-like conditions for observing the effects of this process of standardization disguised as indigenization. In a passage later in the essay concerning the decline of humanistic education in the West, for instance, he observes that the "academic study of Greek, Latin and the Bible" had nearly disappeared from "bourgeois humanistic culture," and he adds, "if I may draw conclusions from my own experiences in Turkey, then it is easy to note corresponding changes in non-European, but equally ancient, cultures" (PWL, 9).

Soon after Auerbach arrived in Istanbul in the summer of 1936 as professor of Romance philology and chair of the faculty of Western languages and literatures at the newly established Istanbul University—which was in the process of being built out of the Darül-fünun (House of Arts and Sciences), the nineteenth-century Ottoman institution of higher learning, now considered by Turkish Republican reformers to be backward and inadequate to the demands of the country's new European identity—he reflected on this process and his own not small role in it in a handful of letters to colleagues and friends in Europe, including Walter Benjamin. Writing to the latter on December 12, 1936, he notes the vertiginous pace and nature of the Republican process of "reform":

> The situation here is not exactly simple, but it is not without charm. They have thrown all tradition overboard here, and they want to build a thoroughly rationalized—extreme Turkish nationalist—state of the European sort. The process is going fantastically and spookily fast: already there is hardly anyone who knows Arabic or Persian, and even Turkish texts of the past century will quickly become incomprehensible since the language is being modernized and at the same time newly oriented on "Ur-Turkish," and it is being written with Latin characters. "Romanologie" is fundamentally a luxury, and I am the only real cultural historian among the newly hired Europeans. And I have to organize instruction in all the Western languages in the university, and all sorts of other things as well. The work is truly

laborious because one has to battle with all the most curious difficulties, misunderstandings, resistances—yet, it is neither practically nor personally uninteresting.[20]

Writing again to Benjamin again a few months later, he displays a clear understanding of the far-reaching cultural and social implications of the language reforms being undertaken so precipitously: "The language reform—at once fantastical ur-Turkish ('free' from Arabic and Persian influences) and modern-technical—has made it certain that no one under 25 can any longer understand any sort of religious, literary, or philosophical text more than ten years old and that, under the pressure of the Latin script, which was compulsorily introduced a few years ago, the specific properties of the language are rapidly decaying. I could report many individual instances from many areas." And Auerbach places these Republican "reforms" of culture and society within a much-larger historical canvas:

[Ataturk] has had to accomplish everything he has done in a struggle against the European democracies on the one hand, and on the other against the old Muslim, pan-Islamist sultan economy, and the result is a fanatical, antitraditional nationalism: a renunciation of all existing Islamic cultural tradition, a fastening onto a fantasy "ur-Turkey," technical modernization in the European sense in order to strike the hated and envied Europe with its own weapons. Hence the predisposition for European exiles as teachers, from whom one can learn without being afraid that they will spread foreign propaganda. The result: Nationalism in the superlative with the simultaneous destruction of the historic national character. This configuration, which in other countries such as Germany, Italy, and indeed also in Russia (?) is not yet a certainty for everyone, steps forth here in complete nakedness. . . . The whole needs to be grasped together this way: I am more and more convinced that the contemporary world situation is nothing other than the cunning of providence to lead us along a bloody and circuitous route to the Internationale of Triviality and Esperanto culture. I thought this already in Germany and Italy, especially in the horrifying inauthenticity of "Blubopropaganda," but here for the first time it has become a certainty for me.[21]

The letters thus reveal Auerbach's serious effort to understand his new surroundings and a remarkable comprehension of their place in world history. The supersonic pace of the developments in Turkey, transforming a multicultural (imperial) state and society into a national one in the course of a few years—Auerbach arrived in Istanbul a mere dozen years after the abolition of the Ottoman Caliphate in 1924—should not conceal their similarity to the catastrophe unfolding in Europe itself, each space characterized by a hypernationalist "militarist modernism," as Mürat Belge has called it.[22] But the historical process that Auerbach describes is in fact twofold: on the one hand, "nationalism in the superlative with the simultaneous destruction of the historic national character" and, on the other, the only seemingly opposite result of the emergence of an "Internationale of Triviality and Esperanto culture." The former process means that the route to the latter is a "bloody and circuitous" one. The largely Hegelian orientation of Auerbach's notion of history is clearly visible even in these brief and informal passages, though he revises its implied sense of inevitable progress with a sense of its "circuitous" nature. And Auerbach seeks to bring into his notion of the historical unfolding events in "the East," even if merely a *near* East of the Euro-Occidental imagination. (The Orient Express, after all, never left the European continent.)

In Istanbul, therefore, Auerbach found himself immersed in the historical process that Kader Konuk, in her fascinating intellectual history of the German-Jewish humanist expatriates' professional life in Istanbul, has called "East West Mimesis," the process of modernization experienced as Europeanization.[23] She sets the émigré milieu against the backdrop of the Kemalist transformation of state and society along European-nationalist lines. Konuk provides new historical heft to the figure of "Auerbach in Istanbul," arguing not only for the links between this setting and the great themes of his subsequent work, including both "Figura" and *Mimesis*, but also for the significance of Auerbach and his cohort's professional activities in the

secularization and Westernization of Turkish culture. Most intrigu-
ingly, she suggests a generalization of the notion of *mimesis* to a
modality of "East West relations" as a whole in the twentieth century,
though in the end it is not clear if she means by this anything other
than what Homi Bhabha designated a long time ago as (colonial) mim-
icry.[24] But while I disagree with Konuk's assessment of the implications of her work for Said's interpretation of Auerbach—she argues
explicitly that she is writing contra Said's reading of Auerbach's
Istanbul exile while taking a rather literalist view of exile as such—and
although she seems sometimes to confuse and collapse into each other
Auerbach's distinct notions of *figura* and mimesis, the former designating in his work a relationship of (symbolic) prefigurement and
fulfillment and the latter a relationship between (literary) language
and social reality, I recognize the significant value of her archival research of the Turkish context for the ongoing Auerbach discussion.

Finally, throughout these letters from Istanbul, Auerbach is aware
of the irony of his own situation as a philologist of *Weltliteratur*,
playing a distinct and visible role in the process of standardization
and Europeanization of the humanistic culture of an Oriental and
Islamic society: "We teach all the European philologies here—
Romance language and literature, English language and literature,
classical philology, German language and literature. We try to influence the instructional life and the library and to Europeanize the
administrative management of scholarship all the way from the instructional grid down to the card catalog. That is naturally absurd,
but the Turks want it, even if they occasionally try to get in the way."[25]
These conditions of his own life thus mirror or encapsulate the larger
historical paradox that the modern European critical humanities, despite their basis, as Auerbach has it, in ideas derived from eighteenth-
century historicism, cannot claim to be standing outside the powerful
social forces of leveling—and let us recall that for Auerbach this
represents a profound loss for human experience—and are in fact
themselves an agent of the process. In this sense, historicism itself,
in a broad sense, both as a theoretical and intellectual tendency and
as a feature of modern social and cultural experience as such, is
embedded in social forces whose process leads in a direction that is
explicitly disavowed in historicist thinking.

It is this set of issues about the fate of culture in the modern world, first experienced and observed in Turkey, that Auerbach addresses in more formal and conceptual terms in "Philology and *Weltliteratur*." Were this historical process to remain unchecked—and to Auerbach it appears to be irreversible—it could produce a result quite unprecedented in the entire history of humanity: "a single literary culture, only a few literary languages, and perhaps even a single literary language." And if such an extreme situation were ever to be actualized, "the notion of *Weltliteratur* would be at once realized and destroyed" (PWL, 3). For Auerbach, therefore, the term *Weltliteratur* references a dialectical process, the activity and attempt to comprehend the social and cultural range of human experience from precisely within the great historical process of its convergence and assimilation—the "approaching unification and simplification," as he called it in the final chapter of *Mimesis* (M, 553). But, true to his historicist leanings, Auerbach poses this question entirely in civilizational terms, unwilling or simply not able in intellectual and conceptual terms to see it as the process of the historical rise of capital in western Europe and its built-in (that is, historically necessary) need and attempt to create a world market, requiring the incorporation of vastly divergent social formations. Thus, he argues that the Soviet Communist model ("Russian-Bolshevist patterns") is more or less one distinct possibility *within* Western civilization when compared with the "basic patterns" of premodern Indian, Islamic, or Chinese civilizations. Putting it a bit more precisely, we might therefore say that the dialectical unfolding of the cultural logic of modern bourgeois society—that is to say Orientalism, in the double sense we have given it in earlier chapters—is reinscribed in Auerbach's essay in civilizational terms, thereby concealing the essential terms of this logic precisely in the process of attempting to reveal it.

I shall return to this question of what is revealed and what concealed in Auerbach's essay. But here we might note that, following Auerbach in this direction, romantic nationalism, whose entire raison d'être in each case is to express the unique expression of the spirit of a distinct people, would have to be understood instead as delivering societies and peoples to a worldwide ensemble that *allows each social entity to be distinct in exactly the same way*, namely, the global system of nation-states. This set of perceptions about the internal logic of nationalisms and nation-states, and in fact all notions of cultural particularity and civilizational uniformity, whose philosophical genealogy, as we shall shortly see, Auerbach traces to Johann Gottfried Herder, inform in more or less explicit ways a great many of his writings, including to a certain extent *Mimesis* itself. Modern nationalism and the kinds of cultural possibilities it represents, which were the social and cultural background of the recent upheaval and devastation on a continental and even global scale, thus constitute a prominent antagonist in Auerbach's essay, which seeks to expose, "with equanimity so that we will not hate whoever opposes us," the structure of claims inherent to this mythos of the modern world (PWL, 7).

And the consequences for our understanding of *Weltliteratur* are equally significant: it emerged precisely alongside the nation-state and nation-form, rather than as a sign of their overcoming. Thus, compared to our contemporary usage, in which the emergence of "world literature" is usually understood as a historical overcoming of self-enclosed "national" literary traditions, Auerbach offers a very different conception. For a range of scholars (such as Damrosch and Moretti) associated with the concept, it is to be understood as antithetical to that of national literature. As we have seen, even Marx and Engels seem to have spoken of world literature in that manner, as a cosmopolitan practice that has overcome national "one-sidedness," but they of course use "nation" in a different sense than we do, signifying a "people" and a place before their induction into the capitalist world economy, rather than the modern nation-form or nation-state. Auerbach's essay thus takes apart the possibility of any such straightforward conception of the historical links between national literatures and world literature.

For Auerbach, the very condition of possibility of the idea of *Weltliteratur* is historicism, the recognition of the multiplicity of aesthetic and cultural norms and value systems historically and across the world, which he considers to be a deeply embedded feature of modern social and cultural life. If, therefore, on the one hand, *Weltliteratur* marks for Auerbach a unifying process, signifying "universal" literature, that which expresses *Humanität* in general, on the other, it always assumes multiplicity and plurality. And philology is the quint-essential science of the historical—that is, the secular, human, and earthly—world, insisting as it does on a historical understanding of the creation of meaning in language. (In that sense, we might say that its status in the humanistic and historical disciplines is for Auerbach analogous to that of mathematics in the natural sciences.) It is only through philology that we can equip ourselves to escape the near-certain advent of bourgeois modernity's historical amnesia. But since philology is in an immediate sense a science of particulars, what would it mean to engage in the philology of *world* literature? What concretely does it mean to say, as Auerbach does, that "our philological home is the earth; it can no longer be the nation" (PWL, 17)?

We shall return to this question at greater length in a moment. What concerns us here is that Auerbach traces the emergence of this feature of modern life—our perception of the irreducible multiplicity of aesthetic values and of values in general—to the rise of philosophical historicism in the late eighteenth century, and, as we shall see, this exclusive focus comes at the cost of understanding the colonial nature of its moment of emergence. Throughout his career from the 1920s on, Auerbach turned his attention repeatedly to the thinkers most often associated with this philosophical historicism, in particular Giambattista Vico and Herder. He returned to this theme for the final time at the end of his career and life in the introduction to the posthumously published *Literary Language and Its Public in Late Latin Antiquity and the Middle Ages* (1965) and spoke of this emergence as the "Copernican discovery" in the field of humanistic studies. It was the one intellectual shift that changed everything in European culture, making possible a capacious concept of humanity, whose diversity could now be perceived in the multiplicity of its "documents": "in aesthetic matters, our historicist capacity for adaptation to the most various forms of beauty is almost boundless; we may make use of it more than once within a few hours or even minutes, during a visit to a museum, in a concert, sometimes in the movies, or leafing through a magazine, or even looking at travel agency advertisements." This form of historical imagination was first "made generally accessible by the activity of the Romantic critics," and "the whole labor of research into early and foreign civilizations done since the beginning of the nineteenth century was and is based on a historicist approach." So comprehensive is this change in Western (and now world) culture that, "just as in Molière's *Bourgeois Gentilhomme*, Monsieur Jourdain's everyday language, to his great surprise, turns out to be prose," most modern individuals "are as little conscious of our historicism as Monsieur Jourdain is of his prose."[26]

I return in a moment to the consequences for Auerbach's argument of the fact that he views philosophical historicism as the condition of possibility (and in fact origin) of "research into . . . foreign civilizations done since the beginning of the nineteenth century." The latter, that is, Orientalism, is, according to the terms of this passage, simply an instantiation or application of the former. But first it is important to understand that Auerbach's attention to the emergence of philosophical historicism in the eighteenth century is directed in part against the received reputation of Herder as the so-called discoverer of this principle or way of thinking. He repeatedly reminds us that Vico formulated some of the ideas associated with historicism several decades earlier and without access to the cultural trends, such as the heritage of German pietism or Jean-Jacques Rousseau's influence, that facilitated the rise of the counter-Enlightenment in Germany: "Herder and his followers started from the conception of the original folk genius as the creator of true poetry: in strong opposition to all theories which based poetry and art on highly developed civilization, good taste, imitation of models, and well-defined rules, they believed that poetry is the work of free instinct and imagination, and that it is most spontaneous and genuine in the early periods of civilization, in the youth of mankind . . . when 'poetry was the natural language of men.'" But Vico had anticipated "the concept of folk genius as a general phenomenon of early poetry," the idea of a sort of collective expression rather than individual authorship, although Herder's thinking on this matter had developed independently of the influence of Vico, whose work was hardly even known to the intelligentsias of England, France, or Germany into the nineteenth century.[27] But juxtaposition of Vico and Herder also has a larger significance for Auerbach than merely a question of the "originality" or priority of the one or the other. To this extent, Auerbach on Vico and Herder differs markedly from Isaiah Berlin on the same two thinkers, for Berlin phrases his discussion of the differences between the two in a largely biographical register, framing Vico as the prior discoverer of philosophical principles and ways of thinking that have subsequently come to be associated with Herder.

The two eighteenth-century thinkers mark for Auerbach distinct trajectories and possibilities of historicist thought into our own times. Auerbach notes that the Herderian historicist "admiration for primitive and early forms of civilization," which is in essence "Nordic" and carries "a certain idyllic, lyrical, and pantheistic connotation," certainly produced a historical understanding of literature and culture, the imperative to understand each period of human history and each society on its own terms that has been a signal achievement in the history of the world. But this "aesthetic historism" was at the same time "a very *dangerous* acquisition of the human mind," since it could lead, as it did especially in Germany, to "an extremely nationalistic attitude toward [one's] own fatherland," the latter coming to be "considered as the synthesis and supreme realization of folk genius."[28] Against Herder's "Nordic" historicist turn to the primitive "spirit" of the nation or people, we might say, Auerbach seems to pit Vico's "Latinate civilizatory" concept of history, to quote Adorno from another but related context, which it is worth examining here briefly even if tangentially. Accused by a listener (in the late 1950s) that he had relied excessively on "foreign words" in a recent radio address, Adorno responded by displacing the question entirely onto the historical situation of German itself within the larger European landscape. He argued that foreign words functioned differently in German than they did in English or French, because in German, "the Latinate civilizatory components did not fuse with the older popular language [as they had centuries ago in the other two languages] but instead were set off from it through the formation of educated elites and by courtly custom," so that "the foreign words stick out, unassimilated. . . . What seems inorganic here is in actuality only historical evidence . . . of the failure of that unification." The writer can thus "take advantage of the tension between the foreign word and the language" for the "beneficial interruption of the conformist moment of language," its deceptive "customary ring of naturalness," and thereby demonstrate "the impossibility of an ontology of language," confronting "even concepts that try to pass themselves off as origin itself with their mediateness, their moment of being subjectively constructed, their arbitrariness." Adorno thus exposes the claim to authenticity made on behalf of the *eigen-* and indigenous element in language in a range of linguistic realms, from ordinary speech to literature and philosophy. But he goes further, to the other end of the modern spectrum, as it were, the opposite mode and implication of the "criterion of intelligibility 'for everyone,'" on the model of "pidgin or Basic English," a language "truly fit for giving commands . . . [as] Europeans once derisively gave orders to their colored servants in the same debased speech they wished their servants would use."[29]

The *spectrum* identified by Adorno here is the one also implicit in Auerbach's reflections on the fate of language, literature, and culture in the twentieth century and its relation to the historicist ways of thinking of the eighteenth, stretching from the "dangerous" myth of the organically distinct and intact *völkisch* speech community to, as he put it to Benjamin from Istanbul, as we have seen earlier, the "Internationale of Triviality and Esperanto culture." The two supposed poles are in fact revealed to be identical, or rather, the same process that accentuates the former is shown to actually lead to the latter. Auerbach's attempt to navigate the map of eighteenth-century philosophy thus represents an attempt to think historically, and we may even say genealogically, about the fate of historicism in the twentieth century. He makes a crucial distinction between Herder and Vico, demonstrating that the latter makes available a form of historicist thinking that does not leave open the possibility—the *danger*—of a fully nationalistic enunciation. If Herder's concept of the organic community and its *Volksgeist* can lead to romantic nationalism and even worse, the virtue of Vico's thought is a more encompassing (and dynamic) humanism, one of whose iterations is his famous hermeneutical formula that, while every cultural product of a human society is produced according to principles that are internal to that society at a given moment in its history, because it is a creation of human beings, it can nevertheless be understood by other human beings. And speaking biographically, we ought to note that the very choice of and commitment to Romance philology, rather than, say, classics, let alone Germanic philology, marks in Auerbach's life an attempt to put at a certain distance the rising nationalistic ambience of German humanistic culture in the pre– and post–World War I period.[30]

Emphasizing Vico's social and cultural situatedness (in Naples) at the margins of eighteenth-century Europe, Auerbach (and, following him, Said) seeks to extract from his work a radically historical humanism, with "the human" understood not as pregiven commonness of nature or experience but rather something that is achieved through social and cultural action by and between divergently situated and constituted individuals and collectivities: "a conception of man united in his multiplicity" (PWL, 4). But this is a form of "historic perspectivism" that is also comparative and worldly, explicitly rejecting the proto-romantic view of cultural complexes as distinct and hermetically self-contained entities. Vico is thus a more secure source for Auerbach for a historicism that can attend to the crisis of European civilization of the mid-twentieth century, the crisis of the nation-state as the basis of modern social and cultural life. But Auerbach gives this humanistic (self-) consciousness of the multiplicity of "the human" a dialectical turn. The philological humanist himself is an agent of the modernity one of whose effects is a leveling out of the heterogeneity that is the human—the very heterogeneity whose memory the philologist seeks to resurrect. And the philologist in the age of Goethe—the age, supposedly, of the "discovery" of human diversity—was as much implicated in this historical process, albeit at an earlier stage—"the period of Goethean humanism was brief indeed"—as the philological humanist in Auerbach's own postwar and postcolonial era (PWL, 3). The convergence with Lévi-Strauss's analysis of the fate of the cultural category of the exotic or authentically other in the postwar and postcolonial era is also a striking one. Like anthropological notions of cultural difference, the philological understanding of linguistic and literary particularity finds itself at a historical crossroads with the rapid decline and disappearance of the colonial world and the hierarchies of knowledge and culture it had both instituted and taken for granted.

A World of Philology

As I noted earlier, the concluding paragraph of Auerbach's essay begins with the categorical assertion that "our philological home is the earth; it can no longer be the nation." It is a remarkable statement, toward which all the lines of argument in the essay seem to have been leading, but it is not, in my view, a conventional expression of a cosmopolitan point of view in the strict sense of that term. The "world" is not a ready-made perspective readily accessible to the humanistic scholar; it can only become available through an active *struggle* with his or her particularistic formation and heritage, a *gain* in perspective that is also a profound *loss* at the same time: "The most priceless and indispensible part of a philologist's heritage is still his own nation's culture and language. Only when he is first separated from this heritage, however, and then transcends it does it become truly effective" (PWL, 17). Auerbach thus views this achieving of a "world" perspective by the displacement of the outlooks offered by one's natal culture as one of the greatest challenges of the historical and philological humanities—and of course "philology" is for him an encompassing term, almost identical with "humanities" as such, and the latter are nothing if not always historical. In making such an effort, Auerbach finally notes, the humanist will "return, in admittedly altered circumstances, to the knowledge that prenational medieval culture already possessed: the knowledge that the spirit [*Geist*] is not national" (PWL, 17; original 49). And it is on this note that Auerbach finally brings "Philology and *Weltliteratur*" to a conclusion by quoting the famous passage from the end of book 3 of the *Didascalicon* of Hugh of St. Victor (Hugo in German), which Said subsequently returned to repeatedly in his writings.

Here is the fuller passage from the Jerome Taylor translation that is cited by Said in such works as *Culture and Imperialism* (Auerbach quotes only the third and fourth sentences reproduced here and in the Latin, left untranslated in the Said translation of the essay; Said typically quotes the second, third, and fourth sentences):[31]

Finally, a foreign soil is proposed, since it too gives a man practice. All the world is a foreign soil to those who philosophize. . . . It is, therefore, a source of great virtue for the practiced mind to learn, bit by bit, first to change about in [*sic*] visible and transitory things, so that afterwards it may be able to leave them behind altogether. The man who finds his homeland sweet is still a tender beginner; he to whom every soil is as his native one is already strong; but he is perfect to whom the entire world is as a foreign land. The tender soul has fixed his love on one spot in the world; the strong man has extended his love to all places; the perfect man has extinguished his. From boyhood I have dwelt on foreign soil, and I know with what grief the mind sometimes takes leave of the narrow hearth of a peasant's hut, and I know, too, how frankly it afterwards disdains marble firesides and paneled halls.[32]

There is something elusive and elliptical about Auerbach's citation of these lines, left at the very end of the essay largely without comment, except in one small but significant way, to which I return shortly. It bears closer reading. What exactly is Auerbach's purpose in leaving us with these words, written probably in the late 1120s by a teacher, theologian, and mystic, from a "didactic" work written to provide an overview and introduction for students at the Abbey of St. Victor to all the fields of knowledge that the author considered important to their education—an introductory medieval textbook, of sorts? One of the effects of Auerbach's citing of Hugh at the conclusion of his essay is to place all that has preceded in a long historical perspective. Earlier in the essay, he had already spoken of the "inner history of the last thousand years" as "the history of mankind achieving self-expression" and argued that "this is what philology, a historicist discipline, treats" (PWL, 5). The passage from Hugh now strengthens the perception that a historical or "philological" understanding of the present crisis requires this longer historical perspective.

Let us begin with some straightforward observations about the passage from the *Didascalicon* and its placement in Auerbach's essay. First of all, we might say that it concerns modes of being in the world or, more precisely, modes of *attachment to place*, if we consider place as a mode and a product of symbolic elaboration. Second, it describes a process in three steps—proceeding "bit by bit"—starting with the orientation that marks the "tender beginner," through that of the "strong soul," and culminating in that of the "perfect man." (I should note that the Latin original merely uses the personal pronoun *ille* and relative pronoun *cui* in these lines, rather than nouns, to refer to the personage undertaking the journey of development, and "soul" and "man" are Taylor's interjections.) In this journey toward perfection, the individual goes through a series of stages, each marked by a distinct orientation, starting with attachment to his or her homeland ("patria"), through an equally strong attachment to every place in the world ("omne solum"), as if every spot on earth were equally the homeland, and finally to experiencing the whole world ("mundum totus") as if it were a foreign land ("exilium") (PWL, 17). If we were to translate the terms of this passage of Hugh's into terms inherent to the historical world of Auerbach's essay—a move he himself seems to call for, as he offers no reading of the passage in its own historical terms—this violation of the very first principle of historicist reading might yield the following: the "tender beginner" displays a (patriotic) love of *nation;* the "strong soul" takes the whole world in a *cosmopolitan* embrace; but the "perfect" one treats every place in the world as a place of *exile.* Love of nation, cosmopolitanism, and exilic imagination are elements in a sort of dialectical process in Auerbach's essay, none of them autonomous from the others and dependent on their determinations.

What Auerbach's cryptic act of citation offers, therefore, literally *in the end,* is exilic imagination and exilic persona (in their relation to the national and the cosmopolitan) as the coordinates of humanism and the humanities. This orientation is not to be confused with detachment, however; it is a mode of being *in* the world characterized by a far more complex process of rooting and uprooting. Following the passage from Hugh of St. Victor, Auerbach thus concludes the essay with the following caution and clarification: "Hugo intended these lines for one whose aim is to free himself from a love of the world. But it is a good way also for one who wishes to earn a proper love for the world" (PWL, 17). To embrace—"to earn a proper love for"—the *whole* world also implies continuously separating oneself from every *particular* "place" within it, from the *symbolic fabrication of place* as such. This is a recipe, in other words, neither for a brooding solipsism, whether communal or individual, nor for the cosmopolitan detachment of a "view from above." Auerbach thus explicitly repudiates notions of an organic link between a language and a people that has been a feature of philology in the era of nationalisms and nation-states. The proximate task of "philology" in Auerbach's expanded sense, therefore, is to break free of the nation-form and find other, less singular modes of situating itself in the world, modes available from the history of Europe itself before the long and slow move away from the medieval world toward modern forms of culture and society, culminating in the establishment of the nation-state as the normative state form throughout the continent and subsequently the world. The final passage of the essay therefore distillates the historical experience of the victims of fascism into the figure of the critical-humanist and philologist as such as an exilic persona. Like *Mimesis*, therefore, as Said noted with respect to that work, "Philology and *Weltliteratur*" too represents an act of "cultural, even civilizational, survival of the highest importance" in the wake of society's self-destruction.[33]

As is well known, in the epilogue to *Mimesis*, Auerbach had already spoken of his eleven-year stay in Istanbul after fleeing from the Third Reich, away from the familiar intellectual world of central Europe, as both a painful separation from and loss of a native world and as an enabling condition for the creation of that unique retrospective look at the expanse of European literary history. It is worth quoting the passage in full:

> There are frequent gaps—that is to say, periods which have not been treated at all, antiquity for example, which I use only by way of introduction, or the early Middle Ages, from which but too little has been preserved. Additional chapters could have been inserted later to deal with English, German, and Spanish texts. I should have liked to treat the *siglo de oro* more extensively; I would especially have liked to add a special chapter on German realism of the seventeenth century. But the difficulties were too great. I may also mention that the book was written during the war and at Istanbul, where libraries are not well equipped for European studies. International communications were impeded; I had to dispense with almost all periodicals, and almost all the more recent investigations, and in some cases with reliable critical editions of my texts. . . . The lack of technical literature

and periodicals may also serve to explain that my book has no notes. Aside from the texts, I quote comparatively little, and that little it was easy to include in the body of the book. On the other hand it is quite possible that the book owes its existence to just this lack of a rich and specialized library. If it had been possible for me to acquaint myself with all the work that has been done on so many subjects, I might never have reached the point of writing. (*M*, 557)

For Said, as is equally well known, *Mimesis* is emphatically "an exile's book."[34] And the passage from the epilogue marks for him Auerbach's recognition of the positive and *productive* role of his exilic experience in Istanbul in the making of the unique historical perspective that is embodied in *Mimesis*—a place of special resonance as the site of historical Europe's Islamic other for anyone, like Auerbach, "trained in medieval and renaissance Roman literatures." Consequently, *Mimesis* "is not, as it has so frequently been taken to be, only a massive reaffirmation of the Western cultural tradition, but also a work built upon a critically important alienation from it."[35] Said's concern here is with exile as a psychic and cultural phenomenon linked to uprooting and displacement, the sundering of ties to a native network of relations and meanings, and not, as Konuk would have it, with whether there were European bookstores and adequate research libraries "for European studies" in Istanbul in the 1930s. Said points to Auerbach's distinctly understated recollection of his loss of homeland and offers a reading of "the drama of this little bit of modesty," the loss of the "authentic presence of culture" in the midst of world historical events coming to be "*symbolized materially* by libraries, research institutes, other books and scholars."[36] But Konuk is also right to argue that "Istanbul" represented not only a place of loss and mourning for Auerbach but also a spectacular richness of location, at the ancient crossroads of civilizations, and, with the ongoing cultural experiments of the Kemalist regime, a rich laboratory-like environment for working out his ideas concerning the fate of humanistic-historicist ways of thinking. And her work has begun the important task of developing an understanding of the ways in which Auerbach's experience in Turkey—his role in feeding the Kemalist enthusiasm for European antiquity, for instance—shaped his major writings of the period.

A detailed study of *Mimesis* along these lines would be a task for another occasion. From the perspective of the question that concerns us here, however—namely, Auerbach's return to and rethinking of the concept of *Weltliteratur* through the historical prism of the European crisis and the problematic of exile—it is important to make a handful of observations. First of all, let us note that in the book's very presentation of "Western literature" as the linguistically and culturally multiple but simultaneously unitary output of a composite civilization, *Mimesis* marks a clear and meaningful departure from notions of organic expressive communities of the Herderian-historicist and primitivist sort. "Europe" is thus a singular but comparative field for the philological humanist. Second, as Auerbach lays it out elaborately in the book's famous first chapter, this composite civilization is not only internally differentiated in linguistic and regional terms but split, *at its very origin*, between "two basic types" or modes of comprehending and representing reality, the Homeric and the Biblical, the legendary and the historical, the pagan and the prophetic. Homeric narrative is leisurely in its unfolding, presents only "foreground," and externalizes everything, leaving nothing hidden, while the Biblical is abrupt, "fraught with background," is psychologically conflicted, and leaves vast areas of intention and motivation "dark and incomplete." As Vassilis Lambropoulos has noted, for Auerbach, Biblical narrative is characterized by "the constant, unrelieved tension between presence and absence, voice and silence, promise and fulfillment, being and becoming."[37] The Israelite God is present precisely in his absence—where he is, for instance, when he commands Abraham to sacrifice Isaac is not a matter the narrative can even begin to address—in sharp contrast with Zeus, who walks among mortals.

On one side, there is the essential freedom of the Homeric tale, its "childlike" simplicity, lack of psychological depth, and legendary (rather than historical) nature, its "delight in physical existence" and the details of ordinary domestic life—as in the episode (in book 19 of the *Odyssey*) of Euryclea's recognition of Odysseus's childhood scar that provides Auerbach's exemplary case of the Homeric—which are treated within the "peaceful realm of the idyllic" and its ability to "bewitch us" or "ensnare us." On the other side, in the "Jewish-Israelitish" approach to human reality, we find "depth" perception of all human events and persons, the unconditional, even "tyrannical," claim to historical Truth, the claim to being universal history, an understanding of human will and motivation as contradictory and conflicted, a depiction of daily life as "permeated with the stuff of conflict, often with poison," an absolutism of overarching purpose, of God's will and Law, and the consequent necessity for interpretation. And it is this approach to human reality that explains the Israelites' unique "concept of God" rather than the other way around. Although the Homeric narratives appear to possess "so much more highly developed" an "intellectual, linguistic, and above all syntactical culture," in the end they are "comparatively simple in their picture of human beings" in the world. Whereas "Homer remains within the legendary with all his material, . . . the material of the Old Testament comes closer and closer to history as the narrative proceeds" (*M*, 23, 7, 12, 15, 13, 16, 12, 14, 22, 8, 13, 18–19).

The origins of European civilization therefore lie outside Europe itself, in the "Near Eastern world," and these two modes, we might say, of being in and knowing the world are not only distinct from each other in every detail but locked in a tense and agonistic relationship. Every subsequent historical European world—early fourteenth-century Florence, for instance, or late sixteenth-century London—can be understood as a new configuration of the two modes, not in the original intact forms but each disaggregated and rearranged in historically new ways. This claim of the irreducibility of the Old Testament tradition to European civilization is of course a remarkable argument to make from the very edge of European Jewish extinction, but it is not based on some notion of a constant Jewishness, whether experience or identity. On the contrary, the "Jewish-Israelitish," while simply one of the distinct modes of understanding and representing reality at the origins of European civilization, linked to a particular historical people, breaks out of the "Jewish religious frame" and is turned into a "general method for comprehending reality" by later historical developments—in the first instance, "in the first century of the Christian era, in consequence of Paul's mission to the Gentiles" (*M*, 8, 16). (This is of course the subject of the long essay "Figura," also written in Istanbul.) Nor is this concept of a composite European civilization identical to the merely compensatory and hence untruthful and clichéd notion of "Judeo-Christian tradition" of the post-Holocaust years. The Judeo-Christian articulation is for Auerbach a place of *antagonism* rather than synthesis, the conflicted stage for the unfolding of Europe's history. It is the tension between the two that is the essence of European civilization, rather than one or the other or a synthesis of the two.

And finally—and this, it seems to me, is the most elusive element in Auerbach's concept of European civilization—the articulation of the Homeric and the Biblical or (following Matthew Arnold), we might say, the Hellenic and the Hebraic, is inherently *unstable* in nature, full of explosive possibilities and dangers at every turn.[38] In the modern era, furthermore, the balance has shifted decisively in favor of the former by way of a vitiation of the latter: "As late as the European Middle Ages it was possible to represent Biblical events as ordinary phenomena of contemporary life, the methods of interpretation themselves forming the basis for such a treatment. But when, through too great a change in environment and through the awakening of a critical consciousness, this becomes impossible, the Biblical claim to absolute authority is jeopardized; the method of interpretation is scorned and rejected, the Biblical stories become ancient legends, and the doctrine they had contained, now dissevered from them, becomes a disembodied image" (*M*, 15–16). What exactly all this might be leading to becomes suddenly clear as, a few pages later, in the midst of a discussion of the differences between "legend" and "history" as modes of writing—the latter's sutured and "difficult" composition across "contradictory motives in each individual," the "hesitation and groping on the part of groups," and "psychological and factual cross-purposes" as against the former's "smoothly" stretched surface from which "all cross-currents, all friction, all that is casual, secondary to the main events and themes, everything unresolved, truncated, and uncertain, which confuses the clear progress of the action and the simple orientation of the actors, has [*sic*] disappeared"—the text turns somewhat jarringly to "the rise of Nationalism Socialism in Germany" (*M*, 20, 19).

In the remaining pages of this chapter in *Mimesis*, it becomes clear that for Auerbach the rise of the Nazis, when understood within the long arc of Europe's history that is charted in the book, represents the victory of "legend" over "history." In fact, the chapter, generally understood to be focused exclusively on some of the earliest documents of European antiquity, spans the entire historical progression that is elaborated in the book as a whole, at least touching on, as we have just seen, late antiquity, the Middle Ages, early modernity, and, finally, the most recent period, which is described in the final chapter of the book as the double moment of modernism and fascism—with the two treated as distinct but related elements—but in the first chapter is simply marked via fascism. What becomes evident in the course of the first chapter is thus that *Mimesis* is not a disinterested literary-historical account of modes or styles of writing, whose main goal would be to make contributions to this or that subfield of European literary history. And the book has of course notoriously been vulnerable to critiques from expertise in one or the other of these subfields. Its larger concern is of a different nature altogether. It wishes to establish that the Jewish element is an indispensible component of Western civilization, but not because the events and personages of the Old Testament represent prophetic prefigurations of those of the New Testament (that is the solution developed by the early Christians as they struggled to differentiate their beliefs and practices from those of their Jewish environment) nor because Christianity is simply the universalization of the monotheist innovation of a tribal ethnonational people from the ancient Near East (which is the characteristic modern, historical, philological, and hence secular explanation). Rather, it is to be seen as such because it represents a mode of being in and understanding the world, a "method" for approaching reality, without whose countervailing force European culture reverts to its "childlike" and "pagan" substratum. Another name for this modern form of unleashed "paganism" in Auerbach's account is, as we have seen, simply "National Socialism." So one implication of Auerbach's discussion of fascism in *Mimesis* seems to be that the pagan and "legendary" element in European civilization needs always to be *tempered* by all that the Biblical complex represents. Auerbach thus establishes here the *primacy* of the Biblical mode of narrative over the Homeric, situating the birth of the West precisely in the establishment of that hierarchy. The epics of the Israelites—and Auerbach insists that the Biblical narratives themselves be considered epics—created a universal civilization when they entered into and harnessed the pagan life-worlds of the eastern Mediterranean region.

What are we to make of this mode of analysis that seems to intrude repeatedly into what otherwise could have been an ambitious but straightforward survey of certain modes and styles of writing in the history of European literatures? Disagreements about the validity or implications of Auerbach's concept of European (literary) history and civilization are certainly possible. Lambropoulos, for instance, has argued that Auerbach in effect makes the Bible the ur-text of the Western tradition, "the originary event in literature," the "background" that haunts the entire history of Western literature. And Biblical interpretation is offered by Auerbach as the generalizable "method" for the reading of literature, making of *Mimesis* a *Biblical reading* of the span of European literary history. Auerbach establishes "the task of literary interpretation . . . as a moral alternative to the pleasures of Greek physical/material understanding (or analysis)." Lambropoulos thus views Auerbach in a strong sense as a partisan figure, arguing that "literature itself is, at its best, Biblical" rather than Greek, so that "now that the world has almost overcome the old Greek influence, the Bible is its true, authentic contemporary."[39] And Porter, while he puts a very different valuation on Auerbach as Jewish figure—speaking admiringly of Auerbach's "Judaizing of philology"—seems essentially to agree with the characterization we find in Lambropoulos.[40]

Lambropoulos's interpretation of Auerbach's (interpretive) concept of (European) literature is, in my view, largely a valid one. But what are we to make of the recurring figures of fascism in *Mimesis*, even in this first chapter whose materials are thought to be so far removed from contemporary historical reality? Lambropoulos himself argues that the mode of reading that Auerbach offers in *Mimesis* is not so much historicist as *figural*, in the sense that Auerbach himself has given to the term. Speaking more precisely, we might say that the former (that is, historicist) mode, as applied in the detailed reading of texts and fragments of texts, is repeatedly interrupted and over-written by the latter (the figural). So a register of reading other than the strictly historicist seems to be invited by the repeated turn in the book, either directly or indirectly and parabolically, to the contemporary conjuncture. We might therefore say that what Auerbach offers is a criticism not of the Hellenic (or even simply Homeric) as such but rather of the *philhellenic* in modern European culture, even if he seems often not to clarify the difference between the two historical realities. In other words, the broader stake for Auerbach is in the modern European, and in particular German, career of ancient Greece and the involvement of this cultural complex in the modern history of the continent, including the most recent developments, which have torn the European world asunder.

Stathis Gourgouris, in his now-classic work on the "institution of Greece," has explicated the role of the post-Enlightenment northern European, and especially German, intelligentsia in the creation of the philhellenic complex and its implications for Greek society it-self in its passage into bourgeois modernity in the nineteenth cen-tury.[41] A cultivated formation *(Bildung)* itself came to be built on a foundation of a sort of new Hellenization. And in the history of emancipation of Jews in the German-speaking lands, *Bildung* ac-quired a crucial role, becoming the key to assimilation into German culture as a means to the acquisition of civil and political rights—hence the fierce attachment of Jews to classical German culture, often even under conditions of extreme duress, and hence the famous figure of the *gebildet* Jew, a figure of course present to an extreme degree in the person of Auerbach himself.[42] The framework intro-duced in the first chapter of *Mimesis* could thus be read at one level as a critique of those historical forms of *Bildung* that had held out the promise of full emancipation and social inclusion to the Helle-nized Jew in Germany. And if this is a correct reading, then this preoccupation with the Hellenic and the Hebraic marks a chilling verdict on the attachment to bourgeois German *Bildung* as the basis for equality, a verdict produced of course from *within* the history of this commitment but from the other side of the civilizational inferno. It seeks to modulate the *optimism* of the whole Kant-Goethe-Schiller heritage and its involvement in the history of the Jewish Question in Germany. In the midst of the inferno unleashed by fascism—a *foregrounding* spectacle, we might say, of false freedom and inauthentic being—Auerbach takes comfort in that other side of Western culture, with its origin in the absent presence of God in the Biblical narrative, which seeks to bind individuals to each other and to the principle of the social bond itself, enjoins mediation, and is the natural antithesis to pagan "naturalness" and "simplicity." What is the meaning of fascism, and why are the Jews among its first victims?—this is the question Auerbach conceals at the core of *Mimesis* from its very beginning. And in "Philology and *Weltliteratur*," Auerbach quietly hints at the suspicion that the growing "standardization" of world culture in the postwar years is not unconnected to the extermination, during the war, of the forms of difference embodied in the Jewish cultures and societies of Europe.[43]

Let us return now to "Philology and *Weltliteratur*" in light of the concept of European civilization that we have encountered in *Mimesis*. Auerbach sums up his case for a new concept of *Weltliteratur* that is appropriate to the present age of declining historical consciousness:

> This conception of *Weltliteratur* and its philology seems less active, less practical and less political than its predecessor. There is no more talk now—as there had been—of a spiritual exchange between peoples, of the refinement of customs and of a reconciliation of races. In part these goals have failed of attainment, in part they have been superseded by historical developments. Certain distinguished individuals, small groups of highly cultivated men [*kleine Gruppen hoher Bildung haben*] always have enjoyed, under the auspices of these goals, an organized cultural exchange: they will continue to do so. Yet this sort of activity has little effect on culture or on the reconciliation of peoples: it cannot stand the storm of opposed vested interests—from which an intensified propaganda emerges—and so its results are immediately dissipated. (PWL, 6)

At one level, Auerbach distinguishes his concept from that derived from the Goethe tradition. It is no longer possible to invest in "hoher Bildung" the hopes for "the reconciliation of peoples." The cultivation of high culture does not necessarily lead progressively to the "refinement" of values in society at large, and an actualization of the cosmopolitan ideal as it has been conceived of in the Western tradition—that is, an actualization of the liberal notion of the possibility of humanity inhabiting the earth as a single, nonantagonistic entity—is not an inevitable outcome of human history. This is a somewhat melancholic admission of the relative powerlessness of humanistic intellectuals with respect to what they themselves might view as progress in society. And of course Auerbach is unable to take the leap of envisioning a humanistic education that seeks to overcome the class-hierarchical landscape of culture in bourgeois society. At another level, however, despite the built-in skepticism of this concept, it is "no less human, no less humanistic, than its antecedent," still allied with the project of the historical realization of the potential of humanity (PWL, 7).

Auerbach is thus an inescapable figure in a genealogy of what Bové calls critical humanism, who appears at the cusp of the reiteration of the traditional humanistic paradigm and the contrary perception that "critical humanism is a situated historical practice enacted within a set of power relations"—power relations, we might add, that extend all the way from the local and institutional to the geopolitical.[44] This is an important insight, which clarifies a number of issues in Auerbach, including his seemingly paradoxical reception in recent years. On the one hand, Auerbach affirms the possibility that the critically engaged humanistic intellectual might yet be able to produce an encompassing survey, "an inner history of mankind" that seeks to preserve at least the memory of human diversity. On the other hand, he himself expresses skepticism about the possibilities for such forms of historical knowledge by proposing a method that, in the final chapter of *Mimesis*, he acknowledges he owes to the narrative "method" of the modernists (*M*, 548). His name for this method is still "synthesis," but it signifies now a practice that is more restrained, more historically self-aware of its own contingent and even ephemeral nature—hence the significance of the notion of starting point or point of departure *(Ansatzpunkt)*. The humanistic scholar, no longer able to assimilate the sum total of the literary materials now available—once again, this is Auerbach's recoding of the loss of centrality of European literatures and of Romance literatures in particular—must proceed instead by locating "a point of departure, a handle, as it were, by which the subject can be seized." The point of departure "must be the election of a firmly circumscribed, easily comprehensible set of phenomena whose interpretation is a radiation out from them and which orders and interprets a greater region than they themselves occupy" (PWL, 14). The perspectivism of the *Ansatzpunkt* thus becomes the means to a new kind of synthesis, a self-consciously partial and "discontinuous history" that seeks to establish *contingently* its own archive across borders and boundaries— of language, nation, continent, civilization, and tradition.[45] While the ultimate goal is still an understanding of the whole, this must be seen as becoming visible only in its movements, to be apprehended only once "all the particulars that make it up are grasped as essences" (PWL, 16). Auerbach thus makes explicit the fact that *Weltliteratur* consists of a certain interplay of the universal and the particular. And philology, which is, of course, above all a method of apprehension of (historical and linguistic) particulars, becomes the privileged mental discipline for a critical humanism seeking to comprehend (the works of) humanity in history. The philologist is thus required to perform an act of imagination that allows for the material to be arranged in novel and unprecedented ways that help to shift the parameters of understanding. In this sense, the very phrase "philology of *Weltliteratur*" is a repudiation of the fragmentation of the humanities into microspecializations and an attempt to restore the possibility of their engagement with the state of the world and with their own conditions of possibility.

But how exactly are we to read Auerbach's somewhat melancholic observation that the "world literatures that were available to Goethe at the end of his life were more numerous than those which were known at the time of his birth" and their number was small "compared to what is available to us today" (PWL, 4)? "We possess," Auerbach further notes, "literatures ranging over six thousand years, from all parts of the world, in perhaps fifty literary languages. Many cultures known to us today were unknown a hundred years ago" (PWL, 8). As I have argued in earlier chapters, Goethe's popularization of the term starting in the late 1820s marked a retrospective look at the writer's own trajectory of engagement with the translations—from Kalidas to Hafez—that modern Orientalism had begun to make available to European literary publics in his lifetime. The backdrop of this personal "discovery" of the Orient is, as I have argued at length, a much-larger historical process, extending from the late eighteenth century to the middle of the nineteenth, in which the availability in the European languages of the works of non-European traditions of writing expanded dramatically. The period marked an expansion and radical transformation of what had hitherto been a largely European "republic of letters" into a global one, incorporating, *at least in theory*, all cultures of writing across the globe. It marked the systematic consolidation of knowledge forms concerned with language and literature precisely by pushing outward the borderlines of the map of literate cultures and extending backward received notions of antiquity. This extended Orientalist "moment" was part of a highly charged historical process, the explosive and violent incorporation of vast populations and civilizational complexes in "the East" into the global imperial system. This political charge is reflected in the polemical register that came to predominate in Said's famous study of the moment. This process of the "discovery," dissemination, and systemization of "Oriental" textual materials, and their codification into "national" traditions, played a significant role in the consolidation of the European empires themselves. As I have already argued at some length, Pascale Casanova's influential work misconstrues this historical moment, viewing it as consisting largely of intra-European developments, rather than as a globally expansionist process that accompanied the growth of the European empires during the Industrial Revolution.

In the passage quoted at the beginning of the previous paragraph, Auerbach uses the term in the plural—world literatures—as he does again in the following sentence about the "historicist humanism" that had been the true goal of philology ever since Vico and Herder (PWL, 4). For *Weltliteratur* in the Goethean sense had *presumed* the existence of historically discrete cultures of writing. Second, and more significantly from our perspective, Auerbach too pays scant attention to this Euro-imperial orientation and determination in the emergence of *Weltliteratur*, noting merely the empirical expansion of the materials available to the philologist when compared with the time of Goethe, the seemingly endless expansion of the "world" itself. He relegates the origins of *Weltliteratur* in the Orientalist refashioning of humanistic knowledge to the realm of the *merely quantitative*—the availability of "more numerous" world literatures. This *numerical multiplication* of the available corpus then becomes the occasion for raising methodological questions that impact philology's erstwhile notions of expertise: "Because . . . of the superabundance of materials, of methods and of points of view, a mastery of that sort has become virtually impossible" (PWL, 4). Furthermore, this quantitative recoding of a (qualitative) historical process has the consequence that the humanistic intention associated with *Weltliteratur*, namely, that it marks a benevolent and nonhierarchical openness in the West toward the rest of the world, is placed beyond the possibility of critical examination. For, as I have already argued, world literature is a concept of bourgeois society, that is to say, fundamentally a concept of exchange and therefore a concept that recodes an opaque and unequal process of appropriation—in this case, of cultural materials—as a transparent one of supposedly free and equal exchange and communication. And the concept of literature—itself refashioned in the Romantic-Orientalist encounter in the process of the "discovery" of non-European materials—provides the supposedly neutral ground on which the appropriation in fact takes place (PWL, 7, 8). Thus, while seeking to refashion the concept of world literature in light of the contemporary turning point in the history of the West and the world, Auerbach in effect absolves the Goethean tradition of its involvement with the modern imperial process and remains ambivalent about the emerging postcolonial contours of the postwar world. Said noted that when Auerbach "takes note of how many 'other' literary languages and literatures seemed to have emerged (as if from nowhere: he makes no mention of either colonialism or decolonization), he expresses more anguish and fear than pleasure at the prospect of what he seems so reluctant to acknowledge. Romania is under threat."[46] This characterization seems a slight exaggeration now, and elsewhere Auerbach speaks more positively of this expansion of literary horizons, notably in "Vico and Aesthetic Historism." All the same, despite (and also of course because of) the humanistic ambition he inhabits and invokes, Auerbach does not seem able to endorse the historical transformation and the unprecedented configurations of the human that this expansion might make possible.

Whether or not this judgment is a correct one, it is important to note explicitly that it is no more and no less than an attempt to demarcate the outer contours and limits of Auerbach's critical practice and therefore an attempt at better examining our own reliance on it and calibrating our engagement with it. Despite Auerbach's variously expressed conservative tendencies—the recurring relapse into subjectivist notions of intuition, individual genius, or creativity, the effort to shore up and reauthorize the edifice of European humanism once it had been put radically into question by the great historical events of the twentieth century, and more broadly the sense of loss that infuses his account of these historical transformations—both Said and Bové consider him an exemplary figure of what it means to inculcate a critical consciousness. This judgment does not rest simply on a form-content, or method-viewpoint, separation. On the contrary, the "contents" of Auerbach's philological humanism are themselves at stake in it. As Bové notes, "even though his project is somewhat too pessimistic and abstract in its objects and methods, Auerbach does point to at least two necessities for contemporary scholarship: to write a discontinuous history as engaged history of the present and to bring the skills of rational, scholarly inquiry to bear on the present social and political conditions out of which all cultural and intellectual discourse emerges."[47] Said posits this mode of engagement with the present and with the possibility of historical transformation against both the formal vacuity of the Anglo-American New Criticism that was contemporary with Auerbach's arrival—in both senses—in America and what he (that is, Said) saw as the guild-like self-referentiality of the culture of theory that came to replace it institutionally. One possible genealogy of Said's requirement of "worldliness" for criticism—an attentiveness to the dense fabric of society and vigilant skepticism toward any claim about an organic, enclosed, and exclusive communal life—thus leads to Auerbach. For the *world* in world literature is to be understood as horizon, ever receding but nevertheless legible in the "works" that are the material of the humanities.[48]

The periodic return of the concept of world literature since its first emergence roughly two centuries ago seems to correspond to periods of expansion and renewed and more intensive integration of the world market and globally extensive bourgeois social order. At its core is thus a dialectic of the universal and the particular, the cosmopolitan and the local.[49] And the "literature" in world literature marks the plane of equivalence and comparability between historically distinct and particular practices of writing. Offered to us as a space for the preservation and consideration of the diversity of human experience, it is nevertheless tied to the runaway train that is capitalist modernization, leveling anything in its path. Auerbach laid out this dialectical element of the concept in these terms: if *Weltliteratur* is ever realized, it will simultaneously have canceled itself. He offers the possibility of inhabiting this dialectic in a not merely affirmative and conformist manner, with an *exilic* philology of *Weltliteratur* against the organicist-nationalist conceptions of language that had emerged from one strand in eighteenth-century historicism and dominated philological practice in the era of nationalisms and nation-states. Neither romantic nationalism of one sort or another, nor the "Internationale of Triviality and Esperanto Culture"—this is the difficult path charted by Auerbach in conceptual terms.

Despite Auerbach's failure to grasp the origin of the concept and practice of world literature itself in the double logic—Orientalism-Anglicism or Orientalism-Occidentalism—of bourgeois world culture, his rethinking of the "philology of *Weltliteratur*" nevertheless offers us a point of entry into the predicament of contemporary culture on a world scale. And this is the point of fulcrum in Auerbach whose lines of force Said seeks to intensify and radicalize. Against the pathos of Auerbach's European-modernist homelessness, Said posits a skeptical yet engaged and *worldly* critical consciousness whose method is this radicalized philology, a "contrapuntal" imagination and practice of philological criticism, linking the figures, forms, and narratives of metropolitan societies to those of the colonial and postcolonial peripheries.[50] Said thus points to a new humanistic practice, reiterated in his final completed work, *Humanism and Democratic Criticism*, whose ultimate goal—perhaps never to be actually reached once and for all—is a new humanism marked by that "proper love for the world" (Auerbach's phrase) that is typical of those who live and act in the world without giving the impression that they possess it.[51] Through such reorientations of intellectual practice (as of social being)—"language without soil," to quote Adorno once again—world literature as a mode of critical thinking may yet be radicalized, a form of reading that seeks to denaturalize the world (as much as language and literature) and explores the possibility of those *noncoercive* forms of knowledge often invoked by Said.[52] The necessity of understanding the relations and structures that constitute literature as a worldwide reality does not bind us to depoliticized and positivistic "distant reading": the notorious problem of the enormity and unmanageability of the archive, of too many particulars, is a nonproblem, as we have seen, a quantitative recoding of the qualitative historical process of their emergence. It would not be correct to argue that the field of literary data "mining" and analysis that Franco Moretti and others have inaugurated produces no knowledge of use to literary scholars and critics, quite to the contrary. But it cannot in itself be considered a variety of criticism per se, that is, a mode of engagement with the (aesthetic) "documents" of cultures and societies as a means of reflecting upon and intervening in the conjunctures of the human world.[53] What is needed for such a purpose is *better* close reading, attentive to the worldliness of language and text at various levels of social reality, from the highly localized to the planet-wide as such. To engage in the "philology"—that is, historically engaged and linguistically attuned criticism—of world literature is to produce critical-historical knowledge of this process, of the concepts and practices, intellectual or scholarly as well as literary, of this worldwide social and cultural assemblage and their modes of embeddedness in the world. You do not need to have read literally everything, to have mastered every particular, in order to give a *general* account of the play of the universal and the particular.

Auerbach's place in the history of the idea that we have been concerned with in this book is thus a troubling and tangential one. He both seizes upon the received notion and offers for it a different eighteenth-century point of reference, reconstellating its elements from the location of the crisis of the European (and world) order in the mid-twentieth century. The preeminent forms of the concept in our own times are more in a line of descent from the forms he placed firmly in the past as inadequate to the historical conditions of his own moment, which, he argued, were dependent upon a conception of Europe and the West that was no longer sustainable. These forms of thinking world literature today betray their own cosmopolitan promise because they obfuscate the antagonisms of our historical moment (and their long history) by promising, implicitly if not explicitly, an easy arrival at the world *polis*: hence the necessity of a fuller treatment of his version of the idea, at an angle to the genealogy of these influential contemporary forms. Auerbach's signature phrase, "our philological home is the earth," thus turns out to be the motto of a homeless (and restless) philology, unable to come to rest even in the European homeland, which it views, with considerable pathos and ambivalence, as a social and cultural formation unable to survive the consequences of its own history—a question that has been urgently reopened, though (for the moment at least) with considerably less violence, in our own times. In his understanding of the fabrication of national and civilizational traditions, at least in the western European setting, this eminently Eurocentric thinker leaves us with an opening for the critical consideration of our own late-bourgeois and (once again) crisis-ridden world from the perspective of those literary and cultural practices and social worlds that are still placed more or less at its margins. Whether or not we ourselves can seize upon *this* notion of world literature for such a transformative and critical purpose in the full sense remains, I think, very much to be seen.

Epilogue: "For a Ruthless Criticism of Everything Existing"

As I HAVE TRIED to show in various ways in the course of this book, the discourse of world literature has since its first emergence been involved in the question of human diversity, providing a cultural cartography of humanity precisely in the midst of the great historical process of the assimilation of human life into an expansionist bourgeois order encompassing the world. This assimilation has itself always been an element in a double process that has as its other facet the production and management of difference. As such, "world literature" seems to resurface from time to time at critical moments in the history of the bourgeois world, moments in which precisely the range of human social and cultural experience comes yet again to be at stake. This is the case with the present discussion, whose background, as I have suggested, is the reintensification of the rule of global capital, and the worldwide dissemination of its neoliberal ideology, in the post-1989 era, which has created zones of consumer capitalism in some of the countries and regions of the former colonized world ruled by local bourgeoisies at least elements of which now consider themselves part of the global ruling class. Notions of the cosmopolitan, the universal, the local, and the particular, which constitute in their mutual articulation the internal mechanics of the concept of world literature, are under new forms of pressure in this historical situation as well. The challenge for *critical* thinking, properly speaking, is therefore how to be always attentive to this longer history and its sedimentations into our own times.

Counterhegemonic critiques of neoliberal capitalism as practice and ideology do not appear to be *inherently* immune to replicating the double cultural logic—what I have called Orientalism-Anglicism—that has accompanied the global expansion of the rule of capital since the Industrial Revolution and the European Enlightenment. This is very often revealed in those moments that are characterized by a purported reassertion of Marxist certainties against "deviations" of one sort or another. The debate that has ensued from the publication of Pradeep Chibber's *Postcolonial Theory and the Specter of Capital*, which seeks to dismiss the entire subaltern studies intervention in order to restore what it considers a universalist social theory, has unfortunately renewed and even intensified this tendency.[1] By way of a final engagement, let us briefly consider an influential (and more important) work of counterhegemonic social and political theory of our times, namely, Michael Hardt and Antonio Negri's *Empire*. The central thesis of this sweeping and immensely imaginative book, which has already become a classic of sorts, concerns the emergence of a single, globally extensive form of sovereignty, which the authors call "Empire" in order to distinguish it from the "imperialism" of the preceding historical era. What is remarkable about the study from our perspective, however, is that the concept of this supposedly global experience of governance—of individuals, bodies, collectivities—is derived entirely and exclusively from the categories of the Western political-theoretical tradition, conceived as a self-enclosed and continuous entity. I quote a key early passage:

> The genealogy we follow in our analysis of the passage from imperialism to Empire will be first European and then Euro-American, not because we believe that these regions are the exclusive or privileged source of new ideas and historical innovation, but simply because this was the dominant geographical path along which the concepts and practices that animate today's Empire developed—in step, as we will argue, with the development of the capitalist mode of production. While the genealogy of Empire is in this sense Eurocentric, however, its present powers are not limited to any region. Logics of rule that

in some sense originated in Europe and the United States now invest practices of domination throughout the globe.[2]

At first sight, these sentences might seem fairly straightforward: they describe a passage from particularity to universality. But they have a far more specific valence as well. The authors deploy one of the most ubiquitous and overdetermined signifiers of the modern era— "Made in Europe," let us say—which marks "the *strength* of Western cultural discourse" in an imperialized world and the "formidable structure of cultural domination" it exercises over the societies it has come to dominate, and they do so with not much more self-consciousness than those nineteenth-century commentators who speculated about the possibilities of bringing natives into the purview of (European) civilization, the prospects for, as I have called it, Enlightenment in the colonies.[3] And this once and for all and total victory of what Hardt and Negri call "Europe" is established by them by what can only be considered a downscaling of their usually high Deleuzian language to a fairly orthodox Marxist analysis. Assertion of the "Made in Europe" formula seems to require this dissimulation of their theoretical investments. Here is another key passage:

> There is at the base of the modern theory of sovereignty, however, a further very important element—a content that fills and sustains the form of sovereign authority. This content is represented by capitalist development and the affirmation of the market as the foundation of the values of social reproduction. Without this content, which is always implicit, always working inside the transcendental apparatus, the form of sovereignty would not have been able to survive in modernity, and European modernity would not have been able to achieve a hegemonic position on a world scale. As Arif Dirlik has noted, Eurocentrism distinguished itself from other ethnocentrisms (such as Sino-centrism) and rose to global prominence principally because it was supported by the power of capital.[4]

The fact that "Europe" has risen over the last half millennium on the back of capital is of course more or less incontrovertible. But what *kind* of concept of the universalizing tendency of capital is this, exactly, and what exactly is it meant to achieve? First, it seeks to establish the (logical) equivalence of all "ethnocentrisms," while simultaneously asserting the historical victory of one, namely, "Eurocentrism," above all the others on the basis of its articulation with capitalism. The claim to (formal) equivalence seems to secure the claim to (actual) preeminence. But more decisively from our perspective here, it appears to place one ethnocentrism, which is primus inter pares in the world of ethnocentrisms, *outside the realm of criticism*. Once successfully sublimated into universalism, Eurocentrism is removed from the historical plane of its emergence in the imperial process and the kinds of social and political conflict, and the modes of resistance and of criticism, that developed in response.

The reliance on the (paraphrased) remark by "Arif Dirlik" is also of interest and appears to be decisive here, so it is perhaps also not irrelevant to try to understand what exactly it is doing in the passage.[5] The reference, it seems to me, works in two registers simultaneously—the name signifies both "historian of China" and "Turkish intellectual," that is, an intellectual of non-Euro-American, Near Eastern (and perhaps even "Muslim") provenance. Hence, as a citation of authority, it is inherently unstable, on the surface a matter of objective (China) scholarship and expertise, but not quite able to conceal the need for a different kind of validation of the claim, namely, one made from a "non-Western" intellectual position. In other words, the authors seem unable not to acknowledge the very possible objection, "postcolonial" in nature, that they wish to dismiss out of hand. If we therefore look at Dirlik's remark itself in this fuller context, it is not a transparent one in the manner that the authors suggest, simply an observation made from the neutral or objective position of "historian of China." On the contrary, it is very much *internal* to the historical process on which it seems to comment from a certain distance, and, more specifically, it shows traces of the equation of modernization with Europeanization that has been a hallmark of Turkish intellectual culture since late Ottoman and (especially) early Republican times and until the rise of political Islam as a political force in the country. Dirlik's own formation took place in the early decades of the Kemalist project, including at Roberts College, which became after 1923 one of the premier institutions for the education of the Republican intelligentsia and political elite. The broader context for his particular take on the question of imperialism (or "Empire") in its relationship to capital in our times is thus the historical process that undergirds this individual formation, namely, the particular trajectory of secularization, modernization, and Europeanization in Turkish political, social, and cultural life since the late Ottoman period, which came into its own in the culture of the Republic established by Kemal Ataturk and his cohort—a history of "East West mimesis," as we have already seen. The position Dirlik enunciates here is thus most meaningfully understood as emerging from *within* the history of Western expansion and domination under capitalism, the "standardization" (Erich Auerbach) of social and cultural forms worldwide, and the various and *varying* responses of the non-European societies affected by that process, but it is used by Hardt and Negri instead to establish the *end* of the self-other dialectic inherent to this historical process.

Furthermore, and more importantly, the notion of the universalism of the logic of "capitalist development," accompanied with what appears to be at least an implicit notion that the diverse societies and regions of the world constitute the undifferentiated *field* for the elaboration of this universalist logic, is made to do the elaborate work of sustaining a hierarchical conception of social and political change in the world—"first in Europe, then elsewhere"—while simultaneously making it disappear from view altogether. If such a structure of thought is implicit in many analyses of imperialism-as-capitalism since Vladimir Lenin's great essay on the subject, it becomes acutely visible in *Empire*. It is thus striking and revealing in this regard that Hardt and Negri's analysis of Empire entirely bypasses the long tradition, painstakingly elaborated in the course of the twentieth century and stretching, say, from Gandhi and Du Bois in its first decade to Said, Guha, and their contemporaries in its final ones, of the critique of empire from perspectives made possible by the experience of imperial subjugation, a critical and *theoretical* tradition, surely, but one that can have only "symptomatic" value for their analysis.[6] What is usually derided as a *cultural* emphasis in Said's understanding of imperialism is in fact something else altogether.

It marks a rejection of such a structure of thought and must not be mistaken for an "idealist" failure to comprehend the determining impact of material and economic forces, as some of his detractors have mistakenly believed. On the other hand, resistance to globalization or criticism of its many attendant concepts and practices, such as world literature, and alternatives to such accounts of the universalization of European forms as we have just seen are not achieved simply by asserting the autonomy of the local. It always also entails an alternative concept of the world as well and, more specifically, as I have argued in Chapter 4, a *general* account of the play of the universal and the particular in the universalizing processes of bourgeois-imperial modernity.

Contemporary theory, in its moments of emergence, was clearly animated by anti-imperialist and antiracist impulses, both in general and in relation to particular contexts of imperial violence and liberationist struggle—the French imbroglio in Algeria with regard to figures like Sartre, Barthes, Foucault, and Derrida and opposition to the U.S. war in Indo-China in the context of the North American appropriation or reigniting of these figures and their work. (And Hardt and Negri's credentials in this regard are obviously unimpeachable.) My concern here is not with anti-imperialism per se as a political position or viewpoint but rather with the ways in which contemporary critical thinking unwittingly replicates logics of a longer provenance in the colonial and postcolonial eras. Such ideas of Europeanness are at work in a range of crises in the world today, from the suffocation of Greek society by a Eurocratic elite to the recent spate of terrorist attacks in a number of European capitals.

As I write these concluding remarks, it is becoming clear that the rulers of Europe will settle for nothing less than the total surrender of Greece, will brook no mere assertion of sovereignty, in the economic crisis that besets the country and the Eurozone monetary union as a whole. The massive transfer of wealth that lies concealed within the so-called bailout of the periphery—a transfer from all European peoples (and, through the IMF, the entire world) to overexposed German and French financial institutions—has created "debt colonies" within Europe itself, above all Greece. This is now clearly evident, above all to the new government of the Left in Greece itself. But what is not so readily understood is the way in which the "colonial" nature of this intra-European situation is apparent in the application to Greece of the very logic of Orientalization and Europeanization—the logic of the process of the universalization of social and cultural forms in capitalism—that we have explored in this book. The crucial difference in this regard in the case of Greece compared to more classically colonial situations like India is the status of the Golden Age that (philhellenic) Europeanist discourse—a sort of Greece-Orientalism, we might call it—attributes to this society, which must face a double alienation in modernity, failing repeatedly and necessarily to live up to that ideal, which "Europe" at the same time can claim as *its* own origin. Stathis Gourgouris has called this distinct form of colonial relation a "colonization of the ideal."[7] In the midst of the Greek crisis, the process of fabrication that I have called "Made in Europe" seems to have been turned inside out or perhaps outside in. The lines of critical thinking to which Hardt and Negri have assigned a simply "symptomatic" valence therefore continue to be indispensible for the critical understanding of the relations of power internal to European society itself, let alone those characteristic of its external career. Indebtedness and the extraction of value, colonial relations and the dynamics of sovereignty, the Anglicist-Orientalist logic of universalization (and indigenization) of social and cultural forms, and the relationship between colonization of the "real" as opposed to the "ideal"—these aspects of the contemporary world made visible in the midst of the crisis of the Eurozone are the appropriate subject matter of any conceptual paradigm invested in critically examining the emergence of world culture (and thus also literature). The wide range of linguistic practices that we label collectively as "English" constitute the vernacular of social movements whenever they challenge the practices of capitalism and the primacy of neoliberal ideas on a transnational level. It is disproportionately in translation from or into English that communication in such terrains typically takes place. So struggles within and against global capitalism now take place (also) on the terrain of linguistic, cultural, and social heterogeneity, even when this fact is not acknowledged in political practice—hence the relevance of translation, or rather a certain politics of translation, both as practice and as paradigm for cultural transactions between and across disparate linguistic and cultural spaces. Our thinking about such movements, if it is not simply to replicate in buried form the antagonisms and inequalities that characterize social relations on a worldwide scale, must account for such practices of translation and the long histories of culture and conflict that continue to inform them.

How, then, do we revisit the concept of world literature today, given these disjunctures and relations of force, at various levels of world literary space, between the global metropolitan languages, societies, and cultures and those of the Global South? We have to move beyond appeals to "diversity" here, because, if we are to take seriously the historical constellation of Orientalism—which made possible, as I have argued, the appearance of the latter group of languages and textual traditions for the first time within the structures and terms of the former—what would be needed is a concept of world literature (and practices of teaching it) that work to reveal the ways in which diversity itself (national, religious, civilizational, continental) is a colonial and Orientalist problematic, one that emerges precisely on the plane of equivalence that is literature. What we have to teach when we teach world literature is precisely the history (and the contemporary workings) of these relations of force and powers of assimilation and the ways in which writers and texts respond to such pressures from a variety of locations in the world. The universalism that is inherent in the task of rethinking the concept of world literature thus has to be confronted with linguistic heterogeneity and the concept itself uncoupled from the effects of standardization and homogenization both within and across languages and cultures that come masked as diversity. In this sense, Said's project at least from *Orientalism* onward implies not a rejection but rather, as I have argued, a radicalization of philology—that is, it calls for a radically historical understanding of language and the forms of its institution in literature, culture, and society. Philology in this sense is thus an indispensable element of the practice of the "secular criticism" of the actually existing world. Continuing elaboration of this *philology after Orientalism* is one of the core and most urgent tasks of the critical literary humanities in our times.

One consequence of this book for contemporary literary studies therefore concerns one of the most powerful elements in the latter's critical toolkit, which has been extensively exported from the North Atlantic countries to the rest of the world: "the Anglophone novel" as both a critical concept and curricular category can only be conceived of as pointing to a *comparative* linguistic, cultural and social field, the heteroglossia inherent to the novel acquiring in this case very specific historical valences due to the form's very origin, in both a diachronic and synchronic sense, in the distinctly colonial politics of language, elements of whose history I have attempted to chart here. It is quite clear to me that, if taken seriously, this reality poses unique challenges to the institutional organization of humanistic knowledge in the university, even if a full discussion of these (among other things) curricular implications of my argument is beyond the scope of this particular work. The task I have set myself here is to examine in a critical and historical fashion two sets of paradigms, the world literary and the Anglophone, and their partially concealed interrelations, which have been effected historically, as I have argued, through the mediation of a third paradigm and cultural field, namely, Orientalism.

As for "readers in the so-called Third World"—Said's phrase!— this book's overarching argument, if correct, implies a call for an abundance of caution and vigilance, a *critical* attitude, properly speaking, toward any claim to autonomy. Historically autonomous action in postcolonial societies such as those of South Asia now requires a healthy dose of skepticism about the social and cultural bases of such historically meaningful action. On the one hand, I hope that this book will strengthen in its own small way those tendencies in Anglophone culture that self-consciously attempt to renounce their own privilege in society, a privilege that, since (we might say), it has been globally endowed, is also a form of subjection. But, on the other hand, the book will offer no easy comfort to those who wish to counter the colonial imbrications of English with the vernacular— language, literature, culture, social imaginary, or social structure— conceived as a space of authenticity and autonomy. Anglophone and vernacular expression and imagination are not so distant from each other as they often claim to be, each inserted, in its own distinct but also crosscutting way, in the historical process of the bourgeois transformation of society over the last two centuries. Of course, this has its own curricular consequences for debates about the nature of "postcolonial education," which must address the Orientalization of language and literature and the terms imposed on culture and society by the Partition. Any attempt to consider, within the field of culture, broadly conceived, a different future must be unsentimental in recognizing and understanding the structures of domination under and against which it struggles to establish itself. It is my hope that this book will be seen as a small individual attempt to contribute to that common goal.

Marx's youthful call for a "ruthless" or even "reckless" form of criticism directed at "everything existing" ["*rücksichtslose Kritik alles Bestehenden*"] has not been historically superseded, because what it describes is the orientation of intellect as such within the dialectic of Enlightenment, that is, within the contradictory and contested logic of bourgeois modernity.[8] But in the early twenty-first century, unlike in the era of liberal capitalism, criticism of culture in its dialectical relation to society cannot merely take the form of ideology critique as traditionally conceived, that is, the identification of the sectional interest of this or that work, form, or element of culture. This book has been concerned with just about the most encompassing cultural concept of our times, the notion of the systematic totality of the expressive productions of nothing less than humanity in its entirety, even though "humanity" or "the human" play little or no explicit role in a number of its most influential elaborations. I have argued that the concept gives form to some fundamental facets of the late capitalist world, the attempt of capital in its present form to induct into its own modes of sociality the very possibility of the international and in fact worldwide. If, on the one hand, the criticism presented here has been directed *against* the hegemonic ambitions of this concept, on the other, it has proceeded from a recognition of the inevitability of thinking *with* it. The effort presented here should therefore be seen as an attempt to delineate the analytical moves— conceptual as well as historical—that are necessary for making it more adequate to radical criticism of the actually existing (as well as emergent) asymmetries and inequalities of the world.

Notes

Acknowledgments

Index

Notes

Prologue

1. See Johann Wolfgang von Goethe, *Conversations of Goethe with Johann Peter Eckermann*, trans. John Oxenford (n. p.: Da Capo Press, 1998), 165–167; Thomas Babington Macaulay, "Minute Recorded in the General Department by Thomas Macaulay, Law Member of the Governor-General's Council, Dated 2nd February 1835," in *The Great Indian Education Debate: Documents Relating to the Orientalist-Anglicist Controversy, 1781–1843*, ed. Lynn Zastoupil and Martin Moir (Richmond, UK: Curzon, 1999), 161–173; Rabindranath Tagore, "World Literature," in *Selected Writings on Literature and Language*, ed. Sisir Kumar Das and Sukanta Chaudhuri (New Delhi: Oxford University Press, 2001), 150; Jorge Luis Borges, "The Library of Babel," in *Labyrinths: Selected Stories and Other Writings*, ed. Donald A. Yates and James E. Irby, trans. James E. Irby (New York: New Directions, 1962), 51–58; Tayeb Salih, *Season of Migration to the North*, trans. Denis Johnson-Davies (London: Heinemann, 1985), 136–138; and Orhan Pamuk, "My Father's Suitcase," *PMLA* 122, no. 3 (2007): 788–796.

2. The now classic argument about the "derivative" nature of anticolonial nationalist discourse is of course Partha Chatterjee, *Nationalist Thought and the Colonial World: A Derivative Discourse* (Minneapolis: University of Minnesota Press, 1992).

3. B. Venkat Mani, "Borrowing Privileges: Libraries and the Institutionalization of World Literature," *Modern Language Quarterly* 74, no. 2 (2013), 250. Also see, Reingard Nethersole, "World Literature and the Library," in *The Routledge Companion to World Literature*, ed. Theo D'haen, David Damrosch, and Djelal Kadir (New York, 2012), 307–315.

4. See David Damrosch, *What is World Literature?* (Princeton: Princeton University Press, 2003); and Franco Moretti, "Conjectures on World Literature," *New Left Review* 1 (2000): 54–68. The latter essay and a number of other

relevant ones have now been collected in Franco Moretti, *Distant Reading* (New York: Verso Books, 2013).

5. Michel Foucault, "Of Other Spaces," *Diacritics* 16 (1986), 26.

6. See Mani, "Borrowing Privileges."

7. See Kenichi Ohmae, *The Borderless World: Power and Strategy in the Interlinked Economy* (New York: Harper Business, 1990).

8. A number of websites track the proliferation of these "people's libraries" worldwide. See, for instance, http://peopleslibrary.wordpress.com and https://www.facebook.com/pages/Occupy-Wall-Street-Library/215569408506718.

9. On the involvement of world literature discourse itself with notions about Westphalia, see Jane O. Newman, "Auerbach's Dante: Poetical Theology as a Point of Departure for a Philology of World Literature," in *Approaches to World Literature*, ed. Joachim Küpper (Berlin: Akademie Verlag, 2013), 39–58.

10. Sandro Mezzadra and Brett Neilsen, *Border as Method, or, the Multiplication of Labor* (Durham: Duke University Press, 2013).

11. Gayatri Chakravorty Spivak, "Can the Subaltern Speak?," in *Can the Subaltern Speak? Reflections on the History of an Idea*, ed. Rosalind Morris (New York: Columbia University Press, 2010), 24.

12. Edward W. Said, *The World, the Text, and the Critic* (Cambridge, MA: Harvard University Press, 1983), 16.

13. Miguel Tamen, review of *On Literary Worlds*, by Eric Hayot, *Modern Philology* 112, no. 1 (August 2014): E1–E4. My thanks to Paul Bové for bringing this review to my attention.

14. A useful (though highly selective) historical account of world literature discourse and practices is provided in Theo D'haen, *The Routledge Concise History of World Literature* (London: Routledge, 2012).

15. On the intertwined histories of world literature and comparative literature, see D'haen, *The Routledge Concise History of World Literature*, 18–21 and 47–73; and Sandra Berman, "World Literature and Comparative Literature," in D'haen, Damrosch, and Kadir, *The Routledge Companion to World Literature*, 169–179.

16. Pheng Cheah, "World against Globe: Toward a Normative Conception of World Literature," *New Literary History* 45 (2014), 303.

17. Frantz Fanon, *Peau noire, masques blancs* (Paris: Éditions du Seuil, 1952), 34, 36; and Fanon, *Black Skin, White Masks* (New York: Grove, 1967), 18, 21; emphasis added.

18. Frantz Fanon, *Sociologie d'une révolution (L'an V de la revolution algérienne)* (Paris: François Maspero, 1972), 75; and Frantz Fanon, *A Dying Colonialism*, trans. Haakon Chevalier (New York: Grove Press, 1967), 90 and 91.

19. Fanon, *Peau noire, masques blancs*, 34; Fanon, *Black Skin, White Masks*, 18.

20. Erich Auerbach, "Philology and *Weltliteratur*" (1952), trans. Maire Said and Edward Said, *Centennial Review* 13, no. 1 (Winter 1969), 3. For the German original, see Erich Auerbach, "Philologie der Weltliteratur," in *Weltliteratur: Festgabe für Strich zum 70. Geburtstag* (Bern: Francke Verlag, 1952), 39–50. All references to the German are to this edition.

21. On the Babel motif in modern theories of language, see Jacques Derrida, "Des Tours de Babel," in *Psyche*, vol. 1 of *Inventions of the Other* (Stanford,

CA: Stanford University Press, 2007), 191–225. For a historical study of the philological preoccupation with the origins of language, see Maurice Olender, *The Languages of Paradise: Race, Ethnicity, and Philology in the Nineteenth Century*, trans. Arthur Goldhammer (Cambridge, MA: Harvard University Press, 2008).

22. David Crystal, *English as a Global Language*, 2nd ed. (Cambridge: Cambridge University Press, 2012), xii.

23. See Ronald A. T. Judy, "On the Politics of Global Language, or Unfungible Local Value," *boundary 2* 24 (Summer 1997): 101–143; and "Some Notes on the Status of Global English in Tunisia," *boundary 2* 26 (Summer 1999): 3–29.

24. Emily Apter, "On Translation in a Global Market," *Public Culture* 13 (2001), 3; Gayatri Chakravorty Spivak, *Death of a Discipline* (New York: Columbia University Press, 2003), xii; and Jonathan Arac, "Anglo-Globalism?" *New Left Review* 16 (July–August, 2002): 35–45.

25. Considerations of the history of theory rarely confront this question. Even in an important volume dedicated to comparative literary studies and globalization, most contributions continue to focus on its emphasis on "difference" rather than its role in the production of "sameness" or standardization. See Haun Saussy, ed., *Comparative Literature in an Age of Globalization* (Baltimore, MD: Johns Hopkins University Press, 2006).

26. Theodor W. Adorno, "On the Question 'What Is German?,'" in *Critical Models: Interventions and Catchwords* (New York: Columbia University Press, 1998), 213.

27. See Edward W. Said, *Orientalism* (1978; repr., New York: Vintage, 2003). Hereafter cited parenthetically in the text as *O*; and Karim Mattar, "The Middle Eastern Novel in English: Literary Transnationalism after Orientalism" (D.Phil. diss. University of Oxford, 2013).

28. For such a "genealogy" of the concept of criticism itself, for instance, see Talal Asad, "Free Speech, Blasphemy, and Secular Criticism," in *Is Critique Secular? Blasphemy, Injury, and Free Speech*, by Talal Asad, Wendy Brown, Judith Butler, and Saba Mahmood (New York: Fordham University Press, 2013).

29. See Moretti, *Distant Reading*; Pascale Casanova, *The World Republic of Letters*, trans. M. B. DeBevoise (Cambridge: Harvard University Press, 2004); and D'haen, *The Routledge Concise History of World Literature*. This is also true of other notable contributions in recent years, like John Pizer, *The Idea of World Literature: History and Pedagogical Practice* (Baton Rouge, LA: Louisiana State University Press, 2006) and Eric Hayot, *On Literary Worlds* (New York: Oxford University Press, 2012).

30. Bryan S. Turner, *Marx and the End of Orientalism* (London: George Allen and Unwin, 1978), 81, 10–11, 7.

31. Among the classic historical studies are Eric Stokes, *The English Utilitarians and India* (Oxford, UK: Clarendon, 1959); and David Kopf, *British Orientalism and the Bengal Renaissance: The Dynamics of Indian Modernization, 1773–1835* (Berkeley: University of California Press, 1969). My argument here is influenced by Rajeswari Sunder Rajan, "After 'Orientalism': Colonialism and English Literary Studies in India," *Social Scientist* 14, no. 7 (July 1986): 23–35.

32. I shall thus retain the term "Anglicism" for the project of *Europeanization* as conceived of in the Anglocentric British Empire.

33. See Gail Minault, "Alois Sprenger: German Orientalism's 'Gift' to Delhi College," *South Asia Research* 31, no. 7 (2011): 7–23, on such ambiguities in one important historical figure.

34. See Edward W. Said, "On Jean Genet's Late Works," *Grand Street* 36 (1990), 38. On Genet and this remarkable essay of Said's, see Stathis Gourgouris, *Does Literature Think? Literature as Theory for an Antimythical Era* (Stanford, CA: Stanford University Press, 2003), 249–291.

35. Even for colonial India, the range is a wide one. For a pioneering set of studies of these phenomena, see Carl A. Breckenridge and Peter Van Der Veer, eds., *Orientalism and the Predicament of Culture* (Delhi, India: Oxford University Press, 1994).

36. See Stathis Gourgouris, *Dream Nation: Enlightenment, Colonization, and the Institution of Modern Greece* (Stanford, CA: Stanford University Press, 1996); and Gourgouris, "Derealizations of the Ideal: Walcott Encounters Seferis," *boundary 2* 39, no. 2 (2012): 181–199.

37. Said's source for this idea is M. H. Abrams, *Natural Supernaturalism: Tradition and Revolution in Romantic Literature* (New York: Norton, 1973).

38. Said, *World, the Text, and the Critic* (Cambridge, MA: Harvard University Press), 16. For a more detailed discussion of this, see Aamir R. Mufti, "Auerbach in Istanbul: The Jewish Question and the Crisis of Postcolonial Culture," *Critical Inquiry* 25, no. 1 (1998): 95–125. On secular criticism and "detranscendentalization," see Stathis Gourgouris, "Transformation, Not Transcendence," *boundary 2* 31, no. 2 (2004): 55–79.

39. Said, *World, the Text, and the Critic*, 13.

40. See, for instance, Asad, "Free Speech, Blasphemy, and Secular Criticism." For a close critical reading of the latter text, see Stathis Gourgouris, *Lessons in Secular Criticism* (New York: Fordham University Press, 2013).

41. Srinivas Aravamudan, *Enlightenment Orientalism: Resisting the Rise of the Novel* (Chicago: University of Chicago Press, 2011), 3.

42. See Edward W. Said, *Culture and Imperialism* (New York: Vintage Books, 1993), 33–35.

43. Karl Marx, "The Future Results of the British Rule in India," in *On Colonialism*, by Karl Marx and Friedrich Engels (Moscow: Progress, 1974), 82.

44. See Ngũgĩ wa Thiong'o, *Decolonizing the Mind* (New York: Heinemann Books, 1986).

45. Any number of the works of, for instance, Galin Tihanov and Karatani Kojin are relevant here, as is the collection *Pour une littérature-monde*, ed. Michel Le Bris and Jean Rouaud (Paris: Gallimard, 2007). Our understanding of the German context will no doubt be much enhanced and transformed by B. Venkat Mani's forthcoming study.

46. For an enormously useful set of revisionist engagements with world-systems theory by scholars in the humanities, see David Palumbo-Liu, Bruce Robbins, and Nirvana Tanukhi, eds., *Immanuel Wallerstein and the Problem of the World: System, Scale, Culture* (Durham, NC: Duke University Press, 2011).

47. On positivism in Moretti, see Tom Eyers, "The Perils of the 'Digital Humanities': New Positivisms and the Fate of Literary Theory," *Postmodern Culture* 23, no. 2 (2013). https://muse.jhu.edu/journals/postmodern_culture/v023

/23.2.eyers.html#f6-text. An early and still pertinent critique of Moretti's use of evolutionary theory, which puts the literary market in the place of nature in physical science, is Christopher Prendergast, "Evolution and Literary History: A Response to Franco Moretti," *New Left Review* 34 (2005): 40–62. On Casanova, See Christopher Prendergast, "Negotiating World Literature," *New Left Review* 8 (2001): 100–121.

48. For a critique, with respect to the literatures of Latin America, of this assumption of correspondence and the attendant claim that literature in the peripheries is always a matter of compromises with metropolitan forms, see Efraín Kristal, "'Considering Coldly . . .': A Response to Franco Moretti," *New Left Review* 15 (2002): 61–74.

49. See Cheah, "World against Globe."

50. See Franco Moretti, ed., *The Novel*, 2 vols. (Princeton, NJ: Princeton University Press, 2007).

51. Mariano Siskind, "The Globalization of the Novel and the Novelization of the Global: A Critique of World Literature," *Comparative Literature* 62, no. 4 (2010): 342. I am citing this article, rather than the fuller chapter in *Cosmopolitan Desires: Global Modernity and World Literature in Latin America* (Evanston, IL: Northwestern University Press, 2014), because aspects of the argument have been, it seems to me, made weaker in the book version, the phrase "world historical globalization of the European bourgeoisie" (338), for instance, being changed in the book to "the globalization of modernity" (28).

52. See Raymond Schwab, *La renaissance orientale* (Paris: Payot, 1950), translated as *The Oriental Renaissance: Europe's Rediscovery of India and the East, 1680–1880* (New York: Columbia University Press, 1984).

53. See Michel Foucault, *The Order of Things* (New York: Vintage Books, 1973), 282–285.

54. See Auerbach, "Philology and *Weltliteratur*"; and Claude Lévi-Strauss, *Tristes Tropiques* (1955; repr., New York: Penguin Books, 1992).

55. Mani, "Borrowing Privileges," 243.

56. These historical details have been gleaned from the official history of the British Library. See P. R. Harris, *A History of the British Museum library, 1753–1973* (London: British Library, 1998).

57. British Library, "George III Collection: The King's Library," http://www.bl.uk/reshelp/findhelprestype/prbooks/georgeiiicoll/george3kingslibrary.html.

58. Q. Mahmudul Haq and Salim Quraishi, *Urdu Language Collections in the British Library* (London: British Library Reference Division, 1984), 5.

59. Ibid., 5–6.

60. See, for instance, *Parliamentary Papers: Accounts and Papers*, vol. 12 (1860).

61. Richard H. Davis, *Lives of Indian Images* (Princeton, NJ: Princeton University Press, 1997), 181; and Saloni Mathur, *India by Design: Colonial History and Cultural Display* (Berkeley: University of California Press, 2007), 133–164.

62. See Davis, *Lives of Indian Images*, 180–181; and Helen Lawson, "The Koh-i-Noor Diamond Will Stay in Britain, Says Cameron as He Rules Out Returning Gem to India on Final Day of Visit," *Daily Mail*, February 21, 2013,

http://www.dailymail.co.uk/news/article-2282104/The-Koh-noor-diamond
-stay-Britain-says-Cameron-rules-returning-gem-India-final-day-visit.html.

63. I cannot resist noting the rather delicious irony that Osama Bin Laden and his estranged family seem to have adopted opposite but equally iconoclastic positions in this regard.

64. See Americo Castro, *The Spaniards: An Introduction to Their History* (Berkeley: University of California Press, 1972).

65. Salman Rushdie, *Shame* (New York: Knopf, 1983), 91. I discuss these matters at length in Aamir R. Mufti, *Enlightenment in the Colony: The Jewish Question and the Crisis of Postcolonial Culture* (Princeton, NJ: Princeton University Press, 2007), esp. chap. 3.

66. See Aziz Ahmed, *Studies in Islamic Culture in the Indian Environment* (Oxford: Oxford University Press, 1964); and Aitzaz Ahsan, *The Indus Saga* (New York: Oxford University Press, 1997).

67. Ashis Nandy, *The Intimate Enemy: Loss and Recovery of Self under Colonialism* (Delhi: Oxford University Press, 1991), ix.

68. See, for instance, Kalpana Dasgupta, "How Learned Were the Mughals: Reflections on Muslim Libraries in India," *Journal of Library History* 10, no. 3 (1975): 241–254.

69. The latest iteration of this idea takes the form of the play "Dara" by the Pakistani playwright Shahid Nadeem, staged at the National Theater in London in early 2015, which takes as its subject matter the trial of Dara by Aurangzeb, highlighting their different conceptions of religiosity, the mystical and the juridico-scriptural, respectively. Contemporary questions about the nature of (Islamic) religiosity in Pakistan and the subcontinent are mapped back onto this early eighteenth-century conflict. Nadeem told a reporter that the entire subsequent history of Hindu-Muslim conflict in the subcontinent, including the Partition of India, could be traced back to this historical event. See Riyaz Wani, "Seeds of Partition were Sown when Aurangzeb Triumphed over Dara Shikoh." *Tehelka* 19, no. 12 (May 9, 2015). http://www.tehelka.com /2015/05/seeds-of-partition-were-sown-when-aurangzeb-triumphed-over -dara-shikoh/.

70. See Lord Teignmouth, *Memoirs of the Life, Writings, and Correspondence of Sir William Jones*, 2 vols. (London: John W. Parker, 1835).

71. See *The King of the World: The Padshahnama, an Imperial Mughal Manuscript from the Royal Library Windsor Castle* (Azimuth, 1997); and the website of the Royal Collection Trust: https://www.royalcollection.org.uk/collection /1005025/the-padshahnama.

72. For a superb ethnographic study of the neo-miniature practice at the NCA, see Virginia Whiles, *Art and Polemic in Pakistan: Cultural Politics and Tradition in Contemporary Miniature Painting* (London: I. B. Taurus, 2010).

CHAPTER 1   *Where in the World Is World Literature?*

1. See Benedict Anderson, *Imagined Communities: Reflections on the Origin and Spread of Nationalism* (London: Verso, 1983), 80.

2. Pascale Casanova, *The World Republic of Letters,* trans. M. B. DeBevoise (Cambridge, MA: Harvard University Press, 2004), 48, 75.

3. See Suzanne Marchand, *German Orientalism in the Age of Empire: Religion, Race, and Scholarship* (Cambridge: Cambridge University Press, 2009), 231.

4. See ibid., 38–52; Bradley L. Herling, *The German Gītā: Hermeneutics and Discipline in the German Reception of Indian Thought, 1778–1831* (New York: Routledge, 2006); and Saverio Marchignoli, "Canonizing an Indian Text? A. W. Schlegel, W. von Humboldt, Hegel, and the Bhagavadgītā," in *Sanskrit and "Orientalism": Indology and Comparative Linguistics in Germany, 1750–1958*, ed. Douglas T. McGetchin, Peter K. J. Park and D. R. SarDesai (Delhi: Manohar, 2004), 248–251.

5. Johann Gottfried Herder, "On the Origin of Language," in *The Origin of Language*, by Jean-Jacques Rousseau and Johann Gottfried Herder (Chicago: University of Chicago Press, 1986), 125, 121.

6. On Herderian historicism in the formation of these two codifiers of twentieth-century anthropology, see Matti Bunzl, "Franz Boas and the Humboldtian Tradition: From *Volksgeist* and *Nationalcharakter* to an Anthropological Concept of Culture," in *Volksgeist as Method and Ethic: Essays on Boasian Ethnography and the German Anthropological Tradition*, ed. George Stocking (Madison: University of Wisconsin Press, 1998), 17–78; Julia E. Liss, "German Culture and German Science in the *Bildung* of Franz Boas," in ibid., 155–184; Michael W. Young, *Malinowski: Odyssey of an Anthropologist, 1884–1920* (New Haven, CT: Yale University Press, 2004); and John H. Zammito, *Kant, Herder, and the Birth of Anthropology* (Chicago: University of Chicago Press, 2000). Michael F. Brown has revisited the uniquely anthropological notion of cultural relativism in "Cultural Relativism 2.0," *Current Anthropology* 39, no. 4 (2008): 363–383.

7. Johann Gottfried Herder, *J. G. Herder on Social and Political Culture* (Cambridge: Cambridge University Press, 1969), 266. See Isaiah Berlin, "The Counter-Enlightenment," in *Against the Current: Essays in the History of Ideas* (Harmondsworth, UK: Penguin Books, 1982), 1–24; Berlin, *Three Critics of the Enlightenment: Vico, Hamann, Herder* (Princeton, NJ: Princeton University Press, 2000); and Berlin, *The Roots of Romanticism* (Princeton, NJ: Princeton University Press, 2001).

8. See, for instance, Liah Greenfeld, *Nationalism: Five Roads to Modernity* (Cambridge, MA: Harvard University Press, 1992), chap. 4.

9. Sarah Lawall, "Introduction: Reading World Literature," in *Reading World Literature: Theory, History, Practice*, ed. Lawall (Austin: University of Texas Press, 1994), 18.

10. See Johann Gottlieb Fichte, *Addresses to the German Nation*, ed. George Armstrong Kelly (New York: Harper Torchbooks1968) 53–58.

11. For an earlier and more extended discussion of nation-thinking, through readings of Fichte's *Addresses to the German Nation*, Walter Scott's *Ivanhoe*, and Heinrich Heine's *The Rabbi of Bacherach*, see Aamir R. Mufti, *Enlightenment in the Colony: The Jewish Question and the Crisis of Postcolonial Culture* (Princeton, NJ: Princeton University Press, 2007), chap. 1.

12. Johann Gottfried Herder, *Another Philosophy of History and Selected Political Writings*, trans. Ioannis D. Evrigenis and Daniel Pellerin (Indianapolis: Hackett, 2004), 5, 9. I have translated the title of this work of Herder's as *Yet Another Philosophy of History for the Education of Mankind*. See Johann Gottfried

Herder, *Auch eine Philosophie der Geschichte zur Bildung der Menschheit*, afterword by Hans-Georg Gadamer (Frankfurt: Suhrkamp Verlag, 1967).

13. Ibid., 29.

14. Ibid., 45, 56, 58.

15. Ibid., 65, 51, 59.

16. See, for instance, Uday Singh Mehta, *Liberalism and Empire: A Study in Nineteenth-Century British Liberal Thought* (Chicago: University of Chicago Press, 1999).

17. See Katie Trumpener, *Bardic Nationalism: The Romantic Novel and the British Empire* (Princeton: Princeton University Press, 1997).

18. Johann Gottfried Herder, "Conclusions Drawn from the Comparison of the Poetry of Diverse Peoples of Ancient and Modern Times," in *Against Pure Reason: Writings on Religion, Language, and History*, ed. Marcia Bunge (Minneapolis: Fortress, 1993), 141, 142.

19. Marchand, *German Orientalism*, 44.

20. See M. H. Abrams, *The Mirror and the Lamp: Romantic Theory and the Critical Tradition* (1953; repr., New York: Oxford University Press, 1971), 78.

21. See Herling, *The German Gītā*; and Marchignoli, "Canonizing an Indian Text?"

22. See William Jones, *Poems, Consisting Chiefly of Translations from the Asiatick Languages* (1772; repr., London: N. Conant, 1777).

23. Abrams, *The Mirror and the Lamp*, 87.

24. Jones, *Poems*, xiii–xiv.

25. Abrams, *The Mirror and the Lamp*, 87. I am grateful to Jennie Jackson for pointing out this passage in Abrams to me. See also Fatma Moussa-Mahmoud, *Sir William Jones and the Romantics* (Cairo: Anglo-Egyptian Bookshop, 1962).

26. Jones, *Poems*, 191, 192, 193, 197, 206, 203, 201–202, 201.

27. Ibid., 163, 170, 163, 166–167, 170, 171, 170, 168.

28. Ibid., 178, 179, 180, 178.

29. See Maryam Wasif Khan, "Translated Orientalisms: The Eighteenth-Century Oriental Tale, Colonial Pedagogies, and Muslim Reform" (Ph.D. diss., University of California, Los Angeles, 2013).

30. See Yopie Prins, *Victorian Sapho* (Princeton, NJ: Princeton University Press, 1999); Virginia Jackson, *Dickinson's Misery: A Theory of Lyric Reading* (Princeton, NJ: Princeton University Press, 2005); and Virginia Jackson and Yopie Prins, "General Introduction," in *The Lyric Theory Reader: A Critical Anthology* (Baltimore: Johns Hopkins University Press, 2013), 1–8.

31. See Thomas Bauer and Angelika Neuwirth, eds., *Ghazal as World Literature I: Transformations of a Literary Genre* (Beirut: Ergon Verlag, 2005).

32. See Muzaffar Alam, "The Culture and Politics of Persian in Precolonial Hindustan," in *Literary Cultures in History: Reconstructions from South Asia*, ed. Sheldon Pollock (Delhi: Oxford University Press, 2003), 131–198.

33. Theodor W. Adorno, "On Lyric Poetry and Society," in *Notes to Literature*, vol. 1, trans. Shierry Weber Nicholsen (New York: Columbia University Press, 1991), 41.

34. Edward W. Said, *Orientalism* (1978; repr., New York: Vintage, 2003), 116–119.

35. See Casanova, *World Republic of Letters*, 40.

36. Ibid., 78.

37. Thomas Carlyle, "The State of German Literature," in *Critical and Miscellaneous Essays* (New York: John B. Alden, 1885), 37. On the curricular use of this extract from Carlyle at one institution in colonial India in the nineteenth century, see Khan, "Translated Orientalisms," 177.

38. Fritz Strich, *Goethe and World Literature* (1945; repr., London: Routledge and Kegan Paul, 1949), 31. See Theo D'haen, *The Routledge Concise History of World Literature* (London: Routledge, 2012), 27–37.

39. See Paul A. Bové, *Intellectuals and Power: A Genealogy of Critical Humanism* (New York: Columbia University Press, 1986).

40. Vinay Dharwadker, "Orientalism and the Study of Indian Literatures," in *Orientalism and the Postcolonial Predicament: Perspectives from South Asia*, ed. Carol Breckenridge and Peter Van der Veer (Philadelphia: University of Pennsylvania Press, 1993), 160.

41. See Stefan Hoesel Uhlig, "Changing Fields: The Directions of Goethe's *Weltliteratur*," in *Debating World Literature*, ed. Christopher Prendergast (London: Verso, 2004), 26–53. See Johann Wolfgang von Goethe, *Conversations of Goethe with Johann Peter Eckermann*, trans. John Oxenford (Boston: Da Capo, 1998), 164–166. On Goethe's reading in Orientalism and travel literature, see Walter Veit, "Goethe's Fantasies about the Orient," *Eighteenth-Century Life* 26, no. 3 (2002): 164–180; and Strich, *Goethe and World Literature*, chap. 9. On Goethe's reading of Hafez and writing of the *Divan*, see Jeffrey Einboden, "The Genesis of *Weltliteratur*: Goethe's *West-Östlicher Divan* and Kerygmatic Pluralism," *Literature and Theology* 19, no. 3 (2005): 238–250.

42. Karl Marx and Friedrich Engels, "*Manifesto of the Communist Party*," in *The Marx-Engels Reader*, 2nd ed., ed. and trans. Robert C. Tucker (New York: Norton, 1978), 476–477. I have replaced Tucker's "what it calls civilisation" with "so-called civilisation" and corrected "nations and peasants" to "nations of peasants."

43. Karl Marx, *Grundrisse: Foundations of the Critique of Political Economy*, trans. Martin Nicolaus (Harmondsworth, UK: Penguin Books, 1993), 408.

44. Marx, *Grundrisse*, 540, 410.

45. Ranajit Guha, *Dominance without Hegemony: History and Power in Colonial India* (Cambridge, MA: Harvard University Press, 1997), 15.

46. Marx, *Grundrisse*, 410.

47. Frantz Fanon, *The Wretched of the Earth*, trans. Constance Farrington (New York: Grove, 1979), 40; and Karl Marx, *Capital: A Critique of Political Economy*, vol. 1, trans. Ben Fowkes (New York: Vintage Books, 1997), 931–932.

48. Karl Marx, "The Future Results of the British Rule in India," in *On Colonialism*, by Marx and Friedrich Engels (Moscow: Progress, 1974), 86.

49. See Said, *Orientalism*, 153–156; Aijaz Ahmad, *In Theory: Nations, Classes, Literatures* (New York: Verso, 1993), chap. 6; and Gilbert Achcar, *Marxism, Orientalism, Cosmopolitanism* (Chicago: Haymarket Books, 2013).

50. See Bryan S. Turner, *Marx and the End of Orientalism* (London: George Allen and Unwin, 1978).

51. See Achcar, *Marxism, Orientalism, Cosmopolitanism*, 73, 81.

52. Said, *Orientalism*, 332.

53. Karl Marx, "The British Rule in India," in Marx and Engels, *On Colonialism*, 36.

54. Ibid., 40, 39, 37; emphasis added.

55. Marx, "Future Results," 82.

56. Ibid., 84–85.

57. See John P. Haithcox, "The Roy-Lenin Debate on Colonial Policy: A New Interpretation," *Journal of Asian Studies* 23, no. 1 (1963): 93–101.

58. The name is a reference to the first Congress of Afro-Asian States, held in 1955 in the Indonesian city of Bandung.

59. See Maxim Gorky, Karl Radek, Nikolai Bukharin, et al., *Soviet Writers' Congress 1934* (London: Lawrence and Wishart, 1977).

60. I address the legacy of Bandung more fully in a work in progress, titled *Edward Said in Jerusalem: Criticism, Secularism, Exile.*

61. See Emily Apter, *Against World Literature: On the Politics of Untranslatability* (London and New York: Verso, 2013); and Lawrence Venuti, "Hijacking Translation: How Comp Lit Continues to Suppress Translated Texts," *boundary 2* (forthcoming).

62. Apter, *Against World Literature*, 2, 3, 20. See Barbara Cassin, ed., *Vocabulaire européen des philosophies: Dictionnaire des intraduisibles* (Paris: Editions du Seuil, 2004). This enormous compendium of the untranslatables of philosophy has itself now been translated; see Barbara Cassin, ed., *Dictionary of Untranslatables: A Philosophical Lexicon*, translation edited by Emily Apter, Jacques Lezra, and Michael Wood (Princeton, NJ: Princeton University Press, 2014).

63. See Jacques Derrida, *Monolingualism of the Other; or, the Prosthesis of Origin*, trans. Patrick Mensah (Stanford, CA: Stanford University Press, 1998).

64. David Damrosch, *What Is World Literature?* (Princeton, NJ: Princeton University Press, 2003), 4.

65. Franco Moretti, "Conjectures on World Literature," *New Left Review* 1 (2000), 54, 55.

66. Mariano Siskind, "The Globalization of the Novel and the Novelization of the Global: A Critique of World Literature," *Comparative Literature* 62, no. 4 (2010): 355.

67. Moretti, "Conjectures on World Literature": 58, 65, 64, 61; emphasis in the original.

68. See Strich, *Goethe and World Literature.*

69. See the pioneering historical studies in Bernard Cohn, *An Anthropologist among the Historians and Other Essays* (New York: Oxford University Press, 1988) and *Colonialism and Its Forms of Knowledge: The British in India* (Princeton, NJ: Princeton University Press, 1996); and Nicholas Dirks, *Castes of Mind: Colonialism and the Making of Modern India* (Princeton, NJ: Princeton University Press, 2001). On the teaching of literature in colonial India, see Gauri Visvanathan, *Masks of Conquest: Literary Study and British Rule in India* (New York: Columbia University Press, 1989).

CHAPTER 2 *Orientalism and the Institution of Indian Literature*

1. See Raymond Schwab, *La renaissance orientale* (Paris: Payot, 1950), translated as *The Oriental Renaissance: Europe's Rediscovery of India and the East, 1680–1880* (New York: Columbia University Press, 1984).

2. See Edward W. Said, "Raymond Schwab and the Romance of Ideas," in *The World, the Text, and the Critic* (London: Faber and Faber, 1984), 252.

3. Recent exceptions include Siraj Ahmed, "Notes from Babel: Toward a Colonial History of Comparative Literature, *Critical Inquiry* 39, no. 2 (Winter 2013): 296–326. Ahmed argues not only that Jones's philology was not the colonial practice that it has been taken to be since Edward Said's brief treatment of him in *Orientalism* but that Jones's understanding of and approach to language was far more humane and less imperialistic than that of Said's. Padma Rangarajan's study, *Imperial Babel: Translation, Exoticism, and the Long Nineteenth Century* (New York, NY: Fordham University Press, 2014), which clearly has overlaps with the argument presented in this chapter, became available to me only after this book had undergone editing, and I regret that an engagement with it will have to await another occasion.

4. Said, "Raymond Schwab," 250. This is a paraphrase of a sentence in Schwab. See Schwab, *The Oriental Renaissance*, 52–57.

5. See ibid., 57–64; and Garland Cannon, "Sir William Jones and the 'Sakuntala,'" *Journal of the American Oriental Society* 73, no. 4 (1953): 198–202.

6. See Bradley L. Herling, *The German Gītā: Hermeneutics and Discipline in the German Reception of Indian Thought, 1778–1831* (New York: Routledge, 2006), 92–93.

7. See ibid., 88–89, 97; and Willi Goetschel, *Spinoza's Modernity: Mendelssohn, Lessing, and Heine* (Madison, WI: University of Wisconsin Press, 2004).

8. See ibid., 15.

9. Dorothy Matilda Figueira, *Translating the Orient: The Reception of Śākuntala in Nineteenth-Century Europe* (Albany: State University of New York Press, 1991), 12. I follow Figueira in transliterating the conventional shortened title of the play as *Śākuntala* and the name of the main female character in it as Śakuntalā.

10. On Anquetil Duperron's importance for Herder, see Herling, *The German Gītā*, 59.

11. Tejaswini Niranjana, "Translation, Colonialism, and the Rise of English," in *Rethinking English: Essays in Literature, Language, History*, ed. Svati Joshi (Delhi: Trianka, 1991), 127, 125.

12. See David Kopf, *British Orientalism and the Bengal Renaissance: The Dynamics of Indian Modernization, 1773–1835* (Berkeley: University of California Press, 1969). The earliest articulation of this notion that I can identify is in a letter of Jones's, written during the process of mastering the Sanskrit text in 1787. See William Jones, *The Letters of Sir William Jones*, vol. 2, ed. Garland Cannon (Oxford: Oxford University Press, 1970), 682; and Garland Cannon, *The Life and Mind of Oriental Jones: Sir William Jones, the Father of Modern Linguistics* (Cambridge, UK: Cambridge University Press, 1990), 274–275.

13. See Rabindranath Tagore, "World Literature," in *Selected Writings on Literature and Language*, ed. Sukanta Chaudhuri, Sisir Kumar Das, and Sankha

Ghosh (New York: Oxford University Press, 2001), 138–150; and Bhavya Tiwari, "Rabindranath Tagore's Comparative World Literature," in *The Routledge Companion to World Literature*, ed. Theo D'haen, David Damrosch, and Djelal Kadir (New York: Routledge, 2012), 41–48. On Tagore and Orientalism, see Amit Ray, *Negotiating the Modern: Orientalism and Indianness in the Anglophone World* (New York: Routledge, 2007), chap. 4.

14. See Tagore, "Shakuntala," in *Selected Writings*, 237.

15. Jawaharlal Nehru, *The Discovery of India* (New York: John Day, 1946), 317. Also see Cannon, *Life and Mind*, xv–xvii; Kopf, *British Orientalism*, 275; pretty much all of Thomas R. Trautmann, *The Aryans and British India* (New Delhi: Yoda, 2004); and Nirad Chaudhuri, *Scholar Extraordinary: The Life of Professor the Rt. Hon. Friedrich Max Müller, P.C.* (London: Chatto and Windus, 1974). For an early attempt to analyze this trope in responses to Said's *Orientalism*, see Rajeswari Sunder Rajan, "After 'Orientalism': Colonialism and English Literary Studies in India," *Social Scientist* 14, no. 7 (1986): 23–35.

16. See Trautmann, *Aryans*, 21–22. For Said's anticipation and refutation of such arguments, precisely with reference to Germany's nonimperial relationship to India, see Edward W. Said, *Orientalism* (1978; repr., New York: Vintage, 2003), 18–19. For the history of German Indology, see Douglas T. McGetchin, Peter K. J. Park, and D. R. SarDesai, eds., *Sanskrit and "Orientalism": Indology and Comparative Linguistics in Germany, 1750–1958* (Delhi: Manohar, 2004); and Suzanne Marchand, *German Orientalism in the Age of Empire: Religion, Race, and Scholarship* (Cambridge: Cambridge University Press, 2009).

17. See Bernard S. Cohn, "The Command of Language and the Language of Command," in *Colonialism and its Forms of Knowledge: The British in India* (Princeton, NJ: Princeton University Press, 1996), 16–56.

18. See Ranajit Guha, *A Rule of Property for Bengal: An Essay on the Idea of Permanent Settlement* (1963; repr., Durham, NC: Duke University Press, 1996). It is a remarkable but hardly noted fact that this book, written at least fifteen years before the publication of Said's *Orientalism*, anticipates elements of its argument in rather uncanny ways. So far as I know, Said was not familiar with the existence of Guha's study when he wrote his own book in the 1970s, which had largely disappeared even from Indian debates after its initial publication by Mouton in 1963, though of course in *Culture and Imperialism* (New York: Vintage Books, 1993), it provides one of the main instances of the latest phase of the global anticolonial "culture of resistance," the phase Said refers to as "the voyage in" (239–261).

19. Amit Ray provides a fine narrative of these scholarly-administrative developments in Calcutta under the tutelage of Hastings. See *Negotiating the Modern*, 29–53. It is one of the smaller ironies of this historical moment that one of the sources Edmund Burke relied on for the ideas about Indian legal reform that made their way into Charles James Fox's ill-fated East India Bill in 1783, which proved to be only the first salvo in the attack on the practices of the East India Company that was to culminate in the trial of Hastings, was none other than Jones, who may well have been the author of the early drafts of some of the sections of the bill that are attributed to Burke. See Garland H. Cannon, "Sir William Jones and Edmund Burke," *Modern Philology* 54, no. 3 (1957): 165–186. On the Hastings trial and Burke's role in it, see Sara Suleri,

The Rhetoric of English India (Chicago: University of Chicago Press, 1992); and Nicholas B. Dirks, *The Scandal of Empire: India and the Creation of Imperial Britain* (Cambridge, MA: Harvard University Press, 2006).

20. See, for instance, Cannon, *Life and Mind*, 229–230; and Nehru, *Discovery of India*, 317.

21. See Trautmann, *Aryans*, 28; and Cannon, *Life and Mind*, 231.

22. On Jones hearing rumors, before his discovery of *Śākuntala*, of the existence of a form of writing called *nāṭaka*, see Cannon, *Life and Mind*, 273–274.

23. On knowledge systems in precolonial India, see "Forms of Knowledge in Early Modern South Asia," a special issue of *Comparative Studies of South Asia, Africa and the Middle East* 24, no. 2 (2004), edited by Sheldon Pollock.

24. Cannon, *Life and Mind*, 137, 142.

25. Sir William Jones, "The Third Anniversary Discourse, on the Hindus, delivered 2d of February, 1786" in *The Works of Sir William Jones, in Six Volumes*, vol. 1 (London: G. G. and J. Robinson, 1799), 21–22.

26. See Canon, *Life and Mind*, 197–198.

27. See Thomas R. Metcalf, *Ideologies of the Raj* (Cambridge: Cambridge University Press, 1997). For a collection of studies of the Aryan thesis into our own times, when it has become entangled in the politics of right-wing Hindu nationalism, see Thomas R. Trautmann, ed., *The Aryan Debate* (Delhi: Oxford University Press, 2005). Unfortunately, and in marked contrast with such historians of ancient India as Romila Thapar, Trautmann remains apologetic and equivocal in face of Hindutva's travesty of historical and archeological evidence and claims. For a more forceful approach, see Romila Thapar, *The Aryan: Recasting Constructs* (Gurgaon, India: Three Essays Collective, 2008).

28. Suleri, *Rhetoric of English India*, 33, 30, 31.

29. For a nuanced historical examination of some of these elements in Jones, see Maryam Wasif Khan, "Translated Orientalisms: The Eighteenth-Century Oriental Tale, Colonial Pedagogies, and Muslim Reform" (Ph.D. diss., University of California, Los Angeles, 2013), esp. chap. 2.

30. Michel Foucault, *The Order of Things* (New York: Vintage Books, 1973), 283.

31. Friedrich von Schlegel, "On the Language and Philosophy of the Indians," in *The Aesthetic and Miscellaneous Works of Friedrich von Schlegel*, trans. E. J. Millington (London: George Bell and Sons, 1900), 456.

32. See Rosane Rocher, "Alexander Hamilton, 1876–1924," *Oxford Dictionary of National Biography*, first published 2004, online ed. January 2008, http://www.oxforddnb.com/view/article/12044.

33. See Partha Chatterjee, *Nationalist Thought and the Colonial World: A Derivative Discourse* (Minneapolis: University of Minnesota Press, 1993); Tapan Raychaudhuri, *Europe Reconsidered* (Delhi: Oxford University Press, 1988); Brian K. Pennington, *Was Hinduism Invented? Britons, Indians, and the Colonial Construction of Religion* (New York: Oxford University Press, 2005); Srinivas Aravamudan, *Guru English: South Asian Religion in a Cosmopolitan Language* (Princeton, NJ: Princeton University Press, 2005); Ray, *Negotiating the Modern*, chap. 3; and Anustup Basu, "Hindutva and Informatic Modernization," *boundary 2* 35 (2008): 239–250.

34. See, among numerous other works, Chatterjee, *Nationalist Thought*; Sudipta Kaviraj, *The Unhappy Consciousness* (Delhi: Oxford University Press,

1995); Nirad C. Chaudhuri, *The Autobiography of an Unknown Indian* (London: Macmillan, 1951); Chaudhuri, *Scholar Extraordinary;* Raychaudhuri, *Europe Reconsidered;* and Kopf, *British Orientalism.*

35. This idea of authenticity is indebted to Aziz al-Azmeh, *Islams and Modernities,* 3rd ed. (London: Verso, 2009), 97–116.

36. Muhammad Iqbal, *Kulliyāt-e Iqbāl Fārsī* (Lahore, Pakistan: Sheikh Ghulam Ali and Sons, 1990), 181. On Goethe and Hafez, see Jeffrey Einboden, "The Genesis of *Weltliteratur:* Goethe's *West-Östlicher Divan* and Kerygmatic Pluralism," *Literature and Theology* 19, no. 3 (2005): 238–250.

37. See Chatterjee, *Nationalist Thought,* chap. 3.

38. Henry Derozio, "Thermopylae," in *Early Indian Poetry in English: An Anthology: 1829–1947,* ed. Eunice de Souza (Delhi: Oxford University Press, 2005), 7, 5. For a fascinating historical study of the presence of the European classics in India during the colonial period, see Phiroze Vasunia, *The Classics and Colonial India* (Oxford: Oxford University Press, 2013).

39. Derozio, "To India—My Native Land," in *Early Indian Poetry in English,* 6. On early editions of Jones's verse, see V. de Sola Pinto, "Sir William Jones and English Literature," *Bulletin of the School of Oriental and African Studies, University of London* 11, no. 4 (1946): 686.

40. See Rosinka Chaudhuri, *Gentlemen Poets in Colonial Bengal: Emergent Nationalism and the Orientalist Project* (Calcutta: Seagull, 2002).

41. See Pennington, *Was Hinduism Invented?*

42. See Vasudha Dalmia, *The Nationalization of Hindu Traditions: Bhāratendu Hariśchandra and Nineteenth-Century Banaras* (Delhi: Oxford University Press, 1997).

43. See ibid., 200–201; and Alok Rai, *Hindi Nationalism* (2001; repr., Hyderabad, India: Orient Longman, 2002), 56–57, 63. I have discussed the grammar of Hindi-Urdu polemics in the late nineteenth century in more detail in chapter 3 of *Enlightenment in the Colony: The Jewish Question and the Crisis of Postcolonial Culture* (Princeton, NJ: Princeton University Press, 2007) and the role of gendered and sexualized figures in the history of the conflict at some length in chapter 4 of that book.

44. See ibid., chap. 3.

45. Ranajit Guha, *Dominance without Hegemony: History and Power in Colonial India* (Cambridge, MA: Harvard University Press, 1997), 132.

46. See Katie Trumpener, *Bardic Nationalism: The Romantic Novel and the British Empire* (Princeton, NJ: Princeton University Press, 1997).

47. For a characteristic argument about Urdu as an allegedly conscious rejection of the indigenous, see Amrit Rai, *A House Divided: The Origins and Development of Hindi-Urdu* (Delhi: Oxford University Press, 1984).

48. See Sheldon Pollock, "The Cosmopolitan Vernacular," *Journal of Asian Studies* 57, no. 1 (1998): 6–37.

49. G. N. Devy, *After Amnesia: Tradition and Change in Indian Literary Criticism* (Hyderabad, India: Orient Longman, 1995), 59. See Suniti Kumar Chatterjee, *Indo-Aryan and Hindi* (1942; repr., Calcutta: Firma K. L. Mukhopadhyay, 1960), esp. chap. 3.

50. The relevant historical literature is an extensive one and exists in several languages, both European and Indian. But see, for instance, Kopf, *British Ori-*

entalism; Sisir Kumar Das, *Sahibs and Munshis: An Account of the College of Fort William* (Calcutta: Orion, 1978); and Muzaffar Alam and Sanjay Subrahmanyam, "The Making of a Munshi," *Comparative Studies of South Asia, Africa and the Middle East* 24, no. 2 (2004): 61–72.

51. See Cohn, "The Command of Language"; and Sadiqur Rahman Kidwai, *Gilchrist and the "Language of Hindoostan"* (New Delhi: Rachna Prakashan, 1972). Gilchrist was a member of the Asiatic Society—he arrived in Calcutta in 1783, a little before Jones's arrival and founding of the society, and he is listed as a member of the society in the first volume of *Asiatick Researches*. See *Asiatick Researches* 1 (1788): 437. Also see John Gilchrist, *The Oriental Linguist: An Easy and Familiar Introduction to the Popular Language of Hindoostan* (Calcutta: Ferris and Greenway, 1798).

52. Alok Rai, *Hindi Nationalism*, 24.

53. An important step has been taken in this direction in Khan, "Translated Orientalisms."

54. Hindi-Urdu words with standard English spellings—like "Hindi" and "Urdu" themselves—are rendered here as English words; others are italicized and transliterated more precisely.

55. See, for instance, Vijayendra Sanatak, *Hindī adab kī tarīkh*, trans. Khursheed Alam (Delhi: Sahitya Academy, 1999), 214.

56. See Amrit Rai, *House Divided*. On Rai's polemical use of Insha, see David Lelyveld, *"Zubaan-e Urdu-e Mu'alla* and the Idol of Linguistic Origins," *Annual of Urdu Studies* 9 (1994): 57–67.

57. Syed Inshallah Khan Insha, *Kahānī Rānī Kētakī aur Kuñvar Uday Bhān kī*, ed. Maulvi Abdul Haq (Aligarh, India: Educational Book House, n.d.), 11–12.

58. On the status of Braj in precolonial North Indian culture, see Allison Busch, *The Poetry of Kings: The Classical Hindi Literature of Mughal India* (New York: Oxford University Press, 2012).

59. I owe this latter point to Rashmi Bhatnagar's superb presentation at MLA 2008 and to our subsequent conversations.

60. This story is told by Christopher King, in *One Language, Two Scripts: The Hindi Movement in Nineteenth Century North India* (New York: Oxford University Press, 1995), 90–91; Alok Rai, *Hindi Nationalism*, 65–66; and Dalmia, *Nationalization of Hindu Traditions*. On performativity in the vernacular in precolonial times, see Sumit Guha, "Transitions and Translations: Regional Power and Vernacular Identity in the Dakhan, 1500–1800," *Comparative Studies of South Asia, Africa and the Middle East* 24, no. 2 (2004): 24–31.

61. On Shukla, see Milind Wakankar, "The Moment of Criticism in Indian Nationalist Thought: Ramchandra Shukla and the Poetics of a Hindi Responsibility," *South Atlantic Quarterly* 101, no. 4 (2002): 987–1014.

62. See Mufti, *Enlightenment in the Colony*, chap. 4.

63. Ranajit Guha, "A Colonial City and Its Time(s)," *Indian Economic and Social History Review* 45, no. 3 (2008): 329, 330, 344, 343, 349, 330.

64. Ibid., 350, 334.

65. See Farman Fatehpuri, *Urdū śu'arā kē tazkirē aur tazkira-nigārī* (Karachi: Anjuman Taraqqi-e Urdu, 1998), 15–19; Muzaffar Alam, "The Culture and Politics of Persian in Precolonial Hindustan," in *Literary Cultures in History: Reconstructions from South Asia*, ed. Sheldon Pollock (Delhi: Oxford University

Press, 2003), 131–198; and Frances Pritchett, "A Long History of Urdu Literary Culture, part 2," in Pollock, *Literary Cultures*, 864–911.

66. See Kamil Zvelbil, "Tamil Literature," in Jan Gonda, ed., *A History of Indian Literature*, vol. 10, facs. 1 (Wiesbaden, 1974); and Cohn, "The Command of Language," 56.

67. See Mehr Afshan Faruqi, *Urdu Literary Culture: Vernacular Modernity in the Writing of Muhammad Hasan Askari* (New York: Palgrave Macmillan, 2012); and Mufti, *Enlightenment in the Colony*, 14–21. On the wide dissemination of perennialist ideas in the early twentieth century, see Mark Sedgwick, *Against the Modern World: Traditionalism and the Secret Intellectual History of the Twentieth Century* (New York: Oxford University Press, 2004).

68. See Sayida Surriya Hussain, *Garcin de Tassy: Biographie et étude critique de ses oeuvres* (Pondichery, India: Institut Francais d'indologie, 1962).

69. The authorship of this work has been put in question in recent decades. See Indra Mukhopadhyay, "Imperial Ellipses: France, India, and the Critical Imagination" (Ph.D. diss., University of California, Los Angeles, 2008), chapter 2.

70. See Margrit Pernau, ed., *The Delhi College: Traditional Elites, the Colonial State, and Education before 1857* (Delhi: Oxford University Press, 2006); and Khan, "Translated Orientalisms."

71. Hussain, *Garcin de Tassy*, 28–31. A caustic contemporary review of this "translation" had already catalogued the many liberties it took with the French original. See "M. de Tassy and Maulawí Karímu-d-dín," *The Benares Magazine* 28 (August 1851): 716–726.

72. See Frances W. Pritchett, "A Long History of Urdu Literary Culture, Part 2," in Pollock, *Literary Cultures*, 864–911.

73. See Muhammad Husain Azad, *Āb-e ḥayāt*, trans. Frances Pritchett and Shamsur Rahman Faruqi (Delhi: Oxford University Press, 2001), 367; Azad, *Āb-e ḥayāt* (Lucknow, India: Uttar Pradesh Urdu Academy, 2003), 451; and Pritchett, "Everybody Knows This Much . . . ," 2–5.

74. Pritchett, "Everybody Knows This Much . . . ," 16, 13, 14.

75. Shamsur Rahman Faruqi, "Constructing a Literary History, a Canon, and a Theory of Poetry," 19.

76. Agha Shahid Ali, *The Veiled Suite: The Collected Poems* (New York: Norton, 2009), 325.

77. Azad, *Āb-e ḥayāt*, 103/77.

78. Azad, *Āb-e ḥayāt*, 57/6.

79. Azad, *Āb-e ḥayāt*, 81/49, 88/56.

80. See Mufti, *Enlightenment in the Colony*, 230–232.

81. See Jeffry Sacks, "Latinity," *CR: The New Centennial Review* 19, no. 3 (2010): 251–286.

CHAPTER 3 *Global English and Its Others*

1. Rashmi Sadana, *English Heart, Hindi Heartland: The Political Life of Literature in India* (Berkeley: University of California Press, 2012), xiv.

2. On literary Republican Turkish and the vicissitudes of the novel form in the language, see Jale Parla, "The Wounded Tongue: Turkey's Language Re-

form and the Canonicity of the Novel," *PMLA* 123, no. 1 (2008): 27–40. For a broader historical analysis of the language reforms and their implications for literature, see Nergis Ertürk, *Grammatology and Literary Modernity in Turkey* (New York: Oxford University Press, 2011); and Emrah Efe Khayyat, "Muslim Literature, World Literature, Tanpınar" (Ph.D. diss., Columbia University, 2014).

3. Erich Auerbach to Walter Benjamin, January 1, 1937, in "Scholarship in Times of Extremes: Letters of Erich Auerbach (1936–1942), on the Fiftieth Anniversary of His Death," *PMLA* 122, no. 3 (2007): 751.

4. See Christopher Ferard, "Turkish Language Reform: The Scottish Connection," *Eurozine*, January 20, 2009, http://www.eurozine.com/articles /2009-01-20-ferrard-en.html.

5. See Vasudha Dalmia, *The Nationalization of Hindu Traditions: Bhāratendu Hariśchandra and Nineteenth-Century Banaras* (Delhi: Oxford University Press, 1997); Alok Rai, *Hindi Nationalism* (2001; repr., Hyderabad, India: Orient Longman, 2002); and Francesca Orsini, *The Hindi Public Sphere, 1920–1940: Language and Literature in the Age of Nationalism* (Delhi: Oxford University Press, 2002).

6. See, for instance, Braj B. Kachru, Yamuna Kachru, and Cecil L. Nelson, eds., *The Handbook of World Englishes* (Oxford, UK: Blackwell, 2006).

7. I am using the following editions here: Al-Tayyib Salih, *Mawsem al-hijra 'ila al-śamāl* (Cairo: Dar al-Hilal, 1969); and Tayeb Salih, *Season of Migration to the North*, trans. Denys Johnson-Davies (London: Heinemann, 1985). I have altered the Johnson-Davies translation as I felt necessary.

8. Johnson-Davies transliterates the last name as Sa'eed. I am using the more familiar English spelling.

9. Salih, *Mawsem al-hijra*, 112; Salih, *Season of Migration to the North*, 136.

10. Salih, *Mawsem al-hijra*, 113–114; Salih, *Season of Migration to the North*, 136–138.

11. Abdallah Laroui, *L'idéologie arabe contemporaine: Essai critique* (Paris: François Maspero, 1967), 4–5.

12. Ibid., 66, 68.

13. Edward W. Said, *Orientalism* (1978; repr., New York: Vintage, 2003), 25, 24.

14. Laroui, *L'idéologie arabe contemporaine*, 68.

15. Salman Rushdie, introduction in *Mirrorwork: Fifty Years of Indian Writing, 1947–1997*, ed. Rushdie and Elizabeth West (New York: Holt, 1997), viii; emphasis in the original.

16. Lord Thomas Babington Macaulay, "Minute Recorded in the General Department by Thomas Babington Macaulay, Law Member of the Governor-General's Council, Dated 2 February 1835," in *The Great Indian Education Debate: Documents Relating to the Orientalist-Anglicist Controversy, 1781–1843*, ed. Lynn Zastoupil and Martin Moir (Richmond, UK: Curzon, 1999), 165.

17. Ranajit Guha, *Dominance without Hegemony: History and Power in Colonial India* (Cambridge, MA: Harvard University Press, 1997), 165.

18. See Gauri Viswanathan, *Masks of Conquest: Literary Study and British Rule in India* (New York: Columbia University Press, 1989).

19. The secondary literature on English in the countries of South Asia is of course enormous. For India, see, for instance, Sadana, *English Heart;* and

Rita Kothari, *Translating India: The Cultural Politics of English*, rev. ed. (New Delhi: Cambridge University Press, 2005). The set of contributions to the debate on English literary education that are contained in *The Lie of the Land: English Literary Studies in India*, ed. Rajeswari Sunder Rajan (Delhi: Oxford University Press, 1993), are still fresh and pertinent. See also Svati Joshi, ed., *Rethinking English: Essays in Literature, Language, History* (Delhi: Triyanka, 1991). For Pakistan, see Tariq Rahman, *Language and Politics in Pakistan* (Karachi: Oxford University Press, 1996).

20. For a whole generation of writers linked to St. Stephen's, for instance, see Aditya Bhattacharjea and Lola Chatterji, eds., *The Fiction of St. Stephen's* (New Delhi: Ravi Dayal, 2000); and Jon Mee, "After Midnight: The Novel in the 1980s and 1990s," in *A History of Indian Literature in English*, ed. Arvind Krishna Mehrotra (New York: Columbia University Press, 2003), 318–336.

21. For an analysis of some of these asymmetries, see Francesca Orsini, "India in the Mirror of World Fiction," in *Debating World Literature*, ed. Christopher Prendergast (London: Verso, 2004), 319–333.

22. See Bishnupriya Ghosh, *When Borne Across: Literary Cosmopolitics in the Contemporary Indian Novel* (New Brunswick, NJ: Rutgers University Press, 2004).

23. On Progressive aesthetics in Urdu, see Aamir R. Mufti, *Enlightenment in the Colony: The Jewish Question and the Crisis of Postcolonial Culture* (Princeton, NJ: Princeton University Press, 2007), chaps. 4 and 5; and Priyamvada Gopal, *Literary Radicalism in India: Gender, Nation and the Transition to Independence* (New York: Routledge, 2005). On Anand's extensive contribution to the discourse on the visual arts and architecture in India, see Annapurna Garimella, ed., *Mulk Raj Anand: Shaping the Indian Modern* (Mumbai: Marg, 2005).

24. See Meenakshi Mukherjee, "The Beginnings of the Indian Novel," in Mehrotra, *History of Indian Literature*, 92–102. For a study of the transition from the reading of English-language novels in colonial India to their original composition, see Priya Joshi, *In Another Country: Colonialism, Culture, and the English Novel in India* (New York: Columbia University Press, 2002).

25. See Leela Gandhi, "Novelists of the 1930s and 1940s," in Mehrotra, *History of Indian Literature*, 175.

26. Virginia Woolf, *Mrs. Dalloway* (New York: Harcourt Brace Jovanovich, 1953), 26, 274. On Anand's relationship to Virginia and Leonard Woolf, see Anna Snaith, "The Hogarth Press and Networks of Anti-Colonialism," in *Leonard and Virginia Woolf: The Hogarth Press and the Networks of Modernism*, ed. Helen Southworth (Edinburgh, UK: Edinburgh University, 2010), 103–127.

27. Mulk Raj Anand, "On the Progressive Writers' Movement," in *Marxist Cultural Movement in India: Chronicles and Documents*, 2nd ed., ed. Sudhi Pradhan (Calcutta: Santi Pradhan, 1985), 5. Anand's recollections of life as a student in London are contained in Mulk Raj Anand, *Conversations in Bloomsbury* (Delhi: Oxford University Press, 1995).

28. Mikhail Mikhailovich Bakhtin, *The Dialogic Imagination: Four Essays*, ed. Michael Holquist (Austin: University of Texas Press, 1981), 272.

29. This was again the case in a newspaper article about the making of the film version of *Midnight's Children*. See Reed Johnson, "Salman Rushdie Be-

queaths 'Midnight's Children' to Film," *Los Angeles Times*, May 5, 2013, http://articles.latimes.com/2013/may/05/entertainment/la-et-mn-salman-rushdie-midnights-children-movie-20130505.

30. Bakhtin, *Dialogic Imagination*, 332.

31. Salman Rushdie, *Midnight's Children* (New York: Penguin Books, 1991), 21–22.

32. Sadana, *English Heart*, 9.

33. Johnson, "Salman Rushdie."

34. I recognize that in making this judgment, I have come somewhat closer to the views of early critics of Rushdie's with whom I had disagreed at the time, in particular Aijaz Ahmed, *In Theory: Classes, Nations, Literatures* (London: Verso, 1992); and Timothy Brennan, *Salman Rushdie and the Third World: Myths of the Nation* (London: Palgrave Macmillan, 1989).

35. The classic study of this problem, by one of Urdu's preeminent poets and novelists, is Fahmida Riaz, *Pakistan: Literature and Society* (New Delhi: Patriot, 1986).

36. See Amit Chaudhuri, ed., *Picador Book of Modern Indian Literature* (London: Picador, 2001).

37. Special correspondent, "Salman Rushdie Hits Back at Jnanpith Winner Bhalchandra Nemade," *Hindu*, February 8, 2015, http://www.thehindu.com/news/national/stung-salman-rushdie-lashes-out-at-jnanpith-winner-bhalchandra-nemade/article6871171.ece.

38. See David Scott, *Conscripts of Modernity: The Tragedy of Colonial Enlightenment* (Durham, NC: Duke University Press, 2004).

39. This line of argument is much indebted to a late-night conversation in Ann Arbor, Michigan, with the great Kannada-language novelist, poet, and critic U. R. Ananthamurthy, who passed away in 2014.

40. See Riaz, *Pakistan*; and Tariq Rahman, *A History of Pakistani Literature in English* (Karachi: Vanguard Books, 1991).

41. For a more detailed treatment of this question, see Mufti, *Enlightenment in the Colony*, chaps. 4 and 5.

42. Salman Rushdie, *Shame* (New York: Knopf, 1983), 91.

43. Along with the theoretical essays collected in *Distant Reading*, the relevant works include Franco Moretti, *Atlas of the European Novel, 1800–1900* (London: Verso, 1999); Moretti, *The Modern Epic: The World System from Goethe to García Márquez* (London: Verso, 1996); and of course, Moretti, ed., *The Novel*, 2 vols. (Princeton, NJ: Princeton University Press, 2006).

44. Mariano Siskind, "The Globalization of the Novel and the Novelization of the Global: A Critique of World Literature," *Comparative Literature* 62, no. 4 (2010): 337, 338.

45. Faiz Ahmed Faiz, *The Rebel's Silhouette*, trans. Agha Shahid Ali (Amherst: University of Massachusetts Press, 1995), 8–9.

46. See Georg Simmel, *The Sociology of Georg Simmel*, ed. Kurt H. Wolff (New York: Free Press, 1964), 118–169.

47. Abir Bashir Bazaz, personal communication, February 2, 2013. Recent scholarship on the Kashmir conflict and its history and sociology includes Chitralekha Zutshi, *Languages of Belonging: Islam, Regional Identity, and the*

Making of Kashmir (New York: Oxford University press, 2004); Mridu Rai, *Hindu Rulers, Muslim Subjects: Islam, Rights, and the History of Kashmir* (Princeton, NJ: Princeton University Press, 2004); and Cabeiri Robinson, *Body of Victim, Body of Warrior: Refugee Families and the Making of Kashmiri Jihadists* (Berkeley, CA: University of California Press, 2013). See also Basharat Peer, *Curfiewed Night: A Frontline Memoir of Life, Love, and War in Kashmir* (London, UK: HarperPress, 2011)

48. See Faiz Ahmed Faiz, *Nuskhahā-e vafā* (Lahore, Pakistan: Kārvāñ, 1989).

49. Faiz, *Rebel's Silhouette*, xxiii.

50. Ibid., xxii. On Shahid and Faiz, see Christi Ann Merrill, "The Lyricism of Violence: Translating Faith in Revolution," *boundary 2* 38, no. 3 (2011): 119–145.

51. For a detailed reading of this poem, see Mufti, *Enlightenment in the Colony*, 213–215.

52. Frantz Fanon, *The Wretched of the Earth*, trans. Constance Farrington (New York: Grove, 1979), 163.

53. I can only note here Nilima Sheikh's stunning engagement with Shahid's work in a series of painted "banners," and that work's interpretation by Kumkum Sangari in a remarkable monograph that serves as a catalogue essay, an adequate treatment of which must await another occasion. See Kumkum Sangari, *Trace Retrace: Paintings, Nilima Sheikh* (Delhi: Tulika Books, 2013).

54. Agha Shahid Ali, "The Blesséd Word: A Prologue," in *The Veiled Suite: The Collected Poems* (New York: Norton, 2009), 171.

55. See Stathis Gourgouris, *Dream Nation: Enlightenment, Colonization, and the Institution of Modern Greece* (Stanford, CA: Stanford University Press, 1996).

56. Hannah Arendt, *The Origins of Totalitarianism* (New York: Harcourt Brace and Company, 1979), 290.

57. Arundhati Roy, "Walking with the Comrades," *Outlook India*, March 29, 2010, http://www.outlookindia.com/article/walking-with-the-comrades /264738. The actual title of the poem is a line from chapter 55 (al-Raḥmān), verse 27, of the Quran: "wa yabqā wajhu rabbik"—"And constant is the face of thy Lord." Roy is referring to the title under which the poem has become popularly known in song form.

58. Shahid, "Homage to Faiz Ahmed Faiz" in *Veiled Suite*, 57–58.

59. Shahid, "In Memory of Begum Akhtar, " in *Veiled Suite*, 53.

60. For a thoroughly revisionist analysis of the erotics of the traditional Urdu poetic tradition, see Shad Naved, "The Erotic Conceit: History, Sexuality and the Urdu Ghazal" (Ph.D. diss., University of California, Los Angeles, 2012).

61. Shahid, "Tonight," in *Veiled Suite*, 374–375.

62. Shahid, "Beyond English," in *Veiled Suite*, 361–362.

63. Shahid, "In Arabic," in *Veiled Suite*, 372–373.

64. Etienne Balibar, *We, the People of Europe?: Reflections on Transnational Citizenship* (Princeton: Princeton University Press, 2003), 109.

65. Sandro Mezzadra, "The Proliferation of Borders," presentation at the Summer Institute on Belonging Differently, Canadian Institute for Advanced

Research, Banff, August 2012. See also Sandro Mezzadra and Brett Neilson, *Border as Method, or, the Multiplication of Labor* (Durham, NC: Duke University Press, 2013). My formulation, "partition as method," is of course indebted to this work.

66. See Chris Parsons, "Whose bright idea was that? Border between India and Pakistan is so brightly lit it can be seen from space," *Daily Mirror* September 6, 2011, http://www.dailymail.co.uk/news/article-2033886/India -Pakistan-border-visible-space.html#ixzz3hkILl3Za.

67. Edward W. Said, *The World, the Text and the Critic* (Cambridge: Harvard University Press, 1984), 16.

68. See Aamir R. Mufti, "The Missing Homeland of Edward Said," in *Conflicting Humanities*, ed. Rosi Braidotti and Paul Gilroy (London, UK: Bloomsbury, 2016).

69. Roy, "Walking with the Comrades."

CHAPTER 4   *"Our Philological Home Is the Earth"*

1. Seth Lerer, introduction to *Literary History and the Challenge of Philology: The Legacy of Erich Auerbach*, ed. Lerer (Stanford, CA: Stanford University Press, 1996), 2.

2. See Erich Auerbach, "Philology and *Weltliteratur*," trans. Maire Said and Edward Said, *Centennial Review* 13, no. 1 (Winter 1969): 1–17; hereafter cited parenthetically in the text as PWL. Because I am interested here in the transmission of the idea of *Weltliteratur* from Auerbach to Said, I shall use the Said translation of this essay throughout this chapter and also refer to the original where necessary (Auerbach, "Philologie der Weltliteratur," in *Weltliteratur: Festgabe für Strich zum 70. Geburtstag* [Bern: Francke Verlag, 1952], 39–50). For all other essays of Auerbach's, I shall refer to the Jane Newman translations in Erich Auerbach, *Time, History, and Literature: Selected Essays of Erich Auerbach*, ed. James I. Porter (Princeton, NJ: Princeton University Press, 2014).

3. Lerer, introduction to *Literary History*, 2.

4. See "Two *Romanisten* in America: Spitzer and Auerbach," in *Grounds for Comparison* (Cambridge, MA: Harvard University Press, 1972), 110–130. Levin was of course the Ph.D. supervisor of Said. Emily Apter has contrasted Spritzer and Auerbach's respective approaches to their Turkish environment, the former, unlike the latter, immersing himself in the host society, by making the effort to learn Turkish, for instance. See *The Translation Zone: A New Comparative Literature* (Princeton, NJ: Princeton University Press, 2005), chap. 3. But the same distinction perhaps applies to their American years as well. While Spitzer became a strident proponent of the development of the humanities in America, Auerbach, as Levin notes, "was content to go his own way, leaving the paperback edition of *Mimesis* to play an exemplary role before an ever-widening audience" (130).

5. Damrosch has written elsewhere about Auerbach; but the emphasis there as well is on *Mimesis*, rather than on Auerbach's essay on *Weltliteratur*. See, for example, Damrosch, "Auerbach in Exile," *Comparative Literature* 47,

no. 2 (1995): 97–117. I must mention, though, that I first read Auerbach—*Mimesis* and the later essay on Vico—in a lecture course of Damrosch's at Columbia in the early 1990s, which remains an enduring debt.

6. See James I. Porter, introduction to Auerbach, *Time, History, and Literature;* and Porter, "Erich Auerbach and the Judaizing of Philology," *Critical Inquiry* 35, no. 1 (Autumn 2008): 115–147.

7. Edward W. Said, *The World, the Text, and the Critic* (Cambridge, MA: Harvard University Press, 1984), 7.

8. See Said, *The World, the Text, and the Critic*, 1–30; and Paul A. Bové, *Intellectuals in Power: The Genealogy of Critical Humanism* (New York: Columbia University Press, 1986), chaps. 3 and 4.

9. See Herbert Lindenberger, "Appropriating Auerbach: From Said to Postcolonialism," *Journal of Commonwealth and Postcolonial Studies* 11, nos. 1–2 (2004): 46–47.

10. See Theodor W. Adorno, "The Essay as Form," in *Notes to Literature*, vol. 1 (New York: Columbia University Press, 1991), 3–23.

11. See R. Radhakrishnan, "In Memoriam," *Politics and Culture*, August 10, 2010, http://politicsandculture.org/2010/08/10/in-memoriam-r-radhakrishnan-2/.

12. See Aamir R. Mufti, "Auerbach in Istanbul: Edward Said and the Question of Minority Culture," *Critical Inquiry* 25, no. 1 (1998): 95–125. A much expanded and revised version of this essay is now at the core of a book manuscript, titled *Edward Said in Jerusalem: Secularism, Criticism, Exile.*

13. For a detailed account of the institutional vicissitudes of Auerbach's career in Germany and especially his dealings with German authorities after the rise of the Nazis to power, see Hans Ulrich Gumbrecht, "'Pathos of the Earthly Progress': Erich Auerbach's Everydays," in Lerer, *Literary History*, 14–35. Gumbrecht argues that Auerbach had developed a "distanced view of European culture" (31) well before his departure from Germany.

14. For a full-scale elaboration of this concept of minority, see Aamir R. Mufti, *Enlightenment in the Colony: The Jewish Question and the Crisis of Postcolonial Culture* (Princeton, NJ: Princeton University Press, 2007).

15. Claude Lévi-Strauss, *Tristes Tropiques*, trans. John and Doreen Weightman (London: Penguin Books, 1973), 38.

16. Lévi-Strauss, *Tristes Tropiques*, 43.

17. This phrase is of course from James Clifford, *The Predicament of Culture: Twentieth-Century Ethnography, Literature, and Art* (Cambridge, MA: Harvard University Press, 1988).

18. The Said translation retains the German term *Weltliteratur*, and I shall follow the same practice in order to highlight the distinctness of Auerbach's conception from the "world literature" of recent U.S.-based discussion.

19. Erich Auerbach, *Mimesis: The Representation of Reality in Western Literature* (Princeton, NJ: Princeton University Press, 2003), 552; hereafter cited parenthetically in the text as *M*.

20. Erich Auerbach to Walter Benjamin, December 12, 1936, in "Scholarship in Times of Extremes: Letters of Erich Auerbach (1936–1942), on the Fiftieth Anniversary of His Death," *PMLA* 122, no. 3 (2007): 749.

21. Auerbach to Benjamin, January 3, 1937, in "Scholarship in Times of Extremes," 751.

22. See Mürat Belge, *Militarist Modernleşme: Almanya, Japonya ve Türkiye* (Istanbul: Iletisim Yayincilik, 2011).

23. See Kader Konuk, *East West Mimesis: Auerbach in Turkey* (Stanford, CA: Stanford University Press, 2010).

24. See Homi K. Bhabha, *The Location of Culture* (New York: Routledge, 1994).

25. Auerbach to Benjamin, January 3, 1937, in "Scholarship in Times of Extremes," 750.

26. Auerbach, *Time, History, and Literature*, 6.

27. Ibid., 37–38, 5.

28. Ibid., 38, 36, 38; emphasis added.

29. Theodor W. Adorno, "Words from Abroad," in *Notes to Literature*, vol. 1, 187, 189, 191.

30. See Paul A. Bové, *Poetry against Torture: Criticism, History, and the Human* (Hong Kong: Hong Kong University Press, 2008), 39; and Konuk, *East West Mimesis*, 26.

31. Edward W. Said, *Culture and Imperialism* (New York: Vintage Books, 1993), 335.

32. See Hugh of St. Victor, *The Didascalicon of Hugh of St. Victor*, trans. Jerome Taylor (New York: Columbia University Press, 1961), 101. Although Said cites the Taylor translation in the passage of *Culture and Imperialism* cited here, he has altered the text in small ways.

33. Said, *The World, the Text, and the Critic*, 6.

34. Edward W. Said, "Introduction to the Fiftieth-Anniversary Edition," in Auerbach, *Mimesis*, xvii.

35. Said, *The World, the Text, and the Critic*, 8.

36. Ibid., 6; emphasis added.

37. Vassilis Lambropoulos, *The Rise of Eurocentrism: Anatomy of Interpretation* (Princeton, NJ: Princeton University Press, 1992), 9.

38. See Matthew Arnold, *Culture and Anarchy and Other Writings*, ed. Stefan Collini (Cambridge, UK: Cambridge University Press, 1993).

39. Ibid., 12, 9, 10, 11.

40. See Porter, "Erich Auerbach and the Judaizing of Philology."

41. See Stathis Gourgouris, *Dream Nation: Enlightenment, Colonization, and the Institution of Modern Greece* (Stanford, CA: Stanford University Press, 1996).

42. I have discussed these matters in much greater detail in chapter 1 of Mufti, *Enlightenment in the Colony*. From the vast secondary literature on the ideal of *Bildung* in the history of Jewish emancipation, see, for instance, George L. Mosse, "Jewish Emancipation: Between Bildung and Respectability," in *Confronting the Nation: Jewish and Western Nationalism* (Hanover, NH: University Press of New England, 1993), 131–145; and David Sorkin, *The Transformation of German Jewry, 1780–1840* (New York: Oxford University Press, 1987).

43. For a significantly different understanding of the relationship of *Mimesis* to the Holocaust, see Malachi Haim Hacohen, "Typology and the

Holocaust: Erich Auerbach and Judeo-Christian Europe," *Religions* 3 (2012): 600–645.

44. Bové, *Intellectuals in Power*, xi.

45. Ibid., 208.

46. Said, *Culture and Imperialism*, 45.

47. Bové, *Intellectuals in Power*, 208.

48. See Said, *The World, the Text, and the Critic*, chaps. 7–9.

49. See Jérôme David, *Spectres de Goethe: Les métamorphoses de la "littérature mondiale"* (Paris: Les Prairies Ordinaires, 2012).

50. See Said, *Culture and Imperialism*.

51. See Edward W. Said, *Humanism and Democratic Criticism* (New York: Columbia University Press, 2004).

52. Adorno, "Words from Abroad," 192.

53. For a more severe criticism than mine along these lines, see Pheng Cheah, "World Against Globe: Toward a Normative Conception of World Literature," *New Literary History* 45, no. 3 (2014): 303–329. Tom Eyers has offered a compelling assessment of the digital and neo-positivistic turn in the literary humanities for its reliance on an impoverished model of the scientific method in "The Perils of the 'Digital Humanities': New Positivisms and the Fate of Literary Theory," *Postmodern Culture* 23, no. 2 (2013). https://muse.jhu.edu/journals/postmodern_culture/v023/23.2.eyers.html#f6-text.

Epilogue

1. See Pradeep Chibber, *Postcolonial Theory and the Specter of Capital* (New York: Verso, 2013). The list of responses to this book is already quite lengthy. One of the best is Timothy Brennan, "Subaltern Stakes," *New Left Review* 89 (2014): 67–87. See also Gayatri Chakravorty Spivak, review of *Postcolonial Theory and the Specter of Capital*, by Pradeep Chibber, *Cambridge Review of International Affairs* 27, no. 1 (2014): 184–203.

2. Michael Hardt and Antonio Negri, *Empire* (Cambridge, MA: Harvard University Press, 2000), xv–xvi.

3. Edward W. Said, *Orientalism* (1978; repr., New York: Vintage, 2003), 25.

4. Hardt and Negri, *Empire*, 85–86.

5. The work that is cited is Arif Dirlik, *The Postcolonial Aura* (Boulder, CO: Westview, 1997).

6. Hardt and Negri, *Empire*, 137–159.

7. Stathis Gourgouris, "Derealizations of the Ideal: Walcott Encounters Seferis," *boundary 2* 39, no. 2 (2012): 182. The fuller version of this argument is presented in Gourgouris, *Dream Nation: Enlightenment, Colonization, and the Institution of Modern Greece* (Stanford, CA: Stanford University Press, 1996).

8. Karl Marx and Friedrich Engels, *Werke*, vol. 1 (Berlin: Dietz Verlag, 1981), 344.

Acknowledgments

THE CORE ARGUMENT of this book was first presented in compressed form in a long article, "Orientalism and the Institution of World Literatures," published in *Critical Inquiry* in 2010. Arguing against the historical myopia of much of the contemporary debate about world literature, it offered a genealogy for the concept that led back to the consolidation in the late eighteenth and early nineteenth centuries of a new philological practice in the work of what I called Calcutta Orientalism. The modes of reading and thinking to emerge out of this conjuncture had profound implications for language, literature, and culture in colonial India, formalizing for the first time some of the logics of social and cultural differentiation and classification, such as the linguistic family tree and the identification of language with religious and national formations, that have been profoundly influential for historical experience in modern times. Two other essays had developed related lines of inquiry. One of them, "Erich Auerbach and the Death and Life of World Literature," was published in 2012 in *The Routledge Companion to World Literature*, edited by Theo d'Haen, David Damrosch, and Djelal Kadir. It concerned Auerbach's refashioning of the nineteenth-century concept of world literature under the historical conditions of the postwar world and Edward Said's use of this renewed practice as his own point of departure for thinking about literary relations on a world scale. The other, "Global

Comparativism," had appeared earlier, in a 2005 special issue of *Critical Inquiry* dedicated to commemorating the life and work of Said soon after his untimely death in 2003. And my introductory contribution to a dossier of *boundary* 2 in 2012 had suggested some points of entry into the question of the status of world literature in the contemporary humanities. The materials from these publications have been thoroughly revised, expanded, and rearranged, and a number of complete sections in each of the chapters and the better part of the prologue and epilogue are being seen here for the first time.

Two teaching experiences—a graduate seminar in the Department of Comparative Literature at UCLA in spring 2011 and a summer seminar for Harvard University's Institute for World Literature at Istanbul Bilgi University in 2012—convinced me of the need for a fuller elaboration of the subject than I had initially attempted. A third group of students at UCLA in spring 2013 helped me enrich these ideas further as I was beginning to compile the materials. I am deeply grateful to all these groups of remarkable students and colleagues in Los Angeles and Istanbul for allowing me to test the ideas that are being presented here, and special thanks are due to David Damrosch (who is one of my former teachers), for the invitation to teach for the institute, which turned out to be a valuable and deeply satisfying experience.

The book has benefited enormously from the input of colleagues at a number of institutions. For those invitations to present my work or for engaging with it on those and other occasions, I must thank especially Jonathan Arac, Rashmi Bhatnagar, Paul A. Bové, Emrah Efe Çakmak, Margaret Cohen, David Damrosch, Stathis Gourgouris, Jennie Jackson, Mina Karavanta, Sanjay Krishnan, Ronald Judy, Kris Manjapra, Karim Mattar, Franco Moretti, Vivan Sunderam, Ram Rahman, Sissy Velisariou, and Milind Wakanker. Stathis and Paul have egged me on almost continuously since I first broached the idea of this book with them and have propped me up from time to time with overblown assessments of its usefulness at moments when I could not quite imagine its audience. These are the unmistakable signs of friendship. My gratitude goes also to the two groups of anonymous readers assembled by my department at UCLA and Harvard University Press, respectively.

Closer to home in Los Angeles, a number of my immediate colleagues have served uncomplainingly as testing ground for the ideas dealt with in the book: I want to acknowledge especially Gil Hochberg, Ali Behdad, Nouri Gana, Efraín Kristal, and Kirstie McClure. Kathy Komar, Katherine King, and Ross Shideler have always been generously accommodating of my many extensions and detours, thus implicitly affirming my work, which is a valuable gift to give to a younger colleague. Efraín's generously shared enthusiasm for my various projects over the years—including one memorable afternoon in the Rue du Faubourg Saint-Antoine in Paris—has always been a source of encouragement, and Kirstie has been a remarkable ready resource on all matters philosophical just three doors away on the third floor of the Humanities Building: to both these brilliant intellectuals and generous colleagues I am most grateful.

A number of dissertations on questions that pertain to the various issues explored here, written by brilliant students I have had the good fortune to work with at UCLA in recent years, have left their mark on the work presented in this book, above all the work of David Fieni, Indra Mukhopadhyay, Neetu Khanna, Shad Naved, Leah Feldman, Maryam Wasif Khan, and Sina Rahmani. With respect to the South Asian materials discussed here, Maryam's work has thrown new light on the questions about the impact of Orientalist ideas and practices on the South Asian vernacular traditions that have been raised in Chapter 2 of this book. Shad's pioneering research on the precolonial poetic practices of northern India have challenged the ease with which we make assumptions about the genealogies of "postcolonial" literatures. And Leah's work on Muslims and Islam in the Russian imperial and Soviet cultural systems helped me broaden in regional and linguistic terms my understanding of the issues concerning Orientalism as knowledge practice that are at the core of this book. This group of young scholars have been among my most important interlocutors over the past several years, and it is with real pleasure that I look forward to their future contributions to their fields of specialization and to the larger discussion about literature as a worldwide assemblage of practices and institutions. A number of highly capable research assistants—Andrea Gyorody in Williamstown, Massachusetts, and, at UCLA, Kirk Sides, Shad,

Ethan Pack, and, finally, Maryam, who exercised almost mystical powers over the interlibrary loan department—have aided my work on the materials of this book, and I am very grateful for their hard work.

Without the generous grant of an Oakley Fellowship from the Sterling and Francine Clark Art Institute and the Frank Oakley Center for the Humanities at Williams College and the repeated support of the Dean of the Humanities, the Academic Senate, and the International Institute at UCLA, the research presented here would have been a far-less-agreeable enterprise. For the incomparable research and writing opportunity in Williamstown—to say nothing of the conviviality!—I thank Michael Ann Holly, Mark Ledbury, and Michael Brown, as well as Frank Oakley, scholar extraordinaire, for his welcome and example.

Mazen Arafat Nomura, Sophie Tremolet, and their daughters, Soumaya and Nourine, have welcomed my family to London on three extended trips that included research for this book at the British Library. Thanks are also due to Neni Panourgiá and to Stathis for their hospitality on two occasions in Galaxidi, an extraordinary place on the earth, possibly still watched over by the gods from Delphi. And the friendship of Pankaj Butalia, Nilofer Kaul, and their son Firdaus, so freely given, grounds my relationship to the city of Delhi, of which I can sometimes dream that it is my own.

I am also grateful to my editor, Lindsay Waters, for encouraging me to write a longer book than I had initially dared to propose—a rare bit of editorial advice in these times. And thanks to both him and to Amanda Peery for being such fierce advocates for the book throughout the process of its completion. And thanks to Hamra Abbas for permission to use for the cover of the book an image from her artwork, *All Rights Reserved* (2006), a brilliant condensation of some of the issues concerning culture and possession, translation and appropriation, and the mobility and immobility of cultural works that I explore here at some length.

Finally, I must acknowledge the most intimate and most cherished debts. Saloni's presence as *world* companion is as ever visible on every page of this book, which is really an attempt to understand the world we have shared for twenty-two remarkable years. For her generosity and patience in the nearly two years it has taken to bring it to completion, she has my undying gratitude. And I thank Jalal for forgiving my many absences during this period and for celebrating with me the submitting of our respective book proposals, one lovely March evening in 2013—a school night!—in West Hollywood. Above all, I thank him for being such a great companion on our world travels and for bringing the beautiful Spanish language into our lives.

My biggest debt to any living person, however, which is literally a lifelong one, is acknowledged in the dedication. This book is offered with much love to my eldest brother, Khalid R. Mufti, Jalal's beloved Taya, who is in Urdu poetry as fish are in water.

Index

Aali, Jamiluddin, 144
Abbas, Hamra, 50–51
Āb-e ḥayāt (Azad), 97, 132, 140–142
Abhijñānaśākuntala. See *Śākuntala* (Kalidas)
Abrams, M. H., 67–68, 100
Achcar, Gilbert, 85, 86
Addresses to the German Nation (Fichte), 62
Ādhā Gāūñ (Raza), 168
Adorno, Theodor, 19, 74, 206, 220–221, 241
After Amnesia (Devy), 121
Against World Literature (Apter), 92, 205
Āg kā daryā (Qurratulain), 143, 176
'Ajā'ib al-āthār fi al-tarājim wa al-akhbār (Jabarti), 29
Algeria, 13–14, 17, 248
Ali, Agha Shahid. See Shahid
All About H. Hatter (Desani), 163, 167
All Rights Reserved (artwork by Abbas), 50–51
"From Amherst to Kashmir" (Ali), 183
Amir Khusrau, 144
Anand, Mulk Raj, 39, 89, 160–162, 169
Anglicism. See Eurocentrism and European culture; Orientalism-Anglicism
Anglophone novel: origins of, 16–18; in Indian vernaculars, 39, 169–172; in

Pakistan, 40, 48, 93, 130, 174–178; as knowledge representation, 53–54, 156–157, 251; Anand and, 89–90, 160–162; social geography of education and, 158–159; Rushdie and, 163–168, 173, 177; Ghosh and, 168; interpretations of, 179–180. See also English language and literature; *specific titles*
Ansatzpunkt, 236
anthropology (discipline), 53–55, 59, 61, 105, 209–210
appropriation, cultural, 43–45, 48–51. See also assimilation
Apter, Emily, 17, 92, 204–205, 275n4
"In Arabic" (Shahid), 197–199
Arabic language and literature, 44, 67–68, 122, 152–154. See also Indian languages and literature; Persian language and literature
Arac, Jonathan, 17, 19
Aravamudan, Srinivas, 28, 110
Arendt, Hannah, 93, 187, 210
Asiatick Researches, 100, 108–109
Asiatic Society, 106, 108, 122
Askari, Muhammad Hasan, 134
assimilation, linguistic and literary, 11–14, 17, 57–59, 79–80, 172. See also appropriation; language
Ataturk, Kemal, 213, 247

Auerbach, Erich: on world literature, 14–15, 78–79, 203–204, 219–220, 234–240; on exilic consciousness of, 41, 203, 207, 225–227, 240; on language reform, 148, 212–214, 221; critical humanism by, 205–206, 208–209, 218, 221–223; personal experiences of, 211–212, 214–215; Konuk on, 214–215; Hugh's *Didascalicon* as quoted by, 223–225; European civilization narratives by, 228–234. *See also* "Philology and *Weltliteratur*" (Auerbach)
authority and authenticity: Turner on, 22; Said on, 26–28, 202; Auerbach on, 40; in Indian literary culture, 111, 172; in Arabic society, 152–154. *See also* colonialism and colonial identity
Azad, Muhammad Husain, 73, 97, 128, 132, 137–143. *See also* literary history
āzādi, 182–183

Babel motif, 2, 15
bākhā (term), 123–125
Balibar, Etienne, 201
Bandung (term), 91–92, 264n58
Bangladesh, 169, 174, 177
Begum Akhtar, 189–190
Benares College incident (1847), 126–127
Bengal Renaissance, 109–110
Benjamin, Walter, 207, 212–213, 221
Berlin, Isaiah, 61, 219
"Beyond English" (Shahid), 195–197
bhadralōk, 109–110
Bhagvat-Geeta, or Dialogues of Kreeshna and Arjoon (Wilkins), 110
Bharatya Janata Party (BJP), 172–173
Biblical narrative of Auerbach, 228–232, 234
Bildung, 233
Black Skins, White Masks (Fanon), 13
Bloomsbury literary culture, 43, 161–163. *See also* London, England
borderless world (term), 5–8, 200–202
Borges, Jorge Luis, 2, 197
bourgeois capitalism. *See* capitalist globalization
Bové, Paul, 78, 205, 207
Braj language and literature, 123–126. *See also* Indian languages and literature
Brick Lane (Ali), 168–169
British India: educational system, 1, 90–91, 103, 114, 121, 128; modern

industrial system of, 23, 88–89, 131; looting of, 44–46; Marx on, 86–87. *See also* East India Company; India
British Library, 41–45, 49. *See also* library, universal
British Museum, 42–43
Burke, Edmund, 64, 103, 106, 266n19
Burnt Shadows (Shamsie), 40, 169, 174, 176

Calcutta, India, 131–132, 162–163. *See also* College of Fort William, Calcutta; East India Company; India
Calcutta Chromosome (Ghosh), 160
Calcutta Orientalism: defined, 30, 37; Sanskritic canonization by, 37–38, 101–104, 106–107, 110; comparative philology in, 104–108; Hinduism and, 110–111. *See also* Orientalism-Anglicism; Sanskritic literature and culture
Cannon, Garland, 105
Capital (Marx), 84
capitalist globalization: defined, 5–6; language of, 12, 96–97; market development in, 81–84; influence on world literature, 90–91, 209–216, 243; Hardt and Negri on, 244–246
Caribbean, 13–14
Carlyle, Thomas, 77, 151
Casanova, Pascale, 20–21, 32–34, 57–59, 75–76, 204
A Case of Exploding Mangoes (Hanif), 174, 176
center-periphery model, 32–34, 95–96
Chatterjee, Partha, 110, 114
Chatterjee, Suniti Kumar, 121
Chattopadhyay, Bankimchandra, 111, 114
Chaudhuri, Amit, 172
chronotope of the indigenous, 37, 47, 74, 107, 112, 129–130. *See also* language
A Code of Gentoo Laws (Halhed), 102, 104
Cohn, Bernard, 103
Colebrooke, Henry Thomas, 104, 111
College of Fort St. George, Madras, 116
College of Fort William, Calcutta, 106, 108, 116, 121–126, 140. *See also* East India Company
"A Colonial City and Its Time(s)" (Guha), 131–132
colonialism and colonial identity: national literature and, 1–4, 90; language acquisition and, 13–14, 135–136; capitalism and, 34–35, 47,

81–84; rise of novels and, 34–35, 95, 130–132; education system of, 90–91, 103, 114, 121, 128; temporal displacement and, 131–132, 162–163. *See also* authority and authenticity; exilic consciousness

colonization of the ideal, 249

Communist International, 89

Communist Manifesto (Marx and Engels), 36, 80–81, 87–88

comparative literature (discipline), 10

"Conjectures on World Literature" (Moretti), 95

Country without a Post-Office (Shahid), 186

critical humanism (discipline): Lévi-Strauss on, 41, 208–209; purpose of, 53–55, 250–252; Auerbach on, 205–206, 208–209, 221–223; Said on, 240–241, 250. *See also* anthropology (discipline); Orientalism-Anglicism; world literature

cultural authority. *See* authority and authenticity

Culture and Imperialism (Said), 223, 266n18

In Custody (Desai), 169–170

Damrosch, David, 4, 32, 94, 204, 275–276n5

Dara Shikoh, 50, 260n69

Daryā-e laṭāfat, 124, 125

Delhi Collection, British Library, 44–45

Delhi College, 136, 137

Delhi Prize and Delhi Prize Agents, 44–45

Derozio, Henry, 113–115

Desani, G. V., 163, 167

Description of the Character, Manners, and Customs of the People of India; and of their Institutions, Religious and Civil (Dubois), 136

D'haen, Theo, 21

Dharwadker, Vinay, 80

Dhūp (Riaz), 144

Didascalicon (Hugh of St. Victor), 223–225

Dirlik, Arif, 245, 246, 247

Discourse on the Origin of Inequality (Rousseau), 60

The Discovery of India (Nehru), 37, 103

dissemination: of English language, 12–13; of world literature, 57–59, 75–76, 237; of ghazals, 72–73; of capitalist globalization, 81–84; distant reading and, 94–96, 241; of Indian literature, 108–109. *See also* assimilation

distant reading, 94–96, 241

Distant Reading (Moretti), 94–96, 204

dōhā genre, 144

Dominance without Hegemony (Guha), 83, 157

East India Bill, 266n19

East India Company, 1, 43–46, 103–104, 134–136, 266n19. *See also* College of Fort William, Calcutta

education system: of British India, 90–91, 103, 114, 121, 128; English and social geography of, 158–159

"Ēk bin-likhī razmīya" (Husain), 176, 177

Empire (Hardt and Negri), 244–246, 247

The Enchantress of Florence (Rushdie), 169

Engels, Friedrich, 36, 80–81, 87–88, 217

English language and literature: multiplicity of, 11, 31; defined, 12; dissemination of, 12–13, 146–148; rise as world literary language, 14–19, 39–40, 92; nationalist political debate on, 172–174; ghazals in, 189–196. *See also* Anglophone novel; world literature

Enlightenment, 42, 61, 63–64, 75–78

Enlightenment Orientalism (term), 28

Eurocentrism and European culture: "universal library," 1–7, 151–152; language and, 11–16; during Enlightenment, 75–78; civilization narratives of, 228–232, 234; universal dominance theory, 244–249. *See also* Orientalism-Anglicism; *specific nations*

exilic consciousness: of Auerbach, 41, 203, 207, 225–227, 240; of Guha, 131–132; of Anand, 162–163; in *Brick Lane*, 168–169; of Shahid, 180, 186, 194–195, 200; of Said, 201–202. *See also* colonialism and colonial identity

Faiz, Faiz Ahmed, 93, 94, 143, 170, 180, 183–186

Fanon, Frantz, 13–14, 84, 153

Faruqi, Shamsur Rahman, 123, 132, 133–134

Fasāna-e 'ajā'ib (Rajab), 128

fascism, 231–232, 234

Figueira, Matilda, 101

Fort William College. *See* College of Fort William, Calcutta

Foucault, Michel, 4, 36

Frederick the Great, 65

French language, 64
"The Future Results of the British Rule in India" (Marx), 84, 86, 88–89

Gandhi, Mahatma, 110, 161–162
Garcin de Tassy, Joseph Héliodore Sagesse Vertu, 134–135, 136
genealogy of literature: Orientalism and, 19–20, 30–31, 35–36, 66–67; philological knowledge revolution, 58–59; Goethe's contribution to, 78, 80; by Auerbach, 239–240
German language and literature, 66, 220, 233–234. See also *specific titles*
German nationalism, 61–62
ghazals: defined, 53, 72, 139; dissemination of, 72–73; of Hafez translated by Jones, 100; of Faiz translated by Shahid, 180, 183–186, 189; in song, 189–190; by Shahid, 189–194. *See also* poetry and poetic composition; Urdu language and literature
Ghosh, Amitav, 160, 168
Gibb, Elias, 148
globalization. *See* capitalist globalization
globalization of the novel (term), 34–35, 95, 130–132, 178–179
Goethe, Johann Wolfgang von: on literature of the East, 1, 3; contemporaries of, 36, 66; *Westöstlicher Diwan*, 85, 99, 112. See also *Weltliteratur* (Goethe)
Goethe and World Literature (Strich), 78
Gourgouris, Stathis, 24, 233, 249
Greece, 6, 248–249
Greek Orientalism, 228–229, 232, 233, 249
Grundrisse (Marx), 82–83
Guha, Ranajit, 83, 103, 118, 131–132, 157, 266n18

ḥabaśī (term), 50
Hafez, 100, 113
Hamann, Johann Georg, 61
"Ham Dēkhēñgē" (Faiz), 188
Hamid, Mohsin, 169, 174
Hamilton, Alexander, 108
Hardt, Michael, 244–246, 247
Heart of Darkness (Conrad), 149
Hebrew language and literature, 59, 60, 65, 71, 198. *See also* Jewish historicism

Herder, Johann Gottfried, 59–66, 79, 101, 217–218, 221
Hindavi (term), 123, 124–125
Hindi language and literature, 117, 119–126, 142, 173. *See also* Indian languages and literature; Urdu language and literature; *specific vernacular*
Hindī sāhitya kā itihās (Shukla), 142
Hindostani/Hindustani (term), 120, 122, 123, 125, 160. *See also* Urdu language and literature
Hindu College, Calcutta, 113–114
Hinduism, 28, 109–111
Hindu society in India, 86–89, 113–119, 127, 172, 260n69. *See also* India
Histoire de la littérature hindouie et hindoustanie (Garcin de Tassy), 135, 136
Histoire de Nader Chah (Jones), 100
historicism of world literature, 75–81, 145, 208, 216, 219–222, 250–251. *See also* world literature
homeopathy of language, 92–93
Homeric narrative of Auerbach, 228–229, 232
Hugh of St. Victor, 79, 223–225
humanism (discipline). *See* anthropology (discipline); critical humanism (discipline)
Humanism and Democratic Criticism (Said), 240–241
Humanität (concept), 61–62, 217–218
Hussain, Sayida Surriya, 136

Imagined Communities (Anderson), 57
India: modern industrial system in, 23, 88–89, 131; Great Rebellion of 1857, 44, 45, 46; nation-thinking in, 110–111; Young Bengal generation, 113–114; class politics of, 118–119, 158–159; temporal displacement from, 131–132, 162–163; Kashmir, 182–183, 186–188. *See also* British India; East India Company; Hindu society in India
"To India-My Native Land" (Derozio), 114–115
Indian languages and literature: indigenization of, 38, 111–120, 126–130; institutionalizing of, 38, 73, 109; awards for, 44–45, 172; Jones on, 67–68; Sanskritic tradition and,

110–112; Iqbal and, 112–113, 170; vernacular literary culture of, 120, 123–127, 162–169, 171–172; Fort William project on, 121–126, 140; rise of the novel in, 130–132, 158, 161; contributions to world literature, 154–156. *See also specific languages and titles*

Indian Orientalism. *See* Calcutta Orientalism

Indian Progressive Writers' Association, 161, 162

indigenization of Indian languages. *See* chronotope of the indigenous; *specific languages*

The Indus Saga (Ahsan), 48

Insha, Inshallah Khan, 123–125

Institutes of Hindu Law, or the Ordinances of Manu, 102

Intellectuals in Power (Bové), 207

Iqbal, Muhammad, 112–113, 170

Iqbal Bano, 188

Islam, 69–70, 85–86, 192–194. *See also* Muslim communities

Islamic militancy, 174, 178, 183, 188, 202

Istanbul, Turkey, 6–7, 26, 148, 212. *See also* Turkey

Jammu and Kashmir Liberation Front (JKLF), 183

Jewish historicism, 214, 229, 233–234. *See also* Hebrew language and literature

jihadi Islamists, 174, 178, 183, 188, 202

Jones, William: on connectedness of language, 36, 105–106; works by, 51, 100, 105, 266n19; on poetic composition, 67–71, 74; on Sanskritic literature, 104. *See also specific works*

Kahānī Rānī Kētakī aur Kuñvar Uday Bhān kī (Insha), 123–125

Kalidas, 101, 102–103, 110

Kashmir, 182–183, 186–188. *See also* India; Pakistan

Kemalist project in Turkey, 148, 213, 214, 227–228, 246–247

kharī bōlī vernacular, 120, 125–127. *See also* Indian languages and literature

King's Library, 43

Koh-i-noor diamond, 45, 46

Konuk, Kader, 214–215, 227–228

Lambropoulos, Vassilis, 228, 232

language: assimilation of, 11–14, 17, 57–59, 79–80, 172; nature of, 60–61, 158–160, 220–222; politics and inadequacies of translation, 92–96, 103, 249–250; family connectedness of, 104–108; global modernization projects, 119–120; reform of, 148, 212–214, 221. *See also specific languages and vernacular*

Laroui, Abdallah, 152–153, 154

Lenin, Vladimir, 89, 247

Lenin Peace Prize, 93

Lerer, Seth, 203, 204

Levin, Harry, 204, 275n4

Lévi-Strauss, Claude, 41, 208–209

library, universal, 1–7, 151–152. *See also* British Library

"Library of Babel" (Borges), 2

L'idéologie arabe contemporaine (Laroui), 152

Linguistic Survey of India (Grierson), 106

literary history: as genre, 54–55, 98, 130–132; of Urdu, 132–137. *See also* Azad, Muhammad Husain

Literary Language and Its Public in Late Latin Antiquity and the Middle Ages (Auerbach), 218

London, England, 101, 131–132, 162–163, 168–169. *See also* Bloomsbury literary culture

Lotus (journal), 91, 93

Lucknow Prize. *See* Delhi Prize and Delhi Prize Agents

lyric reading, 71–74, 180–182. *See also* poetry and poetic composition

Macaulay, Thomas Babington, 1, 23, 27, 155–157

"Made in Europe" theory. *See under* Eurocentrism and European culture

Mānavadharmaśāstra, 102, 110

Mani, B. Venkat, 4, 5

Maps for Lost Lovers (Aslam), 169, 170–171, 176

Marathi language, 172. *See also* Indian languages and literature

Marchand, Suzanne, 58, 65

Marg (journal), 91

market economy. *See* capitalist globalization

Marx, Karl, 36, 80–89, 217

Marx and the End of Orientalism (Turner), 22
Mecca, Saudi Arabia, 46–47
Mehta, Deepa, 166
Mezzadra, Sandro, 7, 201
Midnight's Children (Rushdie), 156, 163–168
Les mille et une nuits (Galland), 101
Mimesis (Auerbach), 203–205, 210–211, 216, 226–228, 231–236
Moor (term), 122
Moretti, Franco, 4, 20–21, 32–34, 94–96, 204
Moth Smoke (Hamid), 169
Moyen Orient (journal), 91
Mrs. Dalloway (Woolf), 162
Mu'allaqāt, 100
Mufti, Aamir R., 53–54, 128, 182
"Mujh sē pahlī sī maḥabbat mērī maḥbūb na māṅg" (Faiz), 184
Muqaddima-e śi'r o śā'irī (Hali), 138
Muslim communities: class politics of India, 118–119, 158–159; East India Company on, 122; Pakistani literature and, 176, 178; in Kashmir, 182–183, 186–188. *See also* Islam

Nadeem, Shahid, 260n69
Naipaul, V. S., 79, 173
na'ī rauśnī movement, 73
Narayan, R. K., 163, 167
National College of Art (India), 51
The Nationalization of Hindu Tradition (Dalmia), 117
national literature: colonial identity and, 1–4, 90; historicism of, 75–78, 98. *See also* world literature; *specific national literatures*
nation-state institution: border transformations of, 5–8, 201–202; British monarchy transition to, 43; nation-thinking and, 61–62, 97, 110–111, 216–217; language reform and, 148, 212–214. See also *specific nations*
Negri, Antonio, 244–246, 247
Nehru, Jawaharlal, 37, 48, 103
Nemade, Bhalchandra, 172
Newton (sculpture by Paolozzi), 42
Nikāt al-śu'arā (Mir), *133*, 137
Nobel Prize, 93
novelization of the global (term), 34, 95. *See also* globalization of the novel (term)

Occupy movement, 6–7
Old Royal Library, 43
one-world literary discourse. *See* world literature
"On the Arts, Commonly Called Imitative" (Jones), 67, 68
On the Language and Wisdom of the Indians (Schlegel), 75
"On the Poetry of the Eastern Nations" (Jones), 67–68
Opisher bela, 131–132
Orientalism (Said), 19–20, 24–28, 56–57, 154. *See also* Said, Edward
Orientalism-Anglicism: defined, 3, 20–23, 30, 33, 99–100, 257n32; genealogy of literature and, 19–20, 30–31, 35–36, 66–67; during Enlightenment, 28, 75–78; emergence of, 37, 237; colonial education of, 90–91, 103, 114, 121, 128; in Greece, 228–229, 232, 233, 249. *See also* Calcutta Orientalism; critical humanism (discipline); Eurocentrism and European culture
Origins of Totalitarianism (Arendt), 210
Orlando (Woolf), 176
In Other Rooms, Other Wonders (Mueenuddin), 174

Pakistan, 50, 174, 177, 260n69. *See also* Kashmir
Pakistani literature, 40, 48, 93, 130, 174–178
Pantheismusstreit (Pantheism controversy), 101
Paolozzi, Eduardo, 42
paramparā, 27–28
Paris, France, 97, 101, 104, 108, 109
A Passage to India (Forster), 167, 169
Payām-e maśriq, 112
Pennington, Brian K., 110, 116
people's library of Occupy movement, 6–7
periphery. *See* center-periphery model
Persian language and literature: British Library collection in, 44; Jones on, 67–68, 71; influences on, 70, 122, 124, 133; translations of, 73, 104, 147–148. *See also* Arabic language and literature; Indian languages and literature
Philhellenic criticism, 233, 249
philology (discipline): comparative, 104–108, 218, 241–242, 250–251;

Auerbach on purpose of, 225–226, 235–237. See also *specific languages*
"Philology and *Weltliteratur*" (Auerbach): reception of, 40, 205; multiplicity and excess in, 94, 222; exilic consciousness in, 203, 207, 225–227; on new concept of *Weltliteratur*, 206–208, 222–223, 234–235; literary historicism in, 208–210, 216, 219–222; on nationalism, 211; personal experience and, 211–212, 214–216; *Didascalicon* in, 223–225. *See also* Auerbach, Erich
pilgrimage sites, 46–47
Poems, Consisting of Translations from the Asiatick Languages (Jones), 67–68
poetry and poetic composition: Herder on, 65, 219; Jones on, 67–71, 74; lyric reading of, 71–74, 180–182; of Faiz, 180, 183–186; Vico on, 219. *See also* ghazals; Shahid; *specific writers and texts*
Pollock, Sheldon, 121
Porter, James, 205, 232
positivistic conception, 33, 54–55, 76, 96, 227, 241
Postcolonial Theory and the Specter of Capital (Chibber), 244
Prison Notebooks (Gramsci), 24
Pritchett, Frances, 132, 137, 138

Qur'an, 134

Ravishing Disunities (ed. by Shahid), 189
Ray, Amit, 110, 266n19
reincarnation, 144, 176
rēkhta genre, 133, 137
The Reluctant Fundamentalist (Hamid), 174
La renaissance orientale (Schwab), 99–100
Rhetoric of English India (Suleri), 106
Riaz, Fehmida, 144, 175, 176, 177
rivāyat (concept), 27–28
Romantic criticism, 42, 75–77, 218–219
Roy, Arundhati, 188, 274n57
Roy, M. N., 89
Royal Library (Windsor), 50
A Rule of Property for Bengal (Guha), 103, 266n18
Rushdie, Salman, 39; on Pakistani distinction, 48, 177; on Indian literary quality, 154–155; works by, 156, 163–169; on life in India, 167; Nemade and, 173

Said, Edward: on social locales, 9; as Orientalized subject, 24–25; criticism by, 25–27, 85, 100–101, 205, 207, 265n3; on authority and authenticity, 27–28, 202, 207; on emergence of historicism, 75, 240–241, 250–251; on criticism of work, 85–86; Hugh's *Didascalicon* as quoted by, 223–224; on critical humanism, 240–241, 250. *See also Orientalism* (Said)
Śākuntala (Kalidas), 101, 102–103, 110
Salih, Tayeb, 2, 149–152, 154
Sanskritic literature and culture: canonization of, 37–38, 101–104, 106–107; British Library collection of, 44; rise in popularity of, 99–100; *Śākuntala* and, 101, 102–103; establishment of, 104–109; as national tradition, 110–112; rise of vernacularization in, 120–121. *See also* Indian languages and literature
The Satanic Verses (Rushdie), 167
Schlegel, Karl Wilhelm Friedrich von, 36, 75, 99, 104, 107–108
Schwab, Raymond, 35, 37, 99–101
Sea of Poppies (Ghosh), 168
Season of Migration to the North (Salih), 149–152, 154
Serampore Baptist mission, Bengal, 116, 122, 123
Shahid (Agha Shahid Ali), 40; Faiz translations by, 180, 183–186, 189; Kashmir and, 182–183, 186–188; on Begum Akhtar, 189–190; "Tonight," 191–194; "Beyond English," 195–197; "In Arabic," 197–199; as exilic poet, 199–200. *See also* ghazals; poetry and poetic composition
Shamsie, Kamila, 40, 169, 174, 176
Shore, John, 50–51
Shukla, Ramchandra, 128, 142
Siskind, Mariano, 34–35, 95, 179
Spitzer, Leo, 204, 275n4
Spivak, Gayatri, 17
Sri Lanka, 174
"The State of German Literature" (Carlyle), 77
Studies in Islamic Culture in the Indian Environment (Ahmed), 48
Sturm und Drang (Storm and Stress) movement, 66
śuddha, 117

Tagore, Rabindranath, 2, 102–103
Tamen, Miguel, 10
"Tanhā'ī" (Faiz), 180, 183–184
Taylor, Jerome, 223–225
tazkira genre, 133, 134, 136–137, 141
"Ṭōbā Ṭēk Siṅgh" (Manto), 155
"Tonight" (Shahid), 191–194
translation, politics and inadequacies of,
    92–96, 103, 249–250
The Translation Zone (Apter), 204–205
Trautmann, Thomas, 267n27
Treatise on the Origin of Language
    (Herder), 60
Tristes Tropiques (Lévi-Strauss), 41,
    208–209
Tunisia, 17
Turāth (concept), 27–28
Turkey, 6, 148, 214–215, 227–228,
    246–247. *See also* Istanbul, Turkey
Turkish language and literature, 67–68,
    148
Turner, Bryan, 22, 85
Twilight in Delhi (Ali), 169

Über die Sprache und Weisheit der Indier
    (Schlegel), 107–108
universalism. *See* Eurocentrism and
    European culture
Untouchable (Anand), 39, 89, 160–162,
    169
Urdu language and literature, 38, 44, 117,
    119–126, 132–141. *See also* ghazals;
    Hindi language and literature; Indian
    languages and literature; *specific
    vernacular*
*Urdu Language Collections in the British
    Library* (pamphlet), 44

vernacular (term), 30, 159
Vico, Giambattista, 218, 219
Vocabulaire européen des philosophies
    (Cassin), 92
Volksgeist, 61, 65, 79, 221. *See also* Herder,
    Johann Gottfried

Wakefield, E. G., 84
Wallerstein, Immanuel, 33
Weltliteratur (concept): Auerbach on,
    14–15, 78–79, 203–204, 234–240;

Goethe on, 14–16, 66, 75–79. *See also*
    "Philology and *Weltliteratur*"
    (Auerbach); world literature
Weltliteratur (Goethe), 14–16, 66, 75–79
Westöstlicher Diwan (Goethe), 85, 99,
    112
What is World Literature? (Damrosch),
    204
The White Tiger (Adiga), 169, 170
Wilkins, Charles, 104, 110, 111
Woolf, Virginia, 162, 176, 272n26
The World, the Text, and the Critic (Said),
    207
world literature: emergence of, ix–xii,
    1–2, 10–11, 48–49; universal library of,
    1–7, 151–152; as a border regime, 8–9,
    200–202; discourse and criticism on,
    9–10, 51–54, 94, 120–121, 250–252;
    Auerbach on *Weltliteratur*, 14–15,
    78–79, 203–204, 219–220, 234–240;
    Goethe on *Weltliteratur*, 14–16, 66,
    75–79; rise of English literary language
    in, 14–19, 39–40, 92; genealogy of
    Orientalism and, 19–20, 30–31, 35–36,
    66–67; rise of novels and, 34–35, 95,
    130–132, 178–179; as academic
    discipline, 54–57, 80, 98; expansion of,
    57–59, 75–76, 237; historicism of,
    75–81, 145, 208, 216, 219–222, 250–251;
    Marx and Engels on, 87–88, 217;
    capitalist globalization and, 90–91,
    209–216, 243; counterhegemonic
    theories, 244–250. *See also* national
    literature; *specific languages*; *specific
    types*; *specific writers*
"World Literature" (Tagore), 102
world republic of letters (term), 38,
    96–97
The World Republic of Letters (Casanova),
    21, 57–59, 204
world-systems theory, 32–33

Yemen, 69–70
*Yet Another Philosophy of History for the
    Education of Mankind* (Herder), 60,
    62–64

Zauq, Ibrahim, 137
Zend Avesta (Duperron), 101–102